CONTEMPORARY CHICANO THEATRE

Contemporary Chicano Theatre

ROBERTO J. GARZA
Editor

UNIVERSITY OF NOTRE DAME PRESS
Notre Dame   London

Library of Congress Cataloging in Publication Data
Main entry under title:

Contemporary Chicano theatre.

1. American drama—Mexican American authors.
2. American drama—20th century. I. Garza, Roberto J.,
1934-
PS628.M4C6   812'.5'408   75-19876
ISBN 0-268-00709-8
ISBN 0-268-00710-1 pbk.

Manufactured in the United States of America

iv

Contents

This anthology of plays is published in connection with the Mexican American Studies Program of the University of Notre Dame, which is under the direction of Julian Samora and is sponsored by a grant from the Ford Foundation.

Preface

This anthology consists of eight plays—all written by Chicano playwrights whose works have been accepted and acclaimed by theatre audiences and critics alike and who are actively involved at the present time in either writing, directing, or teaching drama. The final section of these eight plays was made after the author had collected and critically reviewed all available Chicano drama. As a result, it is the opinion of the author that the plays in this anthology creatively and artistically represent the Chicano Theatre today. Finally, this anthology was edited for those who have little or no knowledge of what Chicano Theatre is as well as for the professional in the fields of drama or Chicano studies. It is one that can be employed as a basic reader or resource reference textbook in the teaching of Chicano Theatre both at the high school and college level.

R.J.G.

Acknowledgments

With pleasure I express my sincerest thanks to my Chicano colleagues who sent me copies of their dramas for consideration to be included in this anthology.

My deepest appreciation and gratitude to my advisor, Dr. Julian Samora, for offering me all the assistance I needed—and who patiently waited for the completion of this work.

And to the National Endowment for the Humanities, my appreciation for making it financially possible for me to carry out this project.

R.J.G.

Historical Antecedents to Chicano Theatre

Exactly when and where the first English-speaking play was presented in what is now the United States is not known. However, Professor George C. D. Odell, in his comprehensive investigation of the *Annals of the New York Stage*, has estimated the date to be between 1699 and 1702.[1]

By this date, Spanish drama in this country was already a flourishing form of religious training and popular entertainment for both Spanish settlers and native Indians. In fact, Spanish dramatic productions can be traced back to the sixteenth century. One of the earliest Spanish-speaking dramatic works to be performed in the United States has been presented on June 24, 1567, in a Spanish mission near what is today the city of Miami, Florida,[2] as part of the celebration of the feast of San Juan Bautista. The Spanish Friars and soldiers of the mission invited the Indians of that region to join them in celebrating this traditional and religious holiday and to witness the presentation of a pastoral play which "depicted the Christian Way of Life."[3]

About thirty years later, on April 30, 1598, this time in the southwestern part of the United States, another Spanish dramatic performance occurred.[4] The occasion for this presentation was not of a religious nature but, rather, was of significant historical importance in the history of the Southwest, for on this day Juan de Onate and his Spanish Conquistadores crossed the Rio Grande River into what is now believed to be the site of El Paso, Texas. Ac-

1

cording to Onate and his Spanish Conquistadores, they had now crossed and entered the "almost unexplored lands north of Mexico,[5] thus beginning the Spanish settlement of what is now the southwestern United States.

There on the banks of El Rio Bravo, Juan de Onate and his soldiers briefly interrupted their long march north to New Mexico to watch the presentation of a play written for the occasion by one of Onate's officers, Captain Marcos Farfan de los Godos, enacted by some of his soldiers. This farcical play was a "take-off" on Onate's conquest to New Mexico.[6]

Months later, having reached their destination, Onate and his soldiers began to work immediately on founding the first Hispano-Mexican pueblo in the Southwest—San Juan de los Caballeros, today known as Santa Fe.[7] By early fall, in 1598, the new Spanish settlement was ready to be dedicated. As had been done in Florida thirty years before, Juan de Onate and his Spanish "colonizers" invited the Indian chiefs of the surrounding area to join them in celebrating the dedication of the new pueblo.

The festivities of the day began by giving thanks to God. Then, throughout the day, the Spanish soldiers amused and entertained their guests with "mock battles, jousting contests, and feats of horsemanship."[8] Toward the end of the day, just before the festivities came to an end, the Spanish settlers took time out to enact a dramatic presentation for their guests. The performance was that of the epic play *Morerias*, which related the "long struggle between the Christians and the Moors from 711 to 1492." This performance probably marked the first presentation of a play in the American Southwest.[9] (This play was to remain among the Spanish traditions of the Southwest. It was later staged under the name of *Moros y Cristianos*.)

Later, as the Indo-Hispano people of the Southwest developed new settlements in that area, they still retained and expanded the "rich varied tradition of religious and secular drama."[10] Dr. Arthur L. Campa states:

> The Spanish colonists in the Southwest have cultivated their traditions more faithfully perhaps than any other linguistic group in the United States. From the San Luis valley of Colorado, down to the Rio Grande Valley in Texas may be found today vigorous remains of sixteenth and seventeenth century folklore.[11]

Exactly when the religious plays were written by the Indo-Hispanos of the Southwest is hard to date, but "because of their being modelled after the Spanish *autos* of the sixteenth century, and due to their form and language, they are strictly seventeenth century at the earliest."[12]

These *pastorelas*, *posadas*, and *autos sacramentales* fall into two categories, or cycles of religious folkdrama. The first cycle is based on the Old Testament and includes the two plays of *Adan y Eva* and *Cain y Abel*. Later another *auto*, *Colquio de la Nueva Conversion y Bautismo de los Cuatro Reyes de Tlaxcala en la Nueva Espana*, was discovered by Dr. S. E. Castaneda. The second cycle is based on the New Testament and begins with the *auto* of *San Jose*, followed in order by *Las Posadas,* eight independent plays, including *Postorelas, Los Reyes Magos, El Nino Perdido,* and *La Passion,* complete the order.[13]

A third category of early drama could be added which would include the historical drama *Los Comanches* based on the defeat of Cuerno Verde at a spot in Colorado now known as Green Horn.[14]

New Mexico was the forerunner in the cultivation of the theatrical arts in the southwestern states. Literature indicates that by the beginning of the eighteenth century there were already dramatic troupes touring the towns in the region presenting their repertoire of religious plays. As time went on, these theatrical groups became quite professional—resulting in the establishment of resident stock companies. However, the new trend of playhouses soon brought to an end the touring troupes.

Although drama arrived there later, the theatrical arts also flourished in California. Records show that the theatre was very much alive in that area in the early part of the nineteenth century, while a later account states that "at the old Pacific capital (Monterrey) the Spanish-Californians were still expressing their own dramatic instincts in a very lively manner at the time of the American occupation in 1848."[15]

Little is known as to what theatrical activity existed during this period outside New Mexico and California. However, it is known that in the latter half of the nineteenth century, Mexican traveling shows known as the *Carpas* and *Tandas* entertained the Mexican-American population along the Rio Grande River.[16] The *Carpa* resembled a Vaudevillian type of theatre. Born of the new nationalistic, proletarian consciousness which grew out of the Mexican Revolution, it consisted:

> of a canvas tent often walled in by detachable wooden panels, a gaudy small stage with bizarre painted drops, lit by a single naked glaring electric bulb. The music is provided by a melancholy orchestra: an ancient upright piano, a trumpet, a bass violin and kettledrums. The "house," simply rows of homemade hard benches, is generally packed with a most colorful crowd composed of people from a variety of types . . .[17]

Las Tandas were in most of the cases an integral part of the *Teatro Carpa.* Basically a *Tanda* was a:

> short musical revue, renewed each week and lasting about an hour. Four tandas were played during the evening. A great emphasis was placed on the presentation of the long-ignored Mexican folklore in dances, sketches and even ballets.[18]

On the road these *Carpas* and *Tandas* were performed in:

> show tents that were drawn by trucks and even on mule carts from suburb to suburb and from village to village, quickly setting up in the main square or out in the middle of the street . . .[19]

These *commedias dell' arte* were attuned to the problems of the common man; they were intended as popular forms of entertainment for the lower classes. For a very inexpensive admission price, the working man or *campesino* could indulge in and savor the great satisfaction of watching the exposé of those corrupt politicians, figures of influence who were his oppressors. In a mixture of rough slapstick, relieved by the "colorful" slang of the lower classes, vaudevillians like El Chaflan, El Chicote, Fernando Soto "Mantequilla," Delia Magana, Don Catarino, Manuel Medel, and the great "Cantiflas," all of whom later became great movie comedians, acted out "slices of life" depicting the pain and beauty of the peasant's life in Mexico.[20]

As the *Teatro Carpas* became more popular with Chicano audiences along *la frontera*, they expanded and enriched their repertoire with satirical skits which "poked fun at the mechinical and inhuman world of the 'American.' "[21]

Unlike the *Pasos* of Lope de Rueda and the farcical interludes or *Entremeses* of Cervantes, which were mostly employed as curtain-raisers and afterpieces to the longer plays and to which the *Teatro Carpa* can be traced generically, the *Teatro Carpa* was always the one and only attraction. It did not have to complement or co-exist with other dramatic forms in order to survive: it existed on its merit, as a theatre for the masses. In this respect, *El Teatro Carpa* had more in common with the *Sainetes* of Ramon De La Cruz or the *Genero Chico* of nineteenth century Spain than with its earlier antecedents.[22]

As a result of the continued migration of Mexican nationals and the influence of Mexican touring groups in this country, several Mexican Folktheatre groups were formed in the southwestern part of the United States. Typical of these groups was the Padua Hills Theatre in Claremont, California which was founded in 1932. This theatre was the:

> playhouse home of the Mexican Players. Their productions, with dialogue in Spanish and English are colorful scenes of Mexican or early California life, enhanced by authentic songs and dances and the beautiful costumes of the different regions. The Theatre is part of a non-profit educational organization dedicated to the promotion of friendship and mutual understanding between Mexico and the United States and to the preservation of the cultural heritage of Mexico and Spanish California. The Players are men and women from Mexico or of Mexican descent who receive their training in the theatrical arts while at Padua Hills.[23]

A traditional and integral part of their repertoire were the performances of the:

> actual celebrations such as the festivals of San Isidro the Virgin of Zapopan in Guadalajara or the Virgin of La Soledad in Oaxaca, the ceremony of Las Canacuas among the Tarascan Indians, a wedding in Tehuantepec, or Las Posadas at Christmas time.[24]

Thus, by the mid-1950s the Mexican Folktheatre came to be an institution— a cultural center for the performing arts of Spanish and indigenous context. But like so many other institutions of this nature, which are dedicated to the

infusion and diffusion of "culture," such groups did little to represent the act-
ual existence of the Chicano in the American society. Their romantic performances reflected nothing of the harsh realities of the oppressed Chicano population. Worse still, this theatre failed to capture and convey that *espiritu* of *La
Raza* which was about to manifest itself.

The period from the mid-1960's to the present is often referred to in literary
circles as *el renacimiento*, or re-birth of Chicano created literature. This could
very well be true, for, although Chicano literary expressions have long existed,
they have either been subdued or have gone unrecognized as such due to their
social, political, educational, and economic implications. Such Chicano scholars
as Americo Paredes, George Sanchez, Julian Samora, and Ernesto Galarza, had
long written critical literature concerning the Chicano in the United States.

However, it was not until October, 1965, that contemporary Chicano dramatic literature came into prominence. As a result of the Chicano *huelgas* in
Delano, California, and as a part of the organizing activities of the United Farm
Workers, Luis Miguel Valdez formed the *Teatro Campesino* to dramatize as
well as give impetus and meaning to the *huelga* in Delano. Valdez's *teatro* in
California was dedicated to the "Organization of the Farmworker" and should
not be confused with *Teatro Campesino* of Mexico of the 1930's, which related problems of health and hygiene to the peasant. The Chicano *Teatro del
Pueblo* (People's Theatre) was to excel even more than its Spanish and Mexican
predecessors in its physical and spiritual commitment to enlighten and change
the behavior and attitudes of its audience.

The dramatic and theatrical creations of Valdez portrayed the *campesino*
as an individual freed from physical and mental oppression. But, more important to the aspiring Chicano writer, the dramatic works of Valdez also represent a symbolic gesture of spiritual liberation from a literary myth. The Chicano can create his own literature! Valdez has been the catalystic force. The
stage has been set for the development of contemporary Chicano literature.

As expected, there soon surge on the literary scene, a *nueva ola* of Chicano
writers. Their literary works were to immediately mark a milestone in every
literary form of contemporary Chicano literature.

The first to break ground was Tomas Rivera. His cuento, 'Y No Se Lo
Trago La Tierra," catapulted contemporary Chicano literature from a regional
to a universal level. Other prose writers to follow Rivera were Rudy Anaya,
Rolando Hinojosa-Smith and many others. Although the literary works of
Anaya and Hinojosa-Smith cannot be considered as cosmic or universal as that
of Rivera's, nevertheless they have cultivated the novel and essay with
equal aplomb. Anaya's novel *Bless Me, Ultima* and Hinojosa-Smith's essays
"Estampas de mi Valle" reflect that romanticism so essential of any literary

movement. In poetry as in drama, both Alurista and Estela Portillo have added the needed dimension to contemporary Chicano literature. Their dramatic and poetic work characterized as powerful, penetrating and at the same time as delicate, serene and senuous has been able to capture el *sentimiento* of the Chicano people and artistically present it in literary form.

The dramatic efforts of Chicano playwrights have remained an important focal point for the expression of Chicano literature. From its inception as a farmworker's companion in the fields and always at his side during the long marches of the *huelga,* the *Teatro Chicano* has evolved into a more versatile, philosophical, and transcendental theatre; it not only depicts the suffering of the *campesino* but also the experience of the young Chicano on our college campuses as well. It is one which is fulfilling its commitment to its audience— *Nuestro Pueblo Chicano.*

NOTES

1. William G. B. Carson, *The Theatre on the Frontier* (Chicago, 1932), p. 5.

2. John E. Englekirk, "En Torno Al Teatro Popular Mexicano," *Hispania* (Spring, 1970), 407.

3. Ibid.

4. Rudy Acuna, *A Mexican-American Chronicle* (New York, 1971), p. 61.

5. Ibid., p. 81.

6. Arthur L. Campa to Roberto J. Garza, October 19, 1972. Personal correspondence.

7. Acuna, p. 81.

8. Ibid., p. 81.

9. Ibid., p. 81.

10. Tomas-Frausto Ybarra, "Teatro Chicano: Two Reports," *Latin American Theatre Review* 4(Spring, 1971), 53.

11. Arthur L. Campa, *Spanish Religious Folktheatre in the Southwest.* 1st Cycle (Albuquerque, 1934), p. 5.

12. Arthur L. Campa, *Spanish Religious Folktheatre in the Southwest.* 2nd Cycle (Albuquerque, 1934), p. 6.

13. Campa, *Spanish Religious Folktheatre in the Southwest.* 1st Cycle, p. 10.

14. Campa to Garza October 19, 1972.

15. Jorge A. Huerta, "Chicano Teatro: A Background," in *Aztlan 2,* no. 2(Fall, 1971), 65.

16. Ybarra, p. 53.

17. Miguel Covarrubias, "Slapstick and Venom," *Mexican Life* 13 (January, 1939), 22.

18. Ibid., p. 22.

19. Ibid., p. 22.

20. Ibid., p. 23.
21. Ybarra, p. 52.
22. Marciano Zurita, *Historia Del Genero Chico* (Madrid, 1920), p. 12.
23. Pauline B. Duel, "Commedia del 'Arte' in a Mexican Folk Theatre: Padeca Hills Theatre, Claremont, California," *Hispania* (Fall, 1969), p. 537.
24. Ibid., p. 538.

Chicano Theatre

Entre todas las formas de arte que sirven
para identificar a una raza, el teatro es,
a ciencia cierta, la mas concluyente.[1]
                              Rodolfo Usigli

The theatre is probably one of the most poignant and potent forms of Chicano artistic expression that attempts to reflect the collective historical, cultural, and social idiosyncrasies of *Nuestra Raza*. It is an artistic manifestation that not only mirrors the "mass struggle of La Raza in the fields and barrios of America"[2] but to an equal extent, exposes that "internal struggle in the very *corazon* of our people"[3] at all social levels. Where our other Chicano literary forms of expression attract and influence the more select groups in society, the theatre is both popular and effective with the masses of *Nuestro Pueble.*[4]

"Defining what is Chicano theatre is very much like defining a Chicano car," says Luis M. Valdez, founder of the *Teatro Campesino*. Underneath those decorative exterior trimmings "that define the car as particularly Raza, lies an unmistakable production of Detroit, an extension of General Motors."[5] Thus, Chicano Theatre is a vehicle which borrows and employs some of the forms and techniques of the European theatre (which in turn was influenced by the Oriental theatre) and of the Mexican Vaudevillian theatres of the *Carpas* and *Tandas* so popular along the frontiers of the southwestern states at the turn of the twentieth century. But there is one thing Chicano theatre is not—a replication of the *gabacho* theatre, for the Chicano theatre is "as beautiful, rasquachi, human, cosmic, broad, deep, tragic, comic, as the Life of La Raza itself.[6]

9

Other writers have compared the *Teatro Chicano* to the "agitprop" type
of theatres so popular and effective during the Depression of the 1930's. These
"agitprop" theatres, more commonly known as "living" or "guerrilla" theatres
are an extension of the "people's" theatres, which are by no means new to
the American theatre tradition. The purpose of such theatre now as in the
"avant-garde Brechtian world"[7] of the 30's is to stimulate social agitation
and promote propaganda among the masses.

The *Teatro Campesino* of Luis Valdez, often referred to as the *Teatro Chicano*, is a cross between Brecht and Cantinflas. Unlike Brecht, who involved
his audience intellectually and:

> encouraged detachment—an emotional coolness—so that the audience
> could take pleasure in understanding what it saw, rather than feeling
> what it saw. . . . He deplored the audience with heart and nerves and
> applauded the audience that tempered its feelings with knowledge and
> observation . . .[8]

Valdez on the other hand encourages physical participation by his audience.
According to Valdez, having spectators take part in his *actos* is "no cute production."[9] Instead, "it is a pre-established, preassumed privilege."[10] Furthermore, adds Valdez, "people must act in *reality* and not only on stage in order
to achieve real change."[11]

Valdez's *Teatro Chicano* is also characterized as being Cantinflesco. Cantinflesco, in the sense that like Cantinflas, who "impersonates the class-conscious
man of the city's lower classes, an inferiority complex hidden under a stubborn individualism and an affected and meaningless wordiness. . . ."[12] The central figures or protagonists (archetypes) in Valdez's *Teatro* almost invariably
personify this type of a character. Like Cantinflas, these archetypes radiate a
roguish or *picaro* type of humor in their actions. But, unlike the dialogue of
Cantinflas, which was characterized by the "masterful use of the relentless
dribble that never achieved a phrase with sense,"[13] Valdez's archetype's manner
of speech is direct and definite. Employing a Spanish that has a strong *Tejano*
influence, his characters convey their social message to their audiences in a
clear, simple, and sensible dialogue.

The basic concept of the Chicano theatre is social. It is one that serves to
"*abrir los ojos y para airear la conciencia del mundo.*"[14] Valdez views his theatre as a force to "demonstrate and educate the campesino in the politics of
survival." Furthermore, its "primary goal is to inform the campesinos of the
possibilities of a better life and to suggest methods of achieving one different
from the trodden existence they know so well."[15] Like Valdez, the majority
of our Chicano dramatists view their roles as that of public servants, whose
special responsibility is to create a theatre which should serve as the "conscience of society."[16] Theirs is a theatre which should depict the social "living
reality" of *La Raza*.

Since "reality" per se is neither a universal nor a definable concept, but, rather, a phenomenon which is personal and subjective for each individual dramatist, it would be expected that the *Teatros Chicanos* would employ various forms, themes, and techniques in relating the various "realities" or human experiences of *La Raza*. Unfortunately, until very recently, most of the Chicano playwrights either imitated or copiously employed the format (and often the content) of Valdez's *Teatro Campesino*.

In the last few years, however, Chicano playwrights have begun to move from the "social-realistic" type of theatre, a theatre which sooner or later always becomes "bogged down in trivial, ephemeral themes."[17] Instead, they are experimenting with a theatre which is both contemporary and cosmic in nature, a theatre in which the Chicano is no longer portrayed as a social animal alone: rather, plays that bring to light *aquellos elementos de la condicion humana que transcienden del hombre.*[18] Less and less is their theatre one which merely mirrors the conventional existence of the Chicano in society: instead, today's theatre "ennobles or elevates the Chicano by holding out to him models of his own potential greatness."[19] These models are, in the majority of the cases, such "transcendental myth figures as the Virgin of Guadalupe, Cuauhtemoc, Moctezuma and other Aztec or Mayan Gods,"[20] for these myths offer optimism and spiritual strength for the growth of La Raza."[21]

Examples of this type of theatre can be found in the works of Alurista, Ysidro Macias, Luis Valdez himself, and a host of others. Valdez's latest dramatic work, *La Carpa Rasquachi* is important to the Chicano theatre not only because it works with this medium, but even more because it marks the beginning of a Chicano National Folkloric Theatre. With the creation of his *Carpa Rasquachi,* which to a certain degree is a synthesis of all his previous work, Valdez has come closer to forming the *Teatro Nacional de Aztlán* he envisioned when he started his *Teatro Campesino* in 1965. The *Teatro Nacional de Aztlán,* "would perform with the same skill and prestige as the Ballet Folklorico de Mexico."[22] "Such a *teatro* could carry the message of La Raza into Latin America, Europe, Japan, Africa—in short all over the world."[23]

Along with the upcoming young Chicano playwrights of *La Nueva Ola* are those of *pensamiento critico* who feel that an effort to re-examine and re-appraise the role of the Chicano theatre is now in order. Through such a self-evaluation, the artist can objectively weigh the merit of his work in retrospect, and can change directions (if necessary) in the development of dimensions which will enhance his future work. Most important, such an examination gives him the opportunity to reorient himself with the goals and role of the theatre; he can consider whether the theatre is one of a utilitarian nature whose primary function is to serve the theatre a practical and immediate purpose for the Chicano community and society or one of a more aesthetic quality.

In assessing the Chicano theatre, the critic should not use the "conventional or "traditional" theatrical yardstick or guidelines. For, unlike the "staged" productions in the "professional" American theatre which are so antiseptic, antibiotic (anti-life), the life situations emerging from the Chicano *teatros* are too real, too full of sudor, sangre, and body smells to be boxed in.[24] "The Chicano *teatro*," is different in that its creators, according to Aisenman,

> . . . are directing their efforts toward a new and different audience that comes into the theatre for fun and revitalization. Theirs is a sociological rather than a literary theatre, dedicated to change at all levels, employing the theatre as a poetic tool to effect that change.[25]

Thus, to a large extent, the *Teatro* is "subject to no other critics except the pueblo itself."[26] And it will be the pueblo who "in the long run, will determine the shape, style, content, spirit, and form of *el Teatro Chicano.*"[27]

In the meantime, like all other theatres, it will go through an evolutionary period—searching, eclectically selecting, and experimenting with those concepts that best serve to exemplify the Chicano "living experience"; but it must be very careful never to become just an imitation of foreign works. It should never exist to reflect *el soplo de la vida* of *Nuestra Raza.*

NOTES

1. R. Vance Savage, "Rodolfo Usigli's Idea of Mexican Theatre," *Latin American Theatre Review,* 4(Spring, 1971), 13.

2. Luis Valdez, *Actos*(Fresno, 1971), p. 3.

3. Ibid., p. 3.

4. Ibid., p. 1.

5. Ibid., p. 1.

6. Ibid., p. 1.

7. Cordelia Candelaria, "Teatro Campesino to Appear at Notre Dame." Press release, University of Notre Dame, March 8, 1973.

8. Edward A. Wright, *Understanding Today's Theater,* 2d ed. (Englewood Cliffs, N.J., 1972), p. 71.

9. Valdez, op.cit., p. 2.

10. Ibid., p. 2.

11. Ibid., p. 2.

12. Covarrubias, op.cit., p. 57.

13. Ibid., p. 57.

14. Valdez, op.cit., p. 2.

15. Savage, op.cit., p. 13.

16. Solomon Tilles, "Rodolfo Usigli's Concept of Dramatic Art," *Latin American Theatre Review* 3(Spring, 1970), 33.

17. Ibid., p. 31.
18. Ibid., p. 33.
19. Ibid., p. 33.
20. Ibid., p. 33.
21. Valdez, op.cit., p. 3.
22. Ibid., p. 3.
23. Ibid., p. 1.
24. Leslie Aisenman, "El Teatro Campesino," *Tenaz*, Los Angeles Free Press (March 31, 1972), p. 7.
25. Valdez, op.cit., p. 3.
26. Ibid., p. 3.

Los Vendidos

LUIS M. VALDEZ

A graduate of San Jose University, Luis M. Valdez has worked with the San Francisco Mime Troupe. Presently he is Drama instructor at the University of California, Santa Cruz.

Prolific, ingenious, and creative are just a few of the many adjectives that would describe his work. As founder of the *Teatro Campesino*, he has inspired and influenced other Chicano playwrights. Since 1966, his *Teatro Campesino* has toured and performed throughout the United States. In 1969 and again in 1972, this *Teatro* was invited to perform in the World Theatre Festival in Nancy, France.

Nationally recognized for his *Teatro Campesino*, he also has been presented with the 1971 Drama Critics Award for production of his *corridos*, the 1970 Los Angeles Drama Critics Circle Award for his *actos* and *mitos*, and the 1968 Obie Award in New York for the creation of a workers' theatre to demonstrate politics of survival.

One of his early *actos*, *Los Vendidos*, has been adopted for a television special. His *Teatro* has also made a film based on "I am Joaquin," the epic poem by Rodolfo "Corky" Gonzales.

Among his many dramatic works are *Actos, Bernabé, The Shrunken Head of Pancho Villa*, and numerous others. He is author of several theatrical reviews and literary articles. For the last two years he has conducted theatre workshops for teatro groups from all over the United States and Latin America.

15

Los Vendidos dramatizes the tactics and acts of intimidation that grape growers and farmers employed on Chicano grape pickers during the *huelgas* in Delano, California. It is a play that displays the dramatist's knowledge and training of classical and contemporary theatre. To convey his message of social injustice against the Chicano laborer, Valdez makes effective use of theatrical techniques used in the Greek mime and contemporary "agitprop" theatres. Also quite obvious in this play is the abundance of Chicano music, dance, and language, ingredients so prevalent in the Spanish theatre of "el genero chico." Combined together, these ingredients make *Los Vendidos* one of the best Chicano plays ever to depict the Chicano struggle for survival in a rural society.

Characters

Honest Sancho
Secretary
Farm Worker
Johnny
Revolucionario
Mexican-American

[*Scene: Honest Sancho's Used Mexican Lot and Mexican Curio Shop. Three models are on display in Honest Sancho's shop: to the right, there is a Revolucionario, complete with sombrero, carrilleras, and carabina 30–30. At center, on the floor, there is the Farm Worker, under a broad straw sombrero. At stage left is the Pachuco, filero in hand.*]

[*Honest Sancho is moving among his models, dusting them off and preparing for another day of business.*]

Sancho: Bueno, bueno, mis monos, vamos a ver a quien vendemos ahora, ¿no? [*To audience.*] ¡Quihubo! I'm Honest Sancho and this is my shop. Antes fuí contratista pero ahora logré tener mi negocito. All I need now is a customer. [*A bell rings offstage.*] Ay, a customer!

Secretary [*Entering*]:   Good morning, I'm Miss Jiménez from—

Sancho: ¡Ah, una chicana! Welcome, welcome Señorita Jiménez.

Secretary [*Anglo pronunciation*]:   JIM-enez.

Sancho: ¿Qué?

Secretary: My name is Miss JIM-enez. Don't you speak English? What's wrong with you?

17

Sancho: Oh, nothing, Señorita JIM-enez. I'm here to help you.

Secretary: That's better. As I was starting to say, I'm a secretary from Governor Reagan's office, and we're looking for a Mexican type for the administration.

Sancho: Well, you come to the right place, lady. This is Honest Sancho's Used Mexican lot, and we got all types here. Any particular type you want?

Secretary: Yes, we were looking for somebody suave—

Sancho: Suave.

Secretary: Debonair.

Sancho: De buen aire.

Secretary: Dark.

Sancho: Prieto.

Secretary: But of course not too dark.

Sancho: No muy prieto.

Secretary: Perhaps, beige.

Sancho: Beige, just the tone. Así como cafecito con leche, ¿no?

Secretary: One more thing. He must be hard-working.

Sancho: That could only be one model. Stop right over here to the center of the shop, lady. [*They cross to the farm worker.*] This is our standard farm worker model. As you can see, in the words of our beloved Senator George Murphy, he is "built close to the ground." Also take special notice of his four-ply Goodyear huaraches, made from the rain tire. This wide-brimmed sombrero is an extra added feature—keeps off the sun, rain, and dust.

Secretary: Yes, it does look durable.

Sancho: And our farmworker model is friendly. Muy amable. Watch. [*Snaps his fingers.*]

Farm Worker [*Lifts up head*]:   Buenos días, señorita. [*His head drops.*]

Secretary: My, he's friendly.

Sancho: Didn't I tell you? Loves his patrones! But his most attractive feature is that he's hard working. Let me show you. [*Snaps fingers. Farm worker stands.*]

Farm Worker: ¡El jale! [*He begins to work.*]

Sancho: As you can see, he is cutting grapes.

Secretary: Oh, I wouldn't know.

Sancho: He also picks cotton. [*Snap. Farm worker begins to pick cotton.*]

Secretary: Versatile isn't he?

Sancho: He also picks melons. [*Snap. Farm worker picks melons.*] That's his slow speed for late in the season. Here's his fast speed. [*Snap. Farm worker picks faster.*]

Secretary: ¡Chihuahua! . . . I mean, goodness, he sure is a hard worker.

Sancho [*Pulls the Farm worker to his feet*] :   And that isn't the half of it. Do you see these little holes on his arms that appear to be pores? During those hot sluggish days in the field, when the vines or the branches get so entangled, it's almost impossible to move; these holes emit a certain grease that allow our model to slip and slide right through the crop with no trouble at all.

Secretary: Wonderful. But is he economical?

Sancho: Economical? Señorita, you are looking at the Volkswagen of Mexicans. Pennies a day is all it takes. One plate of beans and tortillas will keep him going all day. That, and chile. Plenty of chile. Chile jalapenos, chile verde, chile colorado. But, of course, if you do give him chile [*Snap. Farm worker turns left face. Snap. Farm worker bends over.*] then you have to change his oil filter once a week.

Secretary: What about storage?

Sancho: No problem. You know these new farm labor camps our Honorable Governor Reagan has built out by Parlier or Raisin City? They were designed with our model in mind. Five, six, seven, even ten in one of those shacks will give you no trouble at all. You can also put him in old barns, old cars, river banks. You can even leave him out in the field overnight with no worry!

Secretary: Remarkable.

Sancho: And here's an added feature: Every year at the end of the season, this model goes back to Mexico and doesn't return, automatically, until next Spring.

Secretary: How about that. But tell me: does he speak English?

Sancho: Another outstanding feature is that last year this model was programmed to go out on STRIKE! [*Snap.*]

Farm Worker: ¡HUELGA! ¡HUELGA! Hermanos, sálganse de esos files. [*Snap. He stops.*]

Secretary: No! Oh no, we can't strike in the State Capitol.

Sancho: Well, he also scabs. [*Snap.*]

Farm Worker: Me vendo barato, ¿y qué? [*Snap.*]

Secretary: That's much better, but you didn't answer my question. Does he speak English?

Sancho: Bueno . . . no, pero he has other—

Secretary: No.

Sancho: Other features.

Secretary: NO! He just won't do!

Sancho: Okay, okay pues. We have other models.

Secretary: I hope so. What we need is something a little more sophisticated.

Sancho: Sophisti—¿qué?

Secretary: An urban model.

Sancho: Ah, from the city! Step right back. Over here in this corner of the shop is exactly what you're looking for. Introducing our new 1969 JOHNNY PACHUCO model! This is our fast-back model. Streamlined. Built for speed, low-riding, city life. Take a look at some of these features. Mag shoes, dual exhausts, green chartreuse paint-job, dark-tint windshield, a little poof on top. Let me just turn him on. [*Snap. Johnny walks to stage center with a pachuco bounce.*]

Secretary: What was that?

Sancho: That, señorita, was the Chicano shuffle.

Secretary: Okay, what does he do?

Sancho: Anything and everything necessary for city life. For instance, survival: He knife fights. [*Snap. Johnny pulls out switch blade and swings at Secretary.*]

   [*Secretary screams.*]

Sancho: He dances. [*Snap.*]

Johnny [*Singing*] :   "Angel Baby, my Angel Baby . . ." [*Snap.*]

Sancho: And here's a feature no city model can be without. He gets arrested, but not without resisting, of course. [*Snap.*]

Johnny: ¡En la madre, la placa! I didn't do it! I didn't do it! [*Johnny turns and stands up against an imaginary wall, legs spread out, arms behind his back.*]

Secretary: Oh no, we can't have arrests! We must maintain law and order.

Sancho: But he's bilingual!

Secretary: Bilingual?

Sancho: Simón que yes. He speaks English! Johnny, give us some English.
[*Snap.*]

Johnny [*Comes downstage*] :   Fuck-you!

Secretary [*Gasps*] :   Oh! I've never been so insulted in my whole life!

Sancho: Well, he learned it in your school.

Secretary: I don't care where he learned it.

Sancho: But he's economical!

Secretary: Economical?

Sancho: Nickels and dimes. You can keep Johnny running on hamburgers,
Taco Bell tacos, Lucky Larger beer, Thunderbird wine, yesca—

Secretary: Yesca?

Sancho: Mota.

Secretary: Mota?

Sancho: Leños . . . Marijuana. [*Snap; Johnny inhales on an imaginary joint.*]

Secretary: That's against the law!

Johnny [*Big smile, holding his breath*] :   Yeah.

Sancho: He also sniffs glue. [*Snap. Johnny inhales glue, big smile.*]

Johnny: Tha's too much man, ése.

Secretary: No, Mr. Sancho, I don't think this—

Sancho: Wait a minute, he has other qualities I know you'll love. For example, an inferiority complex. [*Snap.*]

Johnny [*To Sancho*] :   You think you're better than me, huh ése? [*Swings
switch blade.*]

Sancho: He can also be beaten and he bruises, cut him and he bleeds; kick
him and he— [*He beats, bruises and kicks Pachuco.*] would you like to try
it?

Secretary: Oh, I couldn't.

Sancho: Be my guest. He's a great scape goat.

Secretary: No, really.

Sancho: Please.

Secretary: Well, all right. Just once. [*She kicks Pachuco.*] Oh, he's so soft.

Sancho: Wasn't that good? Try again.

Secretary [*Kicks Pachuco*]:   Oh, he's so wonderful! [*She kicks him again.*]

Sancho: Okay, that's enough, lady. You ruin the merchandise. Yes, our Johnny Pachuco model can give you many hours of pleasure. Why, the L.A.P.D. just bought twenty of these to train their rookie cops on. And talk about maintenance. Señorita, you are looking at an entirely self-supporting machine. You're never going to find our Johnny Pachuco model on the relief rolls. No, sir, this model knows how to liberate.

Secretary: Liberate?

Sancho: He steals. [*Snap. Johnny rushes the Secretary and steals her purse.*]

Johnny: ¡Dame esa bolsa, vieja! [*He grabs the purse and runs. Snap by Sancho. He stops.*]

[*Secretary runs after Johnny and grabs purse away from him, kicking him as she goes.*]

Secretary: No, no, no! We can't have any *more* thieves in the State Administration. Put him back.

Sancho: Okay, we still got other models. Come on, Johnny, we'll sell you to some old lady. [*Sancho takes Johnny back to his place.*]

Secretary: Mr. Sancho, I don't think you quite understand what we need. What we need is something that will attract the women voters. Something more traditional, more romantic.

Sancho: Ah, a lover. [*He smiles meaningfully.*] Step right over here, señorita. Introducing our standard Revolucionario and/or Early California Bandit type. As you can see he is well-built, sturdy, durable. This is the International Harvester of Mexicans.

Secretary: What does he do?

Sancho: You name it, he does it. He rides horses, stays in the mountains, crosses deserts, plains, rivers, leads revolutions, follows revolutions, kills, can be killed, serves as a martyr, hero, movie star—did I say movie star? Did you ever see *Viva Zapata*? *Viva Villa*? *Villa Rides*? *Pancho Villa Returns*? *Pancho Villa Goes Back*? *Pancho Villa Meets Abbott and Costello*—

Secretary: I've never seen any of those.

Sancho: Well, he was in all of them. Listen to this. [*Snap.*]

Revolucionario [*Scream*]:   ¡VIVA VILLAAAAA!

Secretary: That's awfully loud.

Sancho: He has a volume control. [*He adjusts volume. Snap.*]

Revolucionario [*Mousey voice*]:   ¡Viva Villa!

Secretary: That's better.

Sancho: And even if you didn't see him in the movies, perhaps you saw him on TV. He makes commercials. [*Snap.*]

Revolucionario: Is there a Frito Bandito in your house?

Secretary: Oh yes, I've seen that one!

Sancho: Another feature about this one is that he is economical. He runs on raw horsemeat and tequila!

Secretary: Isn't that rather savage?

Sancho: Al contrario, it makes him a lover. [*Snap.*]

Revolucionario [*To Secretary*]:   ¡Ay, mamasota, cochota, ven pa'ca! [*He grabs Secretary and folds her back—Latin-Lover style.*]

Sancho [*Snap. Revolucionario goes back upright.*]:   Now wasn't that nice?

Secretary: Well, it was rather nice.

Sancho: And finally, there is one outstanding feature about this model I KNOW the ladies are going to love: He's a GENUINE antique! He was made in Mexico in 1910!

Secretary: Made in Mexico?

Sancho: That's right. Once in Tijuana, twice in Guadalajara, three times in Cuernavaca.

Secretary: Mr. Sancho, I thought he was an American product.

Sancho: No, but—

Secretary: No, I'm sorry. We can't buy anything but American-made products. He just won't do.

Sancho: But he's an antique!

Secretary: I don't care. You still don't understand what we need. It's true we need Mexican models such as these, but it's more important that he be *American.*

Sancho: American?

Secretary: That's right, and judging from what you've shown me, I don't think you have what we want. Well, my lunch hour's almost over; I better—

Sancho: Wait a minute! Mexican but American?

Secretary: That's correct.

Sancho: Mexican but . . . [*A sudden flash.*] AMERICAN! Yeah, I think we've got exactly what you want. He just came in today! Give me a minute. [*He exits. Talks from backstage.*] Here he is in the shop. Let me just get some papers off. There. Introducing our new 1970 Mexican-American! Ta-ra-ra-ra-ra-ra-RA-RAAA!

[*Sancho brings out the Mexican-American model, a clean-shaven middle-class type in a business suit, with glasses.*]

Secretary [*Impressed*] :   Where have you been hiding this one?

Sancho: He just came in this morning. Ain't he a beauty? Feast your eyes on him! Sturdy US STEEL frame, streamlined, modern. As a matter of fact, he is built exactly like our Anglo models except that he comes in a variety of darker shades: naugahyde, leather, or leatherette.

Secretary: Naugahyde.

Sancho: Well, we'll just write that down. Yes, señorita, this model represents the apex of American engineering! He is bilingual, college educated, ambitious! Say the word "acculturate" and he accelerates. He is intelligent, well-mannered, clean—did I say clean? [*Snap. Mexican-American raises his arm.*] Smell.

Secretary [*Smells*] :   Old Sobaco, my favorite.

Sancho [*Snap. Mexican-American turns toward Sancho*] :   Eric! [*To Secretary.*] We call him Eric Garcǐa. [*To Eric.*] I want you to meet Miss JIM-enez, Eric.

Mexican-American: Miss JIM-enez, I am delighted to make your acquaintance. [*He kisses her hand.*]

Secretary: Oh, my, how charming!

Sancho: Did you feel the suction? He has seven especially engineered suction cups right behind his lips. He's a charmer all right!

Secretary: How about boards? Does he function on boards?

Sancho: You name them, he is on them. Parole boards, draft boards, school boards, taco quality control boards, surf boards, two-by-fours.

Secretary: Does he function in politics?

Sancho: Señorita, you are looking at a political MACHINE. Have you ever heard of the OEO, EOC, COD, WAR ON POVERTY? That's our model! Not only that, he makes political speeches.

Secretary: May I hear one?

Sancho: With pleasure. [*Snap.*] Eric, give us a speech.

Mexican-American: Mr. Congressman, Mr. Chairman, members of the board, honored guests, ladies and gentlemen. [*Sancho and Secretary applaud*] Please, please. I come before you as a Mexican-American to tell you about the problems of the Mexican. The problems of the Mexican stem from one thing and one thing alone: He's stupid. He's uneducated. He needs to stay in school. He needs to be ambitious, forward-looking, harder-working. He needs to think American, American, American, AMERICAN, AMERICAN, AMERICAN. GOD BLESS AMERICA! GOD BLESS AMERICA! GOD BLESS AMERICA!! [*He goes out of control.*]

[*Sancho snaps frantically and the Mexican-American finally slumps forward, bending at the waist.*]

Secretary: Oh my, he's patriotic too!

Sancho: Sí, señorita, he loves his country. Let me just make a little adjustment here. [*Stands Mexican-American up.*]

Secretary: What about upkeep? Is he economical?

Sancho: Well, no, I won't lie to you. The Mexican-American costs a little bit more, but you get what you pay for. He's worth every extra cent. You can keep him running on dry Martinis, Langendorf bread.

Secretary: Apple pie?

Sancho: Only Mom's. Of couse, he's also programmed to eat Mexican food on ceremonial functions, but I must warn you: an overdose of beans will plug up his exhaust.

Secretary: Fine! There's just one more question: HOW MUCH DO YOU WANT FOR HIM?

Sancho: Well, I tell you what I'm gonna do. Today and today only, because you've been so sweet, I'm gonna let you steal this model from me! I'm gonna let you drive him off the lot for the simple price of—let's see taxes and license included—$15,000.

Secretary: Fifteen thousand **DOLLARS**? For a **MEXICAN**!

Sancho: Mexican? What are you talking, lady? This is a Mexican-**AMERICAN**! We had to melt down two pachucos, a farm worker and three gabachos to make this model! You want quality, but you gotta pay for it! This is no cheap run-about. He's got class!

Secretary: Okay, I'll take him.

Sancho: You will?

Secretary: Here's your money.

Sancho: You mind if I count it?

Secretary: Go right ahead.

Sancho: Well, you'll get your pink slip in the mail. Oh, do you want me to wrap him up for you? We have a box in the back.

Secretary: No, thank you. The Governor is having a luncheon this afternoon, and we need a brown face in the crowd. How do I drive him?

Sancho: Just snap your fingers. He'll do anything you want.

[*Secretary snaps. Mexican-American steps forward.*]

Mexican-American: RAZA QUERIDA, ¡VAMOS LEVANTANDO ARMAS PARA LIBERARNOS DE ESTOS DESGRACIADOS GABACHOS QUE NOS EXPLOTAN! VAMOS.

Secretary: What did he say?

Sancho: Something about lifting arms, killing white people, etc.

Secretary: But he's not suppose to say that!

Sancho: Look, lady, don't blame me for bugs from the factory. He's your Mexican-American; you bought him, now drive him off the lot!

Secretary: But he's broken!

Sancho: Try snapping another finger.

[*Secretary snaps. Mexican-American comes to life again.*]

Mexican-American: ¡ESTA GRAN HUMANIDAD HA DICHO BASTA! Y SE HA PUESTO EN MARCHA! ¡BASTA! ¡BASTA! ¡VIVA LA RAZA! ¡VIVA LA CAUSA! ¡VIVA LA HUELGA! ¡VIVAN LOS BROWN BERETS! ¡VIVAN LOS ESTUDIANTES! ¡CHICANO POWER!

[*The Mexican-American turns toward the Secretary, who gasps and backs up. He keeps turning toward the Pachuco, Farm Worker, and Revolucionario, snapping his fingers and turning each of them on, one by one.*]

Pachuco [*Snap. To Secretary*] :   I'm going to get you, baby! ¡Viva La Raza!

Farm Worker [*Snap. To Secretary*] :   ¡Viva la huelga! ¡Viva la Huelga! ¡VIVA LA HUELGA!

Revolucionario [*Snap. To Secretary*] :   ¡Viva la revolución! ¡VIVA LA REVOLUCION!

[*The three models join together and advance toward the Secretary who backs up and runs out of the shop screaming. Sancho is at the other end of the shop holding his money in his hand. All freeze. After a few seconds of silence, the Pachuco moves and stretches, shaking his arms and loosening up. The Farm Worker and Revolucionario do the same. Sancho stays where he is, frozen to his spot.*]

Johnny: Man, that was a long one, ése. [*Others agree with him.*]

Farm Worker: How did we do?

Johnny: Perty good, look all that lana, man! [*He goes over to Sancho and removes the money from his hand. Sancho stays where he is.*]

Revolucionario: En la madre, look at all the money.

Johnny: We keep this up, we're going to be rich.

Farm Worker: They think we're machines.

Revolucionario: Burros.

Johnny: Puppets.

Mexican-American: The only thing I don't like is—how come I always got to play the godamn Mexican-American?

Johnny: That's what you get for finishing high school.

Farm Worker: How about our wages, ése?

Johnny: Here it comes right now. $3,000 for you, $3,000 for you, $3,000 for you, and $3,000 for me. The rest we put back into the business.

Mexican-American: Too much, man. Heh, where you vatos going tonight?

Farm Worker: I'm going over to Concha's. There's a party.

Johnny: Wait a minute, vatos. What about our salesman? I think he needs an oil job.

Revolucionario: Leave him to me.

[*The Pachuco, Farm Worker, and Mexican-American exit, talking loudly about their plans for the night. The Revolucionario goes over to Sancho, removes his derby hat and cigar, lifts him up and throws him over his shoulder. Sancho hangs loose, lifeless.*]

Revolucionario [*To audience*] :   He's the best model we got! ¡Ajua![*Exit.*]

[*End.*]

Bernabé

LUIS M. VALDEZ

The protagonist, Bernabé, better known as *el tonto* in this play, is the prototype of the proverbial village idiot so popular in world literature. Traditionally, this literary figure has been employed to symbolize such human virtues as purity, truth, innocence and love. Bernabé is no exception. His role is to symbolize man's lost love for Earth. He feels that man, especially the white man, has abused and exploited Earth's natural resources, and that it will take human sacrifice or an act of love to keep man from further destroying Earth. In order to conceive this act of love, Bernabé becomes the sacrificial lamb.

Characters

Bernabé	**Torres**	**La Luna**
La Madre	**El Tío**	**La Tierra**
El Primo	**Consuelo**	**La Sol**

[The action takes place in a rural town in the San Joaquín Valley of California.]

Scene 1

[Near Torres Hotel and Bar, Bernabé and his Madre come walking down the hot sidewalk.]

Madre: ¡Bernabé!

Bernabé: ¿Qué?

Madre: ¡Espérame!   ¡Ay Dios, qué calor!

Bernabé: ¿Qué quiere?

Madre: No te vayas tan recio, hijo. Me dejas atrás.

Bernabé: Pos apúrese, oiga.

Madre: No seas malcriado, Bernabé.

Bernabé: Como muele.

Madre: ¿Qué? Mucho cuidado como le hablas a tu madre, ¿eh? ¿Quieres que la tierra te trague en vida?

31

Bernabé: ¿La tierra?

Madre: Porque eso le pasa a hijos que no respetan a su madre. Se abre la tierra y se los traga en vida gritándole a los cielos.

Bernabé: ¡Chale, a mǐ no!

Madre: Bueno, pa' que veas. Hazle caso a tu madre.

Bernabé: A mǐ me quiere la tierra.

Madre: Vamos [*Bernabé walks off.*] Oye, ¿Pa' dónde vas?

Bernabé [*Pointing uncertainly ahead*] :   ¿Pa' 'onde vamos?

Madre: A la tienda.

Bernabé: ¿La tienda del chino?

Madre: Sǐ, hombre, ¡sǐ! Como me mortificas. Uno de estos dǐas me vas a mandar a la casa de los locos.

Bernabé: Yo no estoy loco.

Madre: Y este sol tan caliente. Ya estoy muy vieja yo para andar en estas calles. [*Stops.*] ¿Sabes qué hijo? Mejor vete tu a la tienda sólo. Traime una botella de alcol. Toma un peso. Y mucho cuidado con ese dinero, hombre. No pierdas el cambio. Quien sabe como le vamos hacer hasta que agarres trabajo. [*Consuelo comes out of hotel with a man.*] ¡Válgame Dios, Bernabé, voltéate!

Bernabé: ¿Porqué? [*The man empties a beer can and throws it down.*]

Madre: ¿Qué te importa? [*She turns him around.*] Viejas sinvergüenzas, ¡Descaradas! Nunca te metas en estas cantinas, Bernabé, si no quieres que se muera tu madre de vergüenza. [*Man exits, Consuelo goes out in opposite direction.*] ¡Andale pues, ya vete a la tienda! [*Starts to go. Bernabé picks up beer can.*]

Bernabé: ¿Oiga, me puedo comprar [*Looks at beer can.*] una nieve?

Madre: ¡No, no, no! ¡Qué nieve ni qué mugre! No hay dinero. Y si ves al Señor Torres, el contratista, pǐdele trabajo. Dile que tu pierna ya está bien. ¡Apurale pues!

[*Bernabé exits and Madre goes off in a different direction. After a short pause, Bernabé re-enters and goes to the hotel entrance. He peeks into the doorway, as El Primo and Torres enter.*]

Primo: Simón, boss, todo salió a toda madre en Tijuana.

Torres: No hubo problemas, ¿eh?

Primo: Chale. Tenǐan la carga lista, les pase la lana, y me vine de volada

Torres: Okay, vamos pa' dentro.

Primo: Orale.

Torres [*Spots Bernabé*] :   Oye, pos mira quien está aquí. Tu primo. ¡Ha!
[*He kicks Bernabé.*]

Bernabé: ¡Ay! Baboso, hijo de la . . .

Torres [*Laughs*] :   No te enojes, Bernabé.

Bernabé: Quihubo.

Torres: ¿Qué estabas mirando, Bernabé? ¿Las viejas? [*To Primo.*] Oye,
Eddie, ¿sabías que tu primo ya se trae una vieja?

Primo: No, ¿deveras, primo?

Bernabé: ¿Cómo sabías?

Torres: Yo sé muchas cosas.

Primo: ¿Quién es?

Torres: ¿Pos quién? Una de las meras viejotas del pueblo. Su mamá. [*Laughs.*]

Primo [*Peeved*] :   Eh, man, no te ríes de mi tía.

Torres: Just kidding, hombre. ¿Qué traes? ¿Cuántas girlfriends tienes ya,
Bernabé?

Bernabé: Una.

Torres: ¿Una nomás? No, hombre, ¿qué no tenías siete?

Bernabé: Más antes.

Primo: ¿Te vas a casar, primo?

Bernabé: Mañana.

Primo: ¿Con quien? ¿La Betty?

Bernabé: No.

Primo: ¿La Mary?

Bernabé: Chale.

Torres: ¿Con quién pues?

Bernabé: Mi novia. [*Laughs.*]

Primo: ¿Y va haber parranda, primo?

Bernabé [*Pause*] :   Vale madre. Mucha parranda.

Torres: ¡Eso es! ¿En dónde?

Bernabé: Aquí.

Torres: ¿Aquí en mi cantina?

Bernabé: No, aquí afuera.

Torres: ¿Aquí en la banqueta?

Bernabé: No, aquí en puro cemento. Aquí donde está la tierra. Y allá en los files. Y en las lomas. Va llover.

Torres [*Laughs*]:   Pues sí, ojalá que llueva cerveza. Bueno, Bernabé, por ahí nos vemos, ¿eh? En la boda.

Primo: Hay te huacho, primo.

Torres [*To Primo*]:   Está más loco. [*They start to exit.*]

Bernabé: ¡Oiga, Torres!

Torres: ¿Qué quieres?

Primo [*Long pause*]:   What is it, primo?

Bernabé [*Searching for words*]:   Quiero estar con mi ruca.

Primo: ¿Tu ruca?

Torres: ¡Ah! ya le agarre! ¿Sabes qué? Como se me hace que éste quiere subir allá arriba.

Primo: ¿Con la Connie?

Torres: Pos luego. Eso es lo que trae. ¿Verdad, Bernabé? ¿Quieres una de mis chamacas?

Bernabé: ¡No!

Torres: ¿Cómo que no? Se te ve, loco. Mira, si me dices lo que quieres, te lo consigo.

Bernabé: ¿Con mi ruca?

Torres: La que quieras.

Bernabé: Quiero un jale.

Torres: ¿Un jale?

Bernabé: En los files.

Primo [*Laughs*]:   ¡Ahora si te frego a tí, Torres! Le tienes que dar chamba. No está ni tan loco el primo, ¿no?

Bernabé [*Laughs*]:   Simón, no estoy ni tan loco.

Torres: ¿Y cómo puedes trabajar con esa pata chueca?

Bernabé: Ya está bien.

Torres: Y tu estás bien loco.

Primo: Aliviánate, boss. Se la jodió trabajando contigo. Besides el primo es muy chambeador. Como el áno pasado—¿cuántos sacos de papa cargabas en la troca, ése? ¿Docientos, quinientos, mil?

Bernabé: ¡Vale madre, mil!

Primo: A thousand sacos, man.

Bernabé: Me los hechaba.

Torres: Huy, ¿pos entonces pa' qué quieres trabajo? Ya debes de estar rico. ¿Qué hiciste con todo el dinero que te pagué?

Bernabé: Compré la tierra.

Torres: ¿Cuál tierra?

Bernabé: Está. Por ahí, y allá, y acá. Toda.

Primo: Comprates un ranchito, ¿eh primo?

Bernabé: No, un ranchote, con mucha tierra. Toda la tierra del mundo. Es mía.

Torres: ¿Tuya?

Bernabé: Mi novia. Nos vamos a casar.

Torres [*Burst out laughing*]: ¡Pinche loco! ¡Vámonos, Eddie! ¡Su novia! ¡Lo que éste necesita es una vieja! [*He exits laughing.*]

Primo: Llévate la suave, Bernabé. [*He exits.*]

[*Long pause. Bernabé looks down at the earth.*]

Bernabé: Tierra, piensan que estoy loco. Pero de todos modos te quiero. [*Looks around.*] Nos vemos a la noche . . . como siempre, ¿eh? [*He exits.*]

Scene 2

[*Bernabé's house. A small unpainted square shack sitting way back on a narrow lot. The action takes place in the bare, grassless front yard.*]

Madre [*Coming out of house*]: ¿Bernabé? Bernabé, ¡ven a cenar! ¡Válgame Dios! ¿dónde está este hombre? ¡Berna - bé!

Primo [*Walking down the street*]: Buenas noches, tía. ¿Qué le pasa? ¿Ya se le perdió Bernabé otra vez?

Madre: No que perdió. Se esconde nomás para mortificarme. ¿No lo haz visto, hijo?

Primo: Esta mañana, cercas de la cantina.

Madre: ¿La cantina?

Primo: Digo, la tienda, tía. ¡La tienda del chino!

Madre: Pues, sí. Lo mandé pa' que me trajiera alcol. Ya tengo una semana
con un dolor de cabeza que no se me quita. Nomás vieras, hijo. Me mortifico
mucho. Ya mero se cumple la renta de la casa, y Bernabé sin trabajo. [*Pause.*]
Tu sí estás trabajando, ¿no hijito?

Primo: Sí, señora, con Torres.

Madre: Ay pos si, ¿no? Dicen que el Señor Torres tiene bastante dinero.

Primo: Pero casi todos los hombres del pueblo están sin trabajo. No va haber
nada hasta que comienza la pisca. Mire, déjeme prestarle diez pesos.

Madre: No, Eduardo, ¿qué diría tu madre? Que no lo permite Dios. Ya bien
conozco a mi hermana. Cuando se trata de dinero, es una lechuza. ¡No, no,
no!

Primo: Aquí está, tía.

Madre: No, hijo, gracias.

Primo: Andale. Pa que se ayude.

Madre: ¡No, no y no!

Primo: Bueno . . .

Madre [*Quickly*]:   Bueno, está bien pues. [*Takes money.*] ¿Y cómo está tu
madrecita?

Primo: Bien, como siempre.

Madre: Gracias a Dios. Bueno, si ves a mijo, me lo mandas pa' la casa, ¿eh?
No sé que le irá pasar. Uno de estos días me lo van a meter a la casa de los
locos, y luego ¿qué voy hacer? [*Exits into the house.*]

Primo: No se apure, tía, adiós. [*Starts to go.*]

Tío [*Entering from the street*]:   ¡Oye, sobrino!   ¡Eddie!

Primo: Orale, tío, ¿cómo ha estado?

Tío: Pos ¿cómo? Bien crudo. Oye, no traes un toztón si quiera para
livianarme? Con unos 35 centavos me compro mi chicolia y ya 'stubo,
¿no? [*Primo gives him money.*]   ¡N'ombre! Eso sí es buen sobrino. Oye,
me fije que le pasates dinero a mi hermanita, ¿eh?

Primo: Unos cuantos bolas, ¿so what?

Tío: No nada, pero te apuesto que ni te dió las gracias, ¿verdad? ¡Sí, no lo
niegues! ¿Qué no te he dicho, Guaro? No le des nada a esa vieja seca,

hombre. No te lo agradece. Mírame a mí. ¡Cuántos años me la pase en los files para mantener a ella, su hijo loco, y tu madrecita que la quiero más que nadie! Tu sabes que cuando voy a tu casa, tu'ama siempre me ofrece una taza de café, un plato de frijoles, vaya, lo que sea ¿verdad? Pero esta otra hermana que tengo, ni un vaso de agua me ofrece. Mejor me dice que me pinte a la fregada porque tiene que cenar Bernabé y no le gusta que lo miren comer. [*Primo laughs.*] ¿No te digo? Así es.

Primo [*Laughs with Tío*]:   ¡Orale pues, tío! ¿Y no ha visto al primo?

Tío: ¿Por que? ¿Ya lo anda buscando esa vieja coyota? ¡Qué caray! Mira, sabes donde anda el pobre loco—pero no se lo digas a su madre, ¿eh? . . . andá allá en el llano detrás de la casa.

Primo: ¿El llano?

Tío: Sí, hombre, el llanito donde juegan los mocosos. Tiene un hoyo que escarbo en la tierra, a allí se mete. Al principio se agarraba a terronazos con los chavalillos, pero ya agarró la maña de esperarse hasta la noche y ahora nadie lo molesta.

Primo: ¿Y cómo sabe todo ésto, tío?

Tío: Lo he visto. Se mete y no sale por una o dos horas enteras.

Primo: ¿Qué hace?

Tío: ¡Pos sabrá Judas! Hasta fuí y me metí al hoyo una vez cuando andaba Bernabé en el pueblo con su madre, pero no vi nada. La pura tierra blandita y calientita. Como que se mete y se revolquea.

Primo: ¿En la tierra?

Tío: ¡Pos que más!

Primo [*Pause*]:   Chale. No puede ser.

Tío: ¿Qué?

Primo: Nada. No está tan loco.

Tío: ¡Seguro que sí está loco! 'Ta bien safado.

Primo: Pero no trastornado.

Tío: ¿Pos quién sabe? ¿Qué se te occure?

Primo: No es nada. Una cosa que nos dijo a mi y a Torres esta mañana. Pero no puede ser.

Tío [*Pause*]:   ¿Pos qué es, hombre? ¿Qué no ves que me tienes aquí de uñas?

Primo: Dijo que la tierra es su novia.

Tío: ¿Novia?

Primo: Y que se van a casar.

Tío [*Pause*]:   Y tu crees que . . . no, hombre, ¡sí no está tan loco!

Primo: ¿No le dije?

Tío: Pero sí está safado ¿eh? [*Pause.*] Bien trastornado. [*Pause.*] ¡Pos mira que loco tan cochino, hombre! ¿Porqué andara haciendo esas cosas?

Primo: ¡Cálmela, tío!

Tío: ¡Es una vergüenza, Guaro! ¡Cómo no es sobrino tuyo—!

Primo: Es primo.

Tío: Pos ahí 'ta, dejara de ser familia. Pero la misma sangre de uno, hombre. ¡Chihuahua! ¿Qué va decir su madre si se da cuenta? Te apuesto que ya sospecha algo.

Primo: ¿La tía?

Tío: Sí, señor. ¿Apoco no conozco a mi hermana?

Madre [*Offstage*]:   Berna-beh!

Tío: ¡Oyela! ¿No te dije?

Madre: ¡Bernabé! Por Dios, sal de ahí!

Primo: Parece que lo halló.

Tío: Pos sí, pobre loco. Ahora le va ir mal.

Madre [*Entering*]:   ¡Ave María Purísima! ¡Virgencita pura, ayúdame!

Tío: ¿Quihubo pues, hermanita, ya no me conoces?

Madre: ¡No me hables ahorita, Teodoro! Traigo muchas mortificaciones.

Tío: Huy, ¿pos cuándo no?

Madre: Te digo que no digas nada, hombre. Tu puedes andar de "wino" y sinvergüenza si quieres, pero yo tengo que apurarme por mijo.

Primo: ¿Ya halló a Bernabé, tía?

Madre: ¡Sí, hijo! ¿Dónde crees que me lo encontré? En un hoyo ¡fíjate! Estaba bien sambutido en la tierra.

Tío: ¿Qué estaba haciendo?

Madre: ¡Qué te importa! Tú aquí muy forongo, y mijo allá corriendo peligro de muerte, ¿verdad?

Tío: ¿Cuál peligro, escandalosa?

Madre: ¡Escandalosa! ¿Escandalosa? Y si la tierra se hubiera caído ensima de mijo, ¿qué le hubiera pasado? ¡Dios mío, se me hubiera sofocado! ¿Qué no entiendes, hombre? ¡Sí el hoyo está bien hondo y obscuro!

Primo: ¿Cómo alcanzo ver al primo, tía?

Madre: Ya venía saliendo, hijo. ¡Gracias a Dios! ¿Me haces el favor de ir a tapar es hoyo ahorita mismo, Eduardo? Antes de que me muera de—

Tío: Mortificación.

Madre: ¡Cállate el hocico! Mejor vete, ¿sabes? ¡Lárgate!

Tío: ¡Lárgate tú! Pos mira, que chirrión.

Madre [*To Bernabé, offstage*] :   ¡Bernabé, ven aquí!

Bernabé [*Offstage*] :   Oh, yo no hice nada.

Madre: ¡Te digo que vengas aquí!

Bernabé: ¿Me va pegar, oiga?

Madre: ¡Vente, Bernabé!

Bernabé: Si me paga, le moto un ching.

Madre [*Gasps*] :   ¡Válgame Dios, Bernabé! [*She grabs him.*] ¡Ahora sí te voy a pegar, por malcriado! [*She beats him.*]

Bernabé: ¡Ay! ¡No! ¡No, mamá!

Tío: Ya pues, ¡déjalo!

Primo: ¡No le pegue, tía!

Madre: Ustedes no se metan en ésto. Bernabé es mijo y tengo el derecho de castigarlo.

Tío: Pero sí ya es hombre.

Madre: No me importa. Soy su madre. Y mientras Dios me preste vida siempre le voy a pegar. ¡Suéltenme!

Bernabé: ¡Yo no hice nada!

Madre: Sí, nada. Ahora me crees ciega, ¿eh? ¿Qué andabas haciendo en ese hoyo? Piensas que no sé lo que haces, ¿verdad? ¡Pero sí sé! ¡Una de estas noches va bajar la luna y te va tragar en vida por cochino!

Bernabé [*With fear*] :   ¡No, 'amá, la luna no!

Madre: ¡Sí, ya verás! ¡Vamos, ándale! ¡Métete a la casa! [*She pushes him into the house.*] Ave María Santisima.

[*Madre exits. Pause.*]

Tío: Pobre loco.

Primo: Lo trata como chabalito.

Tío: Pos así es, hombre. Tu lo mirates—deveras cree que se lo va tragar la luna. Pero tienes razón. Dentro de poco, lo vas a ver en los files como todos los años, sudando y trabajando como un animal. ¿Y tú crees que lo agradece mi hermana? No, hombre, si lo renta como un burro.

Primo: Oiga, tío, ¿cuántos años tiene el primo?

Tío: Pos déjame ver . . . treinta y cuatro, creo. No miento . . . treinta y siete.

Primo: ¿Y cuántas novias a tenido?

Tío: ¿De deveras?

Primo: ¡Simón! [*Pause.*] Ninguna, ¿verdad?

Tío: Eso.

Primo: ¡Orale! Entonces no es locura.

Tío: ¿Qué?

Primo: Lo de la tierra, el hoyo y todo, tío. No se haga. Mire, ¿me ayuda a hacerle un favor al primo?

Tío: ¿Cómo que?

Primo: Pos ya sabe. ¿Conoce a la Consuelo, la que trabaja allí en "Torres Club"?

Tío: ¿La p—?

Primo: ¡Simón, la chavalona!

Tío: No, Guaro, yo ya no me meto en esas cosas.

Primo: No le hace. Mire vaya al Club, y le dice que me espere en un hora. Que el Eddie quiere hablar con ella, ¿me entiende?

Tío: ¿Y por qué no vas tú?

Primo: Porque yo me voy a traer el primo.

Tío: ¿Tu crees que lo va soltar su madre?

Primo: Simón, yo y la tía nos la llevamos suave. Si le digo que voy a llevar a Bernabé a hablar con Torres tocante un jale, no hay pedo. Me lo traigo. ¿Juega?

Tío: Pos que caray, 'ta bien pues. ¡Juega!

Primo: Entonces tenga, héchese unas cuantas heladas mientras nos espera.

Tío: ¡Ay chirrión! ¿qué los tengo que esperar?

Primo: ¿Qué no quiere ver a su sobrino contento?

Tío: ¿Cuál sobrino, tú o el menso aquél?

Primo:　No está ni tan menso, tío. Ya vera. Bueno, trucha pues. El Torres Club, ¿eh? Como a las nueve.

Tío:　¡Epa! Y como se llama la—

Primo:　Consuelo. Tiene unos chamarrotes.

Tío:　Pos sabrás tú, yo no.

Primo:　Orale pues, hay nos watchamos más tarde. I'm going to eat con la tía. [*Starts to exit.*]

Tío:　¡Oye! ¿Y si Bernabé no quiere . . . tú sabes?

Primo:　Entonces el favor es pa' usted, tío. [*Exit.*]

Tío [*Starts to exit*]:　¡Ja! Pa' mí . . . [*Stops. Reconsiders, tilts head, smiles.*] Consuelo, ¿eh? [*Exits.*]

Scene 3

[*Torres Club. Outside in the back alley. Bernabé comes out of the cantina with a beer can. The moon is bright.*]

Bernabé:　¿Tierra? Soy yo. Aquí estamos en el callejón. Hay 'ta la cantina de Torres. Mira—una cerveza. ¿Sabes qué? Mi primo fue y tapo el hoyo donde nos juntábamos solitos. Mi 'ama lo mando. Pero que le hace, ¿verdad? Son puras tablas. ¡Mañana se las quito! Alcabo aquí estás, y allí, y allá. Y aquí merito. 'Tamos juntos todo el tiempo. [*He kisses the earth.*]

[*Torres enters. Sees Bernabé, laughs to himself, shaking his head.*]

Torres:　¡Oye, oye, ya déjala pues!

Bernabé [*Startled*]:　¿Uh?

Torres [*Laughs*]:　No te asustes, loco. Soy yo. ¿Cómo está la novia, bien?

Bernabé:　Simón, bien. [*He rises.*]

Torres:　Fresquesita, ¿eh? Pos que suave. ¡Chichuahua, que calor está haciendo, hombre! Se bajo el sol y sigue lo noche caliente. ¿Qué haces aquí tan tarde?

Bernabé:　Nada.

Torres:　¿Y esa cerveza?

Bernabé:　Me la compro el primo. Veníamos a buscar jale.

Torres:　¿Y dónde está el Eddie? ¿Adentro?

Bernabé:　Hablando con Torres.

Torres:　Oh sí, ¿ch? ¿Y quién soy yo? ¿la luna?

Bernabé: Chale.

Torres: No, ¿verdad? Allá está arriba. Mira que grandotota se ve. ¿No estará celosa? La luna también es mujer, ¿eh? O a la mejor el El hermano de tu ruca. Cuidado, Bernabé, te la va quitar.

Bernabé: Pura madre, ¡nadien me la quita!

Torres: No te enojes pues.

Bernabé: ¡Es mïa!

Torres: Pos dile a los gabachos. A ver si te la entregan.

Bernabé: ¿Cuáles gabachos?

Torres: Los property owners, manito. Los dueños.

Bernabé: Ellos no son nada.

Torres [*Pause*] :   Oye, ¿y si yo quiero la tierra también, qué hago?

Bernabé: ¡Aguántate!

Torres: Pero es mi mamá.

Bernabé: ¿La tierra?

Torres: Pos luego. Es tu jefa también.

Bernabé: ¡La tuya! No es mi jefa.

Torres: Bueno, tu novia pues. Pero mira como la tratan estos rancheros, hombre. La venden cada ves que les da la gana. ¿Miras aquellos files allá? Apenas ayer los compré. Aquï también es mïo. Todos los lotes en esta calle. Y tengo más en el otro lado del barrio, fijate. Pero ¿sabés qué, loco? Te la rento. [*Laughs.*] Pásame lana y te presto la novia.

Bernabé: Oyes Torres, ¡tú estás más loco que yo! [*Laughs.*] Ah que Torres.

Tío [*Enters*] :   ¡Oye tú! ¿Dónde has estado?

Bernabé: Aquï.

Tío: ¿Pos qué traes, hombre? ¿Por qué te salites? [*Spots Torres.*] Oh, buenas noches, Señor Torres.

Torres: Buenas. ¿Qué hay, Teodoro?

Tío: No, nada, este loco. No sé ni pa' que me meti en ésto. Eddie lo Trajo para . . . hacerle un favor. Vamos pa' dentro, ándale. Ya tu primo subió con la vieja. Dijo que te prepares.

Torres: No, hombre. ¿lo van a meter con la Connie?

Tío: Pos sï, si quiere ella.

Torres: ¡Cómo no va querer! Si yo le digo, lo hace.

Tío: Ya está hablando con ella mi sobrino.

Torres: Te vas a rayar, ¿eh Bernabé?

Bernabé: Yo quiero otra birria.

Tío: Ya no hay.

Torres: Déjalo, hombre. Yo se la compro. Vénganse. Conque al fin te vas a casar, ¿eh loco? [*Goes out with Bernabé.*]

Tío: ¡Qué vergüenza! [*Exits.*]

Scene 4

[*Torres Club, upstairs, the hallway of a cheap hotel. Primo enters, his arm around Counsuelo.*]

Primo: Orale, Connie, gracias for doing me this favor, eh?

Consuelo: No es favor, oyes. Me vas a tener que pagar.

Primo: Simón, but the vato's muy especial, you know?

Consuelo: ¿Quién es?

Primo: Mi primo.

Consuelo: ¿Quién?

Primo: Bernabé.

Consuelo: You mean . . . ¿el loquito del pueblo? Sorry, Eddie, lo siento pero yo no.

Primo: ¿Por que no?

Consuelo: Because, porque no. Como sé lo que va hacer. Porque está loco, that's why.

Primo: He's not that loco, chula. Nomás necesita una quebrada.

Consuelo: Well, it's not me, man.

Primo: Mira, ésa, si no es gran cosa. Te pido que le hagas un favor al vato. Es mi primo—sure le falta una canica, but so what? He's got everything else. Andale, chula, nomás por un ratito. Ya le dije que lo ibas a livianar.

Consuelo [*Pause*]:   Dame quince y lo hago.

Primo: Fifteen bolas? Ni que fuera de oro. No, mira, Connie—don't be that way. Besides, todo lo que tengo son nueve grandes, toma. [*Gives her money.*]

Consuelo [*Takes it reluctantly*]:   Bueno, okay. Pero nomás una vuelta y ya'stufas. Where's the loco at?

Primo: Ahí viene con el tío—se hecharon una birria primero.

Consuelo: ¿Tío?

Primo: Teodoro.

Consuelo: ¿Ese winito's your tío?

Primo: Simón, y de bernabé también.

Consuelo: ¿Y no vino su mamá?

Primo: Chale, ¿qué tienes?

Consuelo: Naranjas corazón. Okay, send him in. [*She goes into her room.*]

Tío [*Offstage*]:   ¿Guaro?

Primo: Orale, tío, aquí.

Tío: ¡Hay viene el novio! Viene saboreándose. ¿Ta todo listo?

Primo: Simón.

Tío [*Enters*]:   ¡Híjole la chicharra, hombre! ya era tiempo. ¿On'ta la novia?

Primo: En su cuarto.

Tío: Ah, pos sí, ya lo conozco.

Primo: Se acuerda de sus tiempos, ¿eh tío?

Tío: Huy, ¿pa'que te digo, hombre? Sí yo estrene todo este hotel. Cada día de pago, no salía de aquí. Había unas cosotas aquí en esos tiempos.

Primo: ¿Y Bernabé?

Tío: ¿Pos no venía detrás . . . ? Sí, míralo, hay'stá. ¡Andale! oyes, no te escondas. ¡Vente!

Bernabé: ¿'Pa qué?

Tío: ¿'Pa qué? ¿Pos qué crees? Si aquí está la mera papá. ¿Tienes miedo?

Bernabé: ¡No!

Primo: Andale pues, ése, te está esperando la ruca.

Bernabé [*Enters*]:   ¿Dónde?

Primo: In there. Es la Connie, la que estaba en la barra. La watchates? ¿La petaquia que trai y la piernotas? [*Bernabé laughs.*] Simón que yes, ¿verdad? Ta guenota. Orale pues, métete. Te quiere dar algo.

Bernabé: ¿Qué?

Primo: Tú sabes, loco. [*Bernabé laughs lasciviously.*] Trucha pues, get in there.

[*Bernabé looks at his Primo and Tío. Then hesitantly starts toward Con-*

suelo's room. He reaches the door and is about to go in, when he stops suddenly and turns grinning idiotically.]

Bernabé: Chale.

Primo: Nel, primo, no te chivees. Todo está listo, ¡ándale!

Bernabé: No, me traga.

Tío: ¿Te traga?

Bernabé: La Luna. Por cochino.

Primo: Eso es puro cuento, primo. Tu watchastes a la Connie. ¿Apoco no te gusta?

Bernabé: Simón.

Primo: ¿Entonces?

Bernabé: 'Orita no.

Primo: ¿Porqué no?

Bernabé: No tengo ganas.

Tío: ¿Y no estabas tan listo en la barra?

Bernabé: Quiero otra birria primero.

Tío: Después.

Primo: Tienes que entra ahorita, primo. 'Te está esperando. Besides, ya le pague-20 bolas. ¿Okay?

Bernabé: Mejor no.

Tío: Pero que no oyes, hombre. Ya le pago a la vieja.

Bernabé: Me importa un pito. Yo no quiero esa vieja.

Tío: Bueno, si él no la quiere. [*Pause.*] No la quiere. Llévate el sonzo a la casa, y se acabó.

Consuelo [*At her door*]:   ¿Eddie? ¿Oye, Eddie? ¿Que pasó pues?

Primo: Nada.

Consuelo: Pos dile que se apure. [*She retreats into her room.*]

Primo: ¿Aves? Quiere que entres.

Tío: ¡Y que te apures!

Primo: Come on, ése. Yo sé que sí quieres.

Tío: Seguro que sí quiere. Ta guena la guerca ésa, hombre. Yo no me esperaría tanto.

Bernabé: Entonces métase Ud.

Tío: ¡No seas malcriado! Qué caray, yo ya no puedo con esas cosotas. Toma, héchate un traquito pa' que te de más fuerza. [*Gives Bernabé some beer.*]

Primo: Okay pues, adentro se ha dicho.

Tío: Sea hombre mijo.

[*Bernabé starts to move toward Consuelo's door again. Cautiously he is about to enter, but he stops and beats a retreat.*]

Bernabé: ¡Chale, no puedo!

Tío: ¡Me lleva la . . . que me trajo! Es un burro sin dueño este, hombre.

Primo: Simón, let's go pues.

Bernabé: ¿Pa ónde vamos?

Primo: Pa tu chante.

Bernabé: Nel, yo quiero pistiar.

Primo: Ya pistiamos.

Bernabé: Nomás una.

Tío: N'ombre, éste no quiere mujer. Lo que quiere es ponerse una peda. Vale más que te lo lleves, antes que se emborrache.

Bernabé: Yo no me voy a emborrachar oiga.

Primo: ¡Vámonos, Bernabé!

Bernabé: Nel, yo quiero quedarme aquí.

Tío: Tu madre te está esperando.

Bernabé: Me importa madre. Aquí también me 'stán esperando.

Tío: ¡Entonces métete!

Bernabé [*Pause*]: No . . . me traga.

Primo: Let's go, ése. [*Tries to pull him.*]

Bernabé: ¡No!

Tío: ¡Andale! ¡Agárralo! [*Primo and Tío grab Bernabé.*]

Bernabé: ¡No! ¡Noooo! ¡Quiero pistiar! ¡Quieroo una viejaaa! ¡Quieroo la tierraaa!

[*Consuelo comes out of her room.*]

Consuelo: Oye, oye, ¿what's happening, Eddie?

Primo: Nada. Ya nos vamos.

Consuelo: ¿Que pasó? No va entrar?

Primo: Chale.

Tío: Está safado.

Consuelo: ¿Que pasó, Bernabé? No quieres entrar conmigo. Ya me conoces,
   ¿qué no? Soy Consuelo—la Connie. Aver, dame un abrazo. Andale, hombre
   no te hagas pa'tras. Eddie me dice que te gustan las chavalonas. Is it true,
   ¿eh? Mira—dame tu brazo así . . . ahora lo ponemos aquí. Como novios ¿eh?
   ¿Quieres bailar? Tengo un record player en mi cuarto. Vente, vámonos al
   baile. [*She takes him to the door of her room.*] Y ustedes, ¿qué bobean
   ¡Píntense! ¿Qué no ven que ya nos vamos de honeymoon?

   [*Consuelo laughs and closes the door, pulling in Bernabé with her.*]

Primo: ¡Véngase, tío, le compro una birria!

Tío: ¡Ponle! [*They exit.*]

Scene 5

[*Consuelo's room. A brief silence, then Bernabé screams. Strobe light effect.
   Slow to fast.*]

Consuelo [*Offstage*]:   ¡Bernabé!

Bernabé: ¡Quítate!

Consuelo: Cállate, hombre, ¿qué tienes?

Bernabé: ¡No, mamá, yo no hice nadaaaa!

Consuelo: ¿Qué estás loco?

Bernabé: ¡Mamá! ¡Mamaaaá! [*Comes running out.*]

   [*Consuelo enters, but she looks like the Madre—or at least the Madre dressed
   in Consuelo's clothes. Strobe light flickering.*]

Madre [*As Consuelo*]:   ¿Qué tienes, hombre?

Bernabé: ¡No, nooooo! [*Backs off.*]

Madre: Ya pues, corazón. ¿Qué no quieres entrar conmigo? Soy tu novia.
   [*Changing character back to Madre.*] ¡Pero también soy tu madre y te voy
   a pegar! ¡Por cochino! ¡Vente! ¡Métete al cuarto!

Bernabé: ¡Noooo!

Madre [*Back to Consuelo*]:   ¿Por qué no, honito? ¡Andale! Ya me conoces,
   ¿qué no? Soy Consuelo, la Connie. Eddie me dice que te gustan las
   chabalonas. [*Back to Madre.*] ¡Y por éso te voy a pegar! Soy tu madre,
   y tengo el derecho de castigarte mientras Dios me preste vida! ¿Quieres
   que te trague la tierra? ¡Vente conmigo!

Bernabé: ¡No, noo, no quierooo! ¡Déjeme!

[*Madre drags Bernabé, but he pushes her back into the room. (Lights up. Strobe light gone.) Eddie, Torres, and El Tío come rushing in.*]

Primo: ¿Qué pasa, primo?

Torres: ¿Oye, Connie? ¿Qué parranda se cargan aquí pues?

[*Consuelo comes back in as herself. Bernabé screams.*]

Consuelo: ¡Torres! Get him out of here! ¡Sáquenlo!

Primo: What happen, chula?

Consuelo: ¡I don't know what happen! Está loco, ¿qué no ves?

Bernabé: ¡Yo no hice nada!

Torres: Did he go in at least?

Primo: Sure, he went in.

Tío: Se metió bien contento.

Consuelo [*To Eddie*]:   ¡Te dije, Eddie, te dije!

Primo: Vente, primo. Vámonos pa' tu chante.

Bernabé: ¡No! ¡Nooo! [*Cries out in horror.*] ¡Me pega! ¡Me pega, me pega!

Primo: ¿Quién te pega?

Bernabé [*Points at Consuelo*]:   Mi 'amá.

Tío: ¡Esa no es tu madre, suato!

Consuelo: See what I mean? [*Bernabé screams.*]

Torres: No le hables, mensa.

Consuelo: ¿Y tú, baboso? ¡Todo ésto es tu culpa! ¿Tú crees que me gusta hacer ésto?

Torres: ¡Cállate!

Consuelo: ¿Apoco no me quitas el dinero?

Torres: ¡Métete a tu cuarto! [*He pushes her.*]

Bernabé: ¡No, nooo! ¡Mamá! [*Rushes Torres.*]

Primo: ¡Bernabé, cálmala!

Tío: ¡Estate quieto!

Torres: ¡Sáquenlo pa' fuera!

Primo: We're trying, boss!

Consuelo: ¿Por qué no lo sacas tú, Torres?

Torres: I told you to shut up! [*Pushes her into the room.*]

Bernabé: ¡No, déjala! ¡Déjala!

[*Bernabé leaps on Torres. Primo and Tío try to take him off. Bernabé is crying as he beats on Torres.*]

Primo [*Trying to remove Bernabé*] :   ¡Primo!

Tío: ¡Bernabé!

Bernabé: ¡Es mía! ¡Mi mujer es mía!

Torres: ¡Quítenlo! ¡Get him off of me!

[*Consuelo laughs. Bernabé is hysterical, totally out of it. Primo and Tío succeed on pulling him off Torres.*]

Bernabé: ¡Lo maté! ¡Maté a Torres!

[*Bernabé runs out. Tío starts to run after him. Primo helps Torres to his feet. Consuelo is still laughing.*]

Tío: ¡Bernabé! ¡Vent pa'trás! Bernabé!

Primo: You okay, boss?

Torres: ¡Pos luego! Let me go.

Tío [*To Eddie*] :   ¡Oye! El loco arranco pa' fuera. ¿Se va y le dice a su madre?

Primo: I don't understand what happen to him. ¿Qué le hicites?

Consuelo: Don't ask me, man! No es mi culpa si piensa que soy su mamá.

Tío: ¡Vámonos, Guaro! ¡Se nos va perder!

Primo: Orale, let's go. Sorry, Torres. [*They exit.*]

[*Consuelo and Torres are left behind. Consuelo looks at Torres and starts laughing. A deep bitter laugh, not with a certain satisfaction. She exits into her room.*]

Torres: Go you damn whore. [*Exits.*]

Scene 6

[*El Llano. Night. There is a full moon, unseen, but casting an eery light on the earth. Bernabé is at his pozo, pulling off the boards.*]

Bernabé [*Crying out*] :   ¡Tierra! ¡Maté a Torres! ¡Hijo 'e su tiznada madre, lo maté! [*Pause. Listens for sound.*] Vale más 'sconderme. [*Stops. Fearfully looks at sky, sees moon.*] ¡La luna! ¡Hay viene, ayyy! ¡'Amá, la lunaaaa!

[*Bernabé sobs like a terrified child. Moonlight gathers into a spot focussed on him. Music. La Luna enters, dressed like a Pachuco, 1945 style: Zoot suit, drapes, calcos, hat with feather, small chain, etc.*]

La Luna: Orale pues, ese vato. No te escames. Soy yo, la Luna.

Bernabé [*Wrapping himself into a ball*]:   ¡No, Chale!

La Luna: Control, ése. ¿Qué no eres Chicano? Eres vato loco.

Bernabé [*Looks up slowly*]:   Yo no soy loco.

La Luna: Oh, simón. No lo dije así, carnal. Te estaba cabuliando. Huacha, si no les gusta, pus no te aguitas porque dicen que estás loco, ése. Que tengan pa' que se mantengan. Consafos, putos. Adentro tu sabes que eres Chicano, me entiendes como.

Bernabé: Simón.

La Luna: Pos a toda madre. [*Pause. Reaches into his pocket.*] Oye, ¿no le haces a la grifa? Orale, héchate un tocazo. ¿Traes trolas? Toma. [*Lights joint for Bernabé.*] Alivian el esqueleto, carnal. Yo y tu nos vamos a poner bien locos tonight. Hay te llevo. [*Grabs joint from Bernabé.*] No le aflojes. [*Bernabe gets joint again.*] Ese, ¿miras aquellas estrellas? —hay unas más guenotas. . . . [*Laughs with Bernabé.*] Oye, te huache entrar al Torres Club con tu primo. ¿Cómo te fue?

Bernabé [*Guilty*]:   Bien.

La Luna: Simón, esa Connie es una mamasota, carnal. Pero dime, a la bravota—¿por qué le tubites miedo? [*Bernabé throws joint down.*] No, Chale, no me digas pues. No me importa. Toma, no te aguites. [*Gives him back the joint.*] Oye, Bernabé, ¿sabes qué? Traigo un pedo que averiguar contigo. Se trata de mi carnala.

Bernabé: ¿Tu carnala?

La Luna: Simón, ¿qué te traes con ella?

Bernabé: Nada.

La Luna: No te hagas pendejo, ése. Los huacho juntitos casi casi todas las noches. ¿Me entiendes cómo? Ella me dijo que bajara a periquiar contigo. Se quiere casar loco.

Bernabé: ¿Casar?

La Luna: Contigo. Me la rayo. Huacha, dejame llamarle. Oye, sister, vente, aquí te esperan.

[*Music accompanies the entrance of La Tierra. She emerges from the Pozo. She appears as a soldadera with cartridge belts. Bernabé is spellbound the moment he sees her. Pause. She stares at Bernabé.*]

La Tierra: ¿Quién es?

La Luna: ¿Pos quién? Tu vato loco. Bernabé, ésta es mis carnala, La Tierra.

La Tierra: Buenos noche Bernabé. [*Bernabé makes a slight grunt, smiling idiotically.*] ¿Qué no me conoces?

[*Pause. Bernabé is speechless, embarrassed.*]

La Luna: Orale pues, carnal, dile algo. ¿Apoco le tienes miedo a tu novia?

[*Bernabé struggles to say something. His mind tries to form words. He ends up starting to laugh moronically, from helplessness.*]

La Tierra [*Sharply*]: ¡No, hombre, no te rías! Háblame en serio. Soy la Tierra.

[*Bernabé stares at her. A sudden realization strikes him and turns into fear. He screams and runs.*]

La Luna: ¿Epale, pa' ónde vas, loco? [*He stops Bernabé with a wave of his arm.*] Cálmala, no te tienes que escamar. [*Pulls him toward Tierra.*] Mira a mi carnala, mira que a toda madre se huacha en la moonlight. Te quiere, ¿verdad sister?

La Tierra: Sí es macho.

[*Bernabé is caught in a strange spell. He and La Tierra look at each other for a long moment. La Luna gets restless.*]

La Luna: Bueno, le dijo la mula al freno. ¿Saben qué? Yo voy ir a darme una pasiadita. A ver lo que 'stán chismiando las estrellas. Oye, Bernabé, te cuidas con mi hermana, ¿eh? Llévensela suaves pues.

[*La Luna exits.*]

La Tierra [*Softly*]: ¿Dé que piensas, Bernabé?

Bernabé [*Struggling to say something*]: Maté a Torres.

La Tierra [*Pushing him down*]: ¡H'm que pelado éste! ¿Qué no estabas pensando de mí? No te pares el cuello oyes. Torres no está muerto.

Bernabé: ¿Todavía 'stá vivo?

La Tierra: Pos luego, ¿apoco lo ibas a matar con las manos? Ahorita se está riendo de tí.

Bernabé: ¿Por qué?

La Tierra: Porque me quieres pero no soy tuya. Soy de él.

Bernabé: ¡Cale, eres mía!

La Tierra: ¿Y cómo soy tuya, Bernabé? ¿Cómo y cuándo has luchado por mí? Toda tu vida has trabajado en mis files como un perro ¿y para qué? Para que otros se hagan ricos con tu sudor, para que otros hombres sean mis duenos. Torres me tiene a mi, Bernabé—¿qué es lo que tienes tú? Nada ¿verdad? [*Pause. Bernabé's head is down.*] Mírame, hombre Soy la Tierra. ¿Me quieres de deveras? Porque si tu amor es verdadero entonces yo quiero ser tu mujer. [*Bernabé reaches out to embrace her.*] Pero no tan pronto, pelado. No soy Consuelo, ¿sabes? Si deveras me quieres, tendrás que pelear como los machos. ¿Qué no sabes nada? Muchos hombres han muerto nomás por tenerme. Edes capaz de matar a los que me tienen . . . ¿y no me aman Bernabé?

Bernabé: ¿Matar?

La Tierra: A mis dueños. Entonces seré tuya y harás lo que quieras conmigo. Seré tu mujer. . . . [*She lies down.*] Serás mi esposo.

[*Bernabé goes to her. He lies down beside her and is almost going to embrace her, when La Luna comes back in.*]

La Luna: ¡Orale, párenle ahí! [*Comes over to Bernabé and La Tierra.*] ¿Qué pasa pues, carnal? ¿Qué no te dije que te huacharas con mi hermana? ¿Qué estaban haciendo, eh?

Bernabé [*Rises*]:   ¿Qué te importa?

[*La Tierra rises and stands to one side, observing silently.*]

La Luna: Oye, derepente estás muy bravo.

Bernabé: ¡Vale más que te vayas, Luna!

La Luna: ¡Vale más que no, carnal!

Bernabé: ¡Vete!

La Luna: ¡Míralo, míralo! Muy machote. ¿Qué le hicistes, ésa?

Bernabé: ¡Lárgate! [*Pushes Luna.*]

La Luna: Heh, man, no te caldees. Soy tu camarada, ¿te acuerdas? Casi tu cuñado.

La Tierra: ¡Luna! Déjalo, pobrecito. No estaba haciendo nada.

La Luna: Pura madre, no lo conoces.

La Tierra: Sí lo conozco. Desde el día que nació. Es inocente Es bueno.

Aunque otros se burlan de él. Siempre ha venido a mis brazos buscando mi calor. Lo quiero con un amor intenso que tú no puedes imaginar. Pues tú eres hombre, yo soy mujer. . . . Soy Madre.

La Luna: Simón, que le dije—pura madre.

La Tierra [*Pause*] : Pero también virgen. ¡Déjanos solos!

La Luna: Nel, sister. Primero me dicen que movida se traen. ¿Se van a casar o qué?

La Tierra: Eso depende en Bernabé.

La Luna: ¿Qué dices, loco? ¿Te quieres ranar con mi carnala?

Bernabé: Simón.

La Luna: Pendejo.

La Tierra: ¿Satisfecho?

La Luna: Chale. Todavía necesitan la bendición del Jefe.

La Tierra: Si lo va ha dar.

La Luna: Pos ojalá. Primero tiene que conocer a Bernabé.

Bernabé: ¿Quién?

La Luna: Su papa, loco, mi jefito. El Sol.

Bernabé: ¡Sol!

La Luna: Ya mero llega. Huacha. Está amaneciendo. ¿Sabes qué, ése? Vale más que me dejes hablar primero. Yo y el jefe nos la llevamos suave. Si le digo que eres un Chicano, un camarada mío.

La Tierra: No, Luna.

La Luna: ¿Qué?

La Tierra: El tiene boca. Déjalo que se defienda sólo.

La Luna: Orale, no hay pedo. Pero tu conoces al jefito.

La Tierra: Le vas a tener que pedir mi mano, Bernabé. Si deveras me quieres, no le tendrás miedo a mi papa. Háblale con respeto, pero también con valor. No aguanta a los cobardes.

La Luna: ¡Alalba! ¡Ahí viene! No le mires mucho en la cara, ése. ¡Te ciega!

[*La Tierra and La Luna kneel before the place when the sun is rising. Indígena music: majestic flutes and drums. El Sol rises in the guise of Tonatiuh, the Aztec sun god. He speaks in a resounding voice.*]

La Sol: Buenos días, mis hijos.

La Tierra: Buenos días, papa.

La Luna: Buenos días jefe.

La Sol: Luna. ¿Cómo va mi pleito con las estrellas? ¿Cuidaste mi cielo por toda la noche?

La Luna: Sí, jefe, todo está bien.

La Sol: ¿Y tu hermana? ¿La cuidaste a ella?

La Luna: Sí, señor. ¡Cómo no!

La Sol: ¡Pues como. . . . ¡CALLATE!

La Tierra: ¿Apa?

La Sol: Si mija, ¿cómo estás?

La Tierra: Bien papá.

La Sol: ¿Y toda tu humanidad, esa plaga de infelices mortales que son tus hijos? ¿Siguen todavía con sus avaricias? su envidias? ¿su miedo a la muerte?

La Tierra: Sí, Tata. [*To Bernabé.*] Dale.

Bernabé: ¿Señor! [*Pause.*] Señor de los cielos.

La Sol: ¿Quién me llama?

Bernabé: Soy yo, señor. Aquí abajo.

La Sol: ¿Quién eres tú?

Bernabé: Bernabé.

La Sol: ¿Qué? ¡Mírame!

Bernabé: Bernabé. Vengo a pedirle algo, señor.

La Sol: ¿Qué es?

Bernabé: La Tierra.

La Sol: ¿Mija?

Bernabé: Pa' mi esposa.

La Sol [*Pause*]:   Han pasado muchos años, Bernabé, desde que los hombres se acuerdan quien es el padre de la tierra. En verdad, muy pocos han tenido el valor de pedirme la mano de mija como es debido. ¿Por qué vienes tú?

Bernabé: Soy hombre, señor.

La Sol: ¿Y qué me importa a mí?

Bernabé: La quiero.

La Sol: Muchos hombres la han querido. ¿Apoco crees que eres el primero? Mírala, Bernabé, ésta es la Tierra que ha sido tantas cosas para los hombres: madre, prostituta, mujer. ¿Qué no te da miedo?

Bernabé: No, señor, ¿de qué?

La Sol: De su padre, desgraciado, ¡El Sol!

[*There is a terrifying flash of light and sound. Bernabé runs and hides.*]

La Sol: ¡Miralo, corriendo como un cobarde!   ¡Malora!   ¡Debo de matarte por lo que tu gente le ha hecho a mija!

Bernabé: ¡No fuí yo, señor!

La Tierra: ¡Por favor, Tata, es inocente!

La Luna: Es cierto, Jefe, el vato es Chicano. ¡Nunca ha tenido tierra!

La Sol [*Pause*] :   ¿En qué trabajas, Bernabé?

Bernabé: Trabajo en los files.

La Sol: ¿Eres pobre?

Bernabé: Sí, señor.

La Sol: ¿Entonces comó piensas cuidar a mija?   ¡No tienes dinero!   ¡No tienes poder!

Bernabé: Señor, yo no soy nadie. En el pueblo, la gente dice que estoy loco. Pero sé una cosa, que los ricos están más locos que yo. Venden a la Tierra todo el tiempo, en pedacitos aquí y allá, pero no se puede vender así porque es toda una cosa. Como una mujer, no se debe vender, ¿no?   Es lo que pienso, señor. Si alguien le ha hecho daño a la tierra no son los pobres, son los hombres con dinero y poder. Yo nomás quiero a la Tierra.

La Luna: ¡Orale, te aventates, ése!

La Sol: Dices bien. [*Pause.*] :   Ahora sí entiendo quien eres, Bernabé. Eres el último y el primero. El último de un gran noble linaje de hombres que conocí en tiempos antiguos; y el primero de la raza nueva de los siglos que heredará La Tierra para todos. Tu cara es memoria cósmica, Bernabé: me recuerda de una humanidad entera, de tus mismos ojos, tu piel, tu sangre. Ellos también querían a La Tierra y honraban a su Padre sobre todo lo demás. Eran mis hijos. Penetraron el cerebro humano y las estrellas y encontraron el fuego hambriento que se traga así mismo. Descubrieron lo que ahora sólo un loco comprende; que la vida es muerte, y la muerte es vida. Que la vida no vale nada porque vale todo. Que eres uno, para que seas dos, dos para que seas cuatro, y luego ocho, y entonces diez y seis, y así hasta que eres millones, billones; y luego te vas nuevamente a tu centro y encuentras . . . nada, y entonces llenas el espacio de nada con uno otra vez. ¿Me comprendes, Bernabé?   ¡Tenían el poder del Sol!   [*Pause.*] Si te casas con mija, tendrás este poder. Y serás mi Hijo. ¿Tierra, deveras quieres a este hombre?

La Tierra: Sí, papá.

La Sol: Bernabé, ¿deveras quieres a La Tierra?

Bernabé: Con todo el corazón.

La Sol: ¿Corazón? No, hijo, no con tu corazón. Puedes amarla con tu cuerpo, tu sangre, tu semilla, pero tu corazón me lo daras a mí. ¿Estás listo para morir?

Bernabé: ¡Morir!

La Sol: ¡Para vivir!

[*Bernabé is momentarily stunned and confused. He looks at La Luna and La Tierra, but they say nothing.*]

Bernabé: No quiero morir.

La Sol: Hijo, te ofrezco el poder del Sol. Has sido nada, ahora lo serás todo. Yo soy el comienzo y el fin de todas las cosas. Creed en mí y nunca morirás. ¿Me das tu corazón?

Bernabé: Sí, señor.

La Sol: Que sea así.

[*Bernabe is sacrificed. La Tierra and La Luna lay his body out.*]

La Sol: Bernabé, ¡levántate!

[*Bernabé rises.*]

La Sol: ¡De aquí en adelante serás un nuevo hombre, y tú me ayudarás a conquistar las estrellas! [*Bernabé walks erect.*] Bernabé, la Tierra es virgen y tuya. Sean felizes.

La Tierra: ¡Bernabé!

[*Bernabé and La Tierra embrace.*]

La Luna: Orale. ¡Felicitaciones, ése!   ¡A toda madre!

La Sol: Silencio pues. [*Pause.*] Ya el día se está muriendo. Ha llegado la hora de despedirme. Mis hijos, los dejo con mi bendición. [*Blesses them.*] Luna, cuida mi cielo durante la noche obscura, y dale luz a tu hermana, ¿eh?

La Luna: Sí, jefe, como siempre.

La Sol: Bueno, me voy pues. Bernabé, Tierra, tengan hijos . . . muchos hijos. [*Starts to sink.*]

La Tierra: Buenas noches, papá.

La Luna: Buenas noches, jefe.

Bernabé: Buenas noches, señor.

La Sol [*Sinking fast*]:   Buenas noches . . . Bernabé. [*He is gone.*]

[*There is a silence. La Tierra shivers, then Bernabé and La Luna.*]

La Tierra: Como hace frío.

La Luna: Simón, se fue el jefito. Vale más subirme a mi chante yo también. Orale, novios, ¿qué clase de moonlight quieran? ¿Una luz muy romantic y de aquellas?

La Tierra: No importa, nomás vete.

La Luna.   Mírala, mírala, nomás porque ya se casó otra vez.

Bernabé: Mira, hermano, no andes con insultos. Si antes fuí loco, ahora soy un hombre y la Tierra es mi mujer.

La Luna: Okay, 'ta bien pues. Me tengo que ir al jale de todos modos. [*Looks up.*] Méndigas estrellas, te apuesto que ya traen ansias de meterse al territorio del Jefe. Vale más chequear. Buenas noches pues y llévensela bien suave, ¿eh?

[*La Luna exits.*]

La Tierra: ¿Bernabé? [*She has her back to him.*]

Bernabé: ¿Qué?

La Tierra: Me vas a querer siempre?

Bernabé: Siempre.

La Tierra: ¿Hasta la muerte? [*She turns. Her face is a death mask.*]

Bernabé: Hasta la muerte. [*They embrace.*]

Scene 7

[*Bernabé's house. El Tío comes in quickly, looking over his shoulder. The Madre is at the door of her house.*]

Madre: ¿Teodoro, que pasó? ¿Hallaron a mijo?

Tío: ¿Qué andas haciendo aquí en la calle, hermanita? ¡Métete a la casa, ándale!

Madre: ¿Pa'qué, para mortificarme más?

Tío: ¡El sol está muy caliente!

Madre: No le hace. ¿Qué pasó con mijo? [*Pause.*] ¿Que pasó pues, hombre? ¿Lo hallaron? Mendigo wino, ¿de qué sirves? Bernabé es tu sobrino, pero ni te apura, ¿verdad? Que no te dije que fueras a ver si estca en el pozo.

[*Pause.*] Sí fuistes, verdad? Sabes algo. ¿Qué pasó, hombre? Ay, Teodoro, hay vienen unos hombres. ¡Eduardo viene con ellos! Traen alquién. ¡Bendito sea Dios! [*She starts to run forward.*]

Tío: ¡Quédate aquí, hermanita!

Madre: ¡No, déjame ir! ¡Déjame ir! ¡Es mijo! Sí sabes algo, ¿verdad? ¡Qué pasó! ¡qué pasó!

Tío: Está muerto.

Madre: ¡Ay! [*Gasps. Can't get breath.*]

Tío: Lo hallamos enterrado.

[*A Group of men bring in Bernabé's body. They lay him down. Now the Madre releases a long, sorrowful cry as she leans over Bernabé.*]

Madre: ¡Mijo! ¡Mijito!

Primo [*To one side*]:   It's all my fault, Tío. Fue toda mi culpa.

Tío: No, hijo, no te culpes. Lo querías ayudar. Esto fue por la voluntad de Dios.

[*Freeze.*]

La Raza Pura, or Racial, Racial

RUBÉN SIERRA

Rubén Sierra, a native of San Antonio, Texas, graduated from St. Mary's University with a B. A. degree in drama in 1970. A recipient of a teaching assistantship at the University of Washington (Seattle), he is presently working on an advanced degree in drama at this institution where he is also director of the *Teatro del Piojo*. His dramatic works include *Manolo, The Conquering Father* and *La Raza Pura, or Racial, Racial*. One of his musical variety shows, *Kavalcade of Entertainment*, appeared over KENS-TV (San Antonio, Texas.)

La Raza Pura, or Racial, Racial has been performed several times by St. Mary's University Shoestring Players. This play is presented in 27 vignette scenes which are highly characterized by the use of film and slides.

La Raza Pura, or Racial, Racial is a satirical comedy on the contention that a 'pure race' exists in America. It is because of this belief that prejudice (whether it may be racial, cultural, social, etc.) has become an established and accepted norm in American society. As such, the topic of prejudice and its manifestations is dramatized in this play by depicting the conflict that an Anglo girl and a Mexican-American boy face when they fall in love.

Characters

Agent I	Carlos
Agent II	Bartender
Agent III	Bob
Secretary	Black
Girl	Tri-Colored Girl
Jenny	Irving
Jorge	Darcy
Mrs. Smyth	Stanley Martin
Jenny's Father	Man
Jenny's Mother	Felipe
Billy	Juan
Ralph	Black
Chicano Man	Enrique
Norma	Frank Gomez
Albert	Miss Ruby Bagoonya
Fernando	Miss Garcia
Jim	Miss Gypsy Belle

[*The play takes place in the present or near future. There are several levels of action in* LA RAZA PURA: *1) Film, slides, and soundtracks which are by themselves scenes within the play help to make a statement, set up the action, or comment on the action. 2) ALL-PURPOSE RACIAL AGENCY, a fictional creation of the author for exaggerating and examining just where racial and ethnic prejudice can lead. 3) The real world as we know it, filled with hypothetical situations which given the time and place could and often do happen. The action of the play must be smooth and well timed, and one scene should lead into the other as quickly and as honestly as possible.*]

Scene 1

[*Outside the entrance to the theatre there should be a big sign that reads ALL-PURPOSE RACIAL AGENCY, and the ushers should be dressed in blue blazers with a patch reading the same as the sign. Inside the theatre the decorations should suggest a "fiesta": several pinatas, lots of streamers, Mexican music, and bright colors. Each member of the audience should receive a newsletter, containing a description of every member of the cast, along with various articles and news stories dealing*

61

*with ALL-PURPOSE RACIAL AGENCY. After the audience is seated
and awaits in expectation, there is a quick succession of three gunshots
coming from behind them. At the same time the music stops and the
house goes completely black; we hear a woman scream and voices shouting: "There he goes . . .! Get him . . .!" At the end of this, which should
only last a few seconds, a movie projector starts in a timed sequence with
music, which should be on tape and fed to the audience through four
speakers in each corner of the theatre.*]

Scene 2

[*The stage is divided into three sections: the middle section should be ele-
vated about three feet higher than the other two, and it should have a
large screen as a backdrop visible to the entire audience. The acting area
should have one chair and one desk with a small sign reading RENT-A-
RACE. The other two sections of the stage should have plain walls and
be flexible enough to permit bringing scenery on and off with as little
delay as possible. This scene consists of a film sequence from three to
four minutes in length using either super 8 or 16 mm film. The film can
be selected by the director; however, it should have the following: In an
opening shot a Chicano, overcome with fear and perspiring heavily, is in
an open field, when suddenly he begins running. The camera fades into
a group of men armed with rifles; they are chasing a human prey, the
Chicano (the group can consist of blacks, whites, and others but should
not have any Chicanos). The chase continues until the Chicano is captured and surrounded by the armed men (if there is a stream of water
available, a shot of the water being hit by bullets is effective to show
these men want him dead or alive). As the men surround the Chicano,
a series of three slides with the caption LA RAZA PURA on them
should be superimposed on the screen (this can easily be done by taking
a slide and punching out the title with a simple straight pin; the slides
can be of your choice but the Alamo would serve nicely). In order to
get the maximum effect from the film it should be accompanied with
music such as a piece from "A Few Dollars More."*]

Scene 3

[*This is another film sequence lasting two to three minutes which begins
immediately after the end of the first film. This film should contain
the different faces and places of the poor sections of the city; it should
be well edited and to the point. In order to capture the reality of people
the camera should go into the poverty areas and places of business where*

there are various types of people and things to see. Take shots of people
doing their own thing without being aware of the camera. (Take at least
three times as much film as you will actually use in the theatre during
the play.)]

Scene 4

[As the film ends the lights come up on the middle part of the stage. Seated
behind the desk is a man dressed in a blue blazer and tie with a patch on
the blazer reading ALL-PURPOSE RACIAL AGENCY. He is the typical
young salesman type, deadly serious about his work. On the desk are
papers and a sign reading RENT-A-RACE. A young secretary enters and
approaches Agent I; she has a pad and pencil in her hand and is dressed
in a miniskirt. When she speaks she has a deep Southern accent; she
speaks slowly and as sexy as possible. The agent is articulate and is interested in as much money as he can get by exploiting people.]

Secretary: Sir! [He is startled.] Excuse me, sir.

Agent I: Yes. What is it?

Secretary: The scenes that you wanted for the convention tomorrow between
the Anglo boy and the Chicana girl are ready for your approval.

Agent I: Oh, yes, the scene! Very well, let's have a look at it, and I hope it's
improved from yesterday's mess. This scene is for some very important
clients and I can't afford to have them disappointed. I want results—good,
positive, processed results!

Secretary: I believe they're ready, sir?

Agent I.   But you're not sure?

Secretary: You could probably judge that better than I, sir.

Agent I: In this business you've got to know! No matter what your position
is in this company you must be sure of what you're doing; there's no room
for second guessing. We deal with people, all kinds of people of different
races, colors and cultures, so you must be sure of what you're doing. Do
you understand?

Secretary: Yes sir! Central Headquarters was very explicit on that point during my training period.

Agent I: And what happened?

Secretary: I guess I forgot, sir. I won't let it happen again, I promise!

Agent I: Good! The **ALL-PURPOSE RACIAL AGENCY** needs people who

won't forget, and if they do and do it often, then we just have to make
room for somebody else. How do you think I made it to where I am today?
Because I was tough and I knew people and I knew what made them tick
and how easy it was to make a buck off of them. An honest buck, of course.

Secretary: Of course.

Agent I: Well, we musn't keep Agent III and the girl waiting any longer,
should we?

Secretary: No sir! [*Pause.*] And thank you, sir, for being so helpful.

Agent I: Don't mention it! Oh, and how about dinner at my place, say about
sevenish?

Secretary: Yes sir! [*She exits and lights come up on stage left.*]

Agent I [*Watching secretary as she walks away swaying back and forth*]:   Ah,
jes! Juicy little morsel.

[*On stage left is Agent III, an Anglo in his midtwenties, and a girl who re-
sembles a Chicana, also in her midtwenties; they are acting out a scene
very seriously and straightforward.*]

Girl: I want to very much, but it isn't possible.

Agent III [*Taking her hand*]:   I don't see why it has to be! We've known
each other for over three years; that ought to mean something, shouldn't
it?

Girl: It's not that! It's because of my parents.

Agent III: Oh! They won't accept me because I'm an Anglo. Does it bother
you?

Girl: I wouldn't date you if it did!

Agent I: Wait a minute! It's got to be more soap-opera-ish! That's what sells!
You're not fooling anybody playing it so seriously! You've got to get to
the meat of the matter; that's where it counts! Boy meets girl, she's different
but they still fall in love, then the parents step in and break it off, simple
and succinct! It's an ethnic problem, not Romeo and Juliet! The scene has
got to be real, but the audience must not know that; you've got to fool
them as best you can! I want to give our clients their money's worth; like
feeding a baby, you give him a little, he likes it and he comes back for more.
Okay? Let's do it from the top!

Agent III: Excuse me, sir?

Agent I: Yes, Three, what is it?

Agent III: I've done lots of crazy things since I've been working for the ALL-
PURPOSE RACIAL AGENCY, but why this?

Agent I: Money! That's why! Let me tell you something you may or may not know, and that is that people are funny sometimes, kind of stupid actually. At times they want to see things as they are, but as times they want to make believe. What we're trying for our audience is to give them a situation which doesn't happen in everyday life, an Anglo falling in love with a Chicana. Not very likely, and even if it did happen it probably wouldn't be accepted anyway, not by the Chicanos and surely not by the Anglos. So we depict the situation like it might be if it did happen, and we have a little fun and make a little money, simple as that.

Agent III: Yes, sir, I understand: in a way you're saying prejudice can be rewarding—financially.

Agent I: Now you've got the idea!

Girl: Can we get on with the scene; it's getting late and I've got a bus to catch.

Agent I: By all means, and if you do a good job, tomorrow I'll throw in a little bonus for both of you. [*He smiles and exits.*]

[*Agent III and the girl repeat the scene, but this time they exaggerate their lines and actions, melo-dramatic to the nth degree.*]

Girl: [*Bringing hand to forehead*] I want to very much, but it isn't possible!

Agent III [*Taking her hand and placing it on his heart*] :   I don't see why it has to be? We've known each other for over three years; that ought to mean something, shouldn't it?

Girl [*Giving him her back*] :   It's not that! It's because . . . because of my parents!

Agent III [*Hanging his head*] :   Oh! They won't accept me because I'm an Anglo! [*Grasping her hands and bringing her to him.*] It doesn't bother you, does it?

Girl [*Pulling him closer*] :   I wouldn't date you if it did!

[*As they embrace there is a black out.*]

Scene 5

[*As soon as we go into black out the projector and music begin, and we see another film sequence lasting approximately three to four minutes. In this film for the first time we see Jenny, an Anglo girl, and Jorge, a Chicano boy; they are in their early twenties. This film should be shot somewhere in a park with trees and grass and possibly a fountain or brook with running water. Several shots show the couple as they meet and begin to discuss what takes place in the following scene. Ideally it*

should be a sunny day, and the camera should capture some close-ups
and also some slow-motion shots of both the boy and the girl.]

Scene 6

[*As the film finishes, the lights come up on stage right where there on a*
bench is Jenny; she appears upset and worried about something. Jorge
enters.]

Jorge: Jenny!

Jenny [*Turning to Jorge*] :   Jorge, I'm glad you came.

Jorge: What's the matter?

Jenny [*Motioning beside her*] :   Sit down! [*He sits and she takes his hand.*]
You know how I feel about you Jorge. I'd do anything for you—you know
that?

Jorge: And I'd do the same!

Jenny: Yes, I know. [*Pause.*] How long have we known each other?

Jorge: Since junior high, why?

Jenny: That's a long time for two people, isn't it?

Jorge: I suppose. But what are you getting at?

Jenny: It's my parents. I don't know what to do anymore!

Jorge: What do you mean?

Jenny: You know how they've been against us seeing each other, ever since
we were kids.

Jorge: So what?

Jenny: My father especially. I don't know why but that's just the way he is.

Jorge: Whatever you're trying to tell me, I can tell it's not going to be something I want to hear.

Jenny: And it's something I don't want to say.

Jorge: Well, then don't!

Jenny: They've forbidden me from seeing you anymore.

Jorge [*Standing up*] :   And?

Jenny: That's just it. What am I going to do? Go against my parents and
sneak around behind them and continue to see you till I run out of lies to
tell them. What do I do?

Jorge: But I love you, Jenny!

Jenny: I love you! But it doesn't make it any easier for me because I love my parents also, and I don't want to hurt them.

Jorge: Aw, Jenny! What can I say?

Jenny: I want them to accept you and understand you, not to hate you!

Jorge: I don't want them to hate me either, but I don't want to lose their daughter no matter what it takes.

Jenny: What are we going to do?

Jorge: What if we wait awhile, and see what happens—maybe things will work themselves out. My parents left it up to me. Though they're not too crazy about the idea of me falling for a "gringa," they still don't want to stand in my way. Chances are your parents will see things out a little differently than they do now, if we wait.

Jenny: That's not good enough. You know my dad's a redneck from the word go! That's just the way he is, the way he was brought up.

Jorge: So what makes you so different, "gringa"?

Jenny: Some crazy "wetback" Chicano I know, who just swept me off my feet with that latin-lover approach. [*Laughing.*] I've been corrupted ever since; I've seen the light!

Jorge: You know for being so intelligent you sure have a stupid father!

Jenny: Jorge!

Jorge: Just kidding; not stupid, just a little dumb.

Jenny: And you're so smart?

Jorge: I fell in love with you, didn't I?

Jenny: With logic like that who can argue? [*They embrace and kiss. After a moment Jenny pulls away.*] You make me feel so happy, Jorge!

Jorge: I hope so!

Jenny: So what, now?

Jorge: Well, you could marry me!

Jenny: Yes, I could, but it wouldn't solve the problem; it would only make it worse.

Jorge [*Sitting down on bench*]: When I was a kid, I used to tell myself I would never marry anybody but a Chicano, no matter what. So what happened to that firm conviction? I don't know. That's all I can say, I don't know. I used to hate the Anglo because I blamed him for the suppression that the Chicano had faced for hundreds of years and is still facing. But it's bigger than that. It goes much further than just the Anglo; it's society and what it's done to people, not just the Chicano, but the Indian and the Black and the Asian. I don't hate anymore; I feel sorry, I pity the fact that some-day society will wake up and find they've been living a lie, a lie which will someday destroy them if things don't change. What's worse than that, us getting married? No, I don't think so! [*Pause.*] We'll just have to make the best of it, simple as that! Well, what do you say?

Jenny: I have a Chicano philosopher for a boyfriend, and I just can't fight the fact that I love him and don't want to lose him no matter what, that's what I say.

Jorge: Then that settles it, so let's not hear anymore talk about you not see-ing me anymore! We'll find a way, and if we don't we'll make one! [*They kiss as the stage goes to black.*]

Scene 7

[*As the stage goes into black, a recording begins playing over the speakers, accompanied with slides of people young and old, of all colors, and creeds. The voice should be soft, appealing, but firm.*]

Tape: What you just saw could happen to anyone, regardless of race, creed, color, or ethnic background! Two people sharing something . . . something so nebulous as love. Why should parents come in the way of their children's happiness? Why should society never bend its values and why should it im-pose them without really examining just why they exist? [*Pause.*] Together-ness . . . that's a nice thought! Maybe it's a solution to the problem. [*Pause.*] I wonder. . . .

Scene 8

[*This scene takes place on center stage in the Rent-a-Race department of the ALL-PURPOSE RACIAL AGENCY with Agent I, the secretary and Mrs. Smyth, a typical high-society woman who is bigoted but who wants to impress her friends by giving a party and have a few choice ethnics to add a little color and spice to the gala occasion.*]

Secretary [*Enters and finds Agent I napping at his desk*]:   Sir! [*Agent I jumps.*] Excuse me, sir, but Mrs. Smyth is here to see you.

Agent I [*Looking at calendar*]:   Ah, yes, Mrs. Smyth, wife of moneybags Smyth! Well, show her in, show her in!

Secretary: Yes sir!

Agent I: And please try not to be so overzealous when you say "sir"! Especially when I'm catching a few winks!

Secretary: No sir!

Agent I: What?

Secretary: I mean, yes sir, I won't be so . . . overzealous . . . when I say . . . sir, sir!

Agent I: Very good! Now if you wouldn't keep Mrs. Smyth waiting any longer!

Secretary: Of course, sir! [*She exits and Agent I straightens out his tie. Mrs. Smyth enters.*]

Agent I [*Very suave*]: Good afternoon, may I be of service?

Mrs. Smyth [*Cold and aloof*]: Yes. I'm having a small dinner party for about 200 people, and my sister, the Duchess de Baloncy, suggested your agency to me. She says that to be *in* I would have to come and see you about my guest list. If you know what I mean?

Agent I: Of course, Mrs. Smyth.

Mrs. Smyth: I wouldn't want *anyone* to say that I'm prejudiced, and so I want one of your . . . *people* to attend my party.

Agent I: Well, it's our custom to use at least three of our people at any one party. These ethnic groups tend to be unsociable when left alone . . . don't you agree?

Mrs. Smyth [*Unconcerned*]: Whatever you advise. I'm sure *you're* more experienced in these matters. I suppose I must take all three.

Agent I: Would you care to see our color chart? We want to make sure you have exactly what you want!

Mrs. Smyth: Color chart?

Agent I [*Picking up chart*]: Yes, now here we have our Chicano line! I must mention that we consider Messkins our speciality! [*Pause.*] Ah, here we are! [*Showing chart to Mrs. Smyth.*] First of all we have Tijerina Off-White. This style leans to the conservative side, but it's a good color. Then, of course, there is Acapulco Gold, a most popular color! Chavez Beige, Fuentes Tan, and Gonzalez Brown. We also have Messkin-Indian Red, this color has excellent potential! Then we have Chicano Cream, which is a little browner than most browns. And, of course, Plain Old Brown, which has a lovely shine to it! Now which do you prefer?

Mrs. Smyth: Oh, dear me! So many interesting colors to pick from. Are you sure I need all three?

Agent I: Oh, it's a must! For flair and color and combination and mystical intrigue!

Mrs. Smyth [*Looking at chart*]:   Acapulco Gold sounds good! Gonzalez Brown has a nice ring to it, and let me see . . . Plain Old Brown for a traditional effect, wouldn't you say?

Agent I: By all means, Mrs. Smyth! We must think traditional, shouldn't we?

Mrs. Smyth: By all means!

Agent I [*Smiling*]:   Now as to type. Are there any particulars you might want to look at? [*She nods her head no.*] Very well! I'll show you our array of models, and when you see something you like feel free to say so! [*He picks up another chart.*] First of all there is our "Frito Bandito," who won't do much . . . but he'll eat all the dip. Then we have our most requested model . . . "The Jaime Bond Secret Agent" model, who will seduce all the women at the party. For all your hippie friends we have the "Juan Frijol" model, who will entertain you with his guitar. Then, of course, there is "lupe." the sweet little peasant who will sit in the corner and make tortillas to your little heart's content! If you want to add an additional bit of spice to the party, we of course have our "Greaser" model, who will insult anyone at will. And if you wish not to be too obvious about your integrated guest list, we have the "Vendido" model who *Looks* like an *Anglo* but *Smells* like a *Messkin!*

Mrs. Smyth [*Looking him over from head to toe*]:   My, you are well stocked, aren't you?

Agent I [*Flushed*]:   Well, ahh . . . yes.

Mrs. Smyth: I can't make up my mind; they all look the same to me. Why don't you pick them for me!

Agent I: Since this is your first time to use our service I suggest you take it easy; the stronger models have an odor that takes some getting used to! Why don't you take Lupe, Jaime Bond Secret Agent, and Vendido?

Mrs. Smyth: Fine, fine! I'll need them a week from Friday at 7:30 at 869 Rednecked Road . . . and, here, charge it to my Bank-A-Merricard!

Agent I: Yes, of course! And if we can help you in any way please give us a call! And remember our motto, "Want to have a party that's great, let us help you integrate!"

[*The lights fade slowly out.*]

Scene 9

[*The stage goes into black from Scene 8. As it does so, the following mono-logue begins, accompanied by slides. The slides should be used only to highlight what is being said.*]

Monologue: Satire is a way of laughing at ourselves and seeing the falacy we commit when we choose to be different. However, oftentimes we fail to accept or understand the meaning of what we see, hear, and feel. Seeing our own mistakes as other people see them gives us an opportunity to pause and reexamine what we are and attain a new insight into what we really are.

Scene 10

[*Lights come up on stage right which is set to look like a living room; it needs only to be suggested. Seated opposite of each other are Jenny's parents; the father can be reading some sort of magazine, and the mother can be knitting or some such thing. Jenny enters.*]

Jenny [*Looking at parents and gaining courage to say what she wants to say*]: Mom. [*Pause.*] Dad. [*Pause.*] I'd like to talk to you.

Dad: If it's about you and that friend of yours, I don't want to hear another word about it. I've told you how I feel and that should be sufficient.

Jenny [*Pleading*]:   Daddy, you've got to face this: Jorge and I are in love and we want your permission to get married.

Dad [*Angry*]:   Permission to get married? You really want to ruin your life, don't you? No daughter of mine is going to lower herself by marrying some damn greaser!

Jenny: He's not a "greaser"!

Dad: Have you taken a close look at him lately? He's nothing but a wetback, and he ought to go back where he belongs!

Jenny: This is where he belongs!

Dad: The hell he does!

Mom: Listen to your father, Jenny! He knows what he's talking about.

Jenny: Daddy, why can't you understand he's no different than you are!

Dad: His kind is no good, Jenny! He just wants to marry you so he can say, "Hey, look everybody! I got myself a white girl!" That's all he wants! He wants to raise himself up, and he wants to use you as insurance.

Jenny: How can you say that? Jorge loves me and I love him, and the only thing either of us wants is to make a life together and raise a family and be happy for the rest of our lives.

Dad: You're not marrying anybody unless I say you can, do you understand?

Jenny: By the time your prejudice wears off I'll be an old maid! And, besides, you can't stop me from marrying Jorge; I'll marry him with or without your permission!

Mom: My dear, your father is right. What sort of life would you have with a boy with his background and what would our friends say?

Jenny: It's not the least bit important what your friends have to say about this. Most of them are bigots anyway! The only thing of any importance is what Jorge and I want for each other, and nobody's going to stop us from getting that!

Mom: You're mixed up my dear, so why get excited? He couldn't possibly provide for you, now could he?

Jenny [Angry]:   Oh, for the love of God, think about me for a minute! Doesn't my happiness mean anything to you?

Dad: Of course it does! And that's why we don't want you marrying some nobody! What kind of life could he possibly give you? Could he give you the same comforts you've known all your life? And what kind of position could he ever hold in society?

Jenny: What can I do to make you see the fact that all I need to make me happy is being with Jorge. That's all that I want! Besides, Jorge is no ordinary individual: he's bright, ambitious, and he has a wonderful future ahead of him. Can't you accept that and just let me live my own life?

Mom: Jenny, now you know that we want only the best for you, but we don't think that young boy is good enough for you!

Dad: Enough about this Jorge business; I don't want to hear another word about it!

Mom: Why don't you find yourself a nice American boy? Then you can be really happy!

Jenny: All right, now I don't need to have your blessing or permission because no matter what happens I'm going to marry Jorge, and you or anyone else will not be able to stop me! [*She starts to exit.*]

Dad: Just a minute, young lady! You would go against the wishes of your parents to marry a greaser? We'll just see how far you can get.

Jenny: Thank you, father, for the understanding that you've given me. I hope you never regret your selfishness! [*She runs out.*]

Dad: Jenny! Wait. . . !

Mom: Let her go! She won't listen; she's made up her mind!

[*The lights slowly fade out.*]

Scene 11

[*The stage is in total darkness and over the loudspeakers we hear a short cut from a Beatles song, "Happiness is a warm gun. . . ." The lights come up and we are in the front area of the stage between the audience and the stage, a stand-up sign reading "Bus Stop" can be seen. From stage left a Chicano in his early twenties enters. Whistling a tune, he stops and looks around; he is waiting for a bus. About this time two young Anglo toughs in their late teens enter and stop about 10 or 15 feet from the Chicano.*]

Ralph: I tell you I can smell one a block away; they've all got that wet, fishy smell. Ha! ha! ha!

Billy: Yeah! I know what you mean: all those Messkins are alike . . . just a bunch of wetback greasers!

Ralph: There ain't one who's worth the flour they make their tortillas out of!

Billy: Hey, Ralph, standing by the bus stop, a real genuine grea-ser! [*The Chicano overhears but attempts to ignore them.*]

Ralph: Why don't we have a little fun, Billy Boy!

Billy: Hey, yeah, let's go hassle him!

Ralph [*Walking up to the Chicano*]: Hey greaser! Got a cigarette?

Chicano [*Not looking at him*]: I don't smoke.

Ralph: Hey, Billy Boy, the greaser don't smoke!

Billy: I wonder what he does do?

Chicano: Haven't you guys got anything better to do?

Ralph: Aw-w. He wants us to quit bothering him! Are we bothering you, huh, greaser?

Chicano: Yeah, you're bothering me!

Billy: [*Harassing him*]: Bother . . . bother . . . bother!

Ralph: Hey, greaser, is that right that all Messkins sell their sisters real cheap?

Chicano [*Angered*]: Wait a goddamn minute! You better watch what you say!

Ralph: Go to hell and take your mother with you!

Chicano: Keep it up and see if I don't put my foot in your mouth!

Ralph: Hey, Billy Boy, the greaser's trying to get rough!

Billy: Well, come on spic, I'm here too!

Chicano: Baboso!

Billy: What'd he say?

Ralph: Who knows? I don't speak Messkin; nobody that's anybody does!

Chicano: You dumb jackass! Spanish is taught in every school in the city; you're just too stupid to know the difference!

Ralph [Tauntingly]:   What do we have here? An educated Spic! Say, I'll bet you went to that college for poor greasers!

Billy [Playing along]:   What school's that, Ralph?

Ralph: You know, PEON U! [*They laugh.*]

Chicano: You're going to keep putting down Chicanos, huh?

Ralph: Yeah! What are you going to do about it?

Chicano [Trips and knocks Ralph to the ground]:   I'm going to let you join them!

Billy: Hey, greaser, you can't do that!

Chicano: Shut your fat mouth, Gringo!

Billy: You can't talk to me like that. . . .

Chicano: Little man doesn't like being called names, eh? Chicanos don't like it either!

Ralph [Getting up]:   Let's fix this guy, Billy Boy!

Billy [Moving towards Chicano]:   It'll be a pleasure!

[*At this point a strobe light comes on in order to slow down and magnify the action. The fight should be planned carefully to avoid injury.*]

Chicano: Come on and try!

[*Billy moves at him, as the Chicano side steps, blocks his punch, and counters with an uppercut to the stomach. Billy doubles up and the Chicano follows with a forearm smash to the back of his neck; Billy goes to the ground. In the meantime Ralph moves in.*]

Ralph: You filthy Spic. You're going to get yours!

[*They struggle; both exchange blows. Billy gets up slowly and pulls out a gun. Ralph gets in a blow to the chin and knocks the Chicano down. As he tries to get up, Billy fires the pistol and hits the Chicano in the chest. He falls back and dies. The strobe light stops and we go back to regular lighting.*]

Billy [*Drops gun*]: God! [*Crying.*] I didn't mean to do that. I just wanted to scare him! How'll we get out of this!

Ralph [*Trying to remain calm*]: Easy! Self-defense! He came here starting to argue and pushing us around; then you thought he was going for a gun or a knife!

Billy [*Searching through the Chicano's pockets*]: But he doesn't have a gun, [*Pause.*] not even a pocket knife!

Ralph: Listen! I said you thought he was going for a weapon; that's what it looked like to me. And you know how these greaser hoods are with concealed weapons—every other one's a walking arsenal. That's why there are so many shootings and knifings around here. But this time one of 'em got a taste of his own medicine.

Billy [*Calming down*]: Yeah, that's what happened!

Ralph: Come on! Let's split! [*Billy picks up the gun and they run out.*]

[*Slow black out.*]

Scene 12

[*This series of slides should begin and end with the slide of a young Chicano boy about ten years of age, and the following poem should be rendered from the standpoint of a child. The poem is the author's "Brown Eyed Boy."*]

> Brown-eyed boy, don't look away!
> Brown-eyed boy, don't hide your face!
> Brown-eyed, brown-skinned boy,
> Why are you afraid?
>
> Where's your mother, brown-eyed boy?
> She is . . . oh! I didn't know!
> But, brown-eyed boy, get off the streets!
> Brown-eyed, brown-skinned boy,
> Don't be so sad!
>
> Where's your father, brown-skinned boy?
> You don't know . . . oh!

But, brown-skinned boy, don't get in trouble!
Brown-eyed, brown-skinned boy,
You'll be all right!

Hey, brown-eyed boy, where'd you get your tan?
You were . . . oh! I see.
But, brown-eyed boy, what's wrong with you?
Brown-eyed, brown-skinned boy,
Can I help you?

Wanna play with me?
You can't . . . oh!
Where do you live, brown-eyed boy?
Brown-eyed, brown-skinned boy,
Please don't cry!

Where are you going, brown-skinned boy?
Don't worry!
I'll be your brother,
Brown-eyed, brown-skinned boy.

Scene 13

[*On stage left there are two youths, an Anglo boy and a Black girl.*]

Norma: I wonder what's keeping Fernando?

Albert: Who knows? He's probably still looking for a poem to use for our Spanish class.

Norma: I guess.

Albert: Have you got one yet?

Norma: Yeah, but I wanted Fernando to help me with it.

Albert: First he helps me; then he helps you.

Norma: Gee, Albert, you're so generous!

Albert: I try, Norma, I try.

Norma: I'll bet you do.

Albert: Don't worry; he'll help both of us, just wait and see!

Norma: I know he will. [*Pause.*] I bet when he does his tomorrow it'll be dynamite, with that flair for the dramatic.

Albert: Can you just picture it. "Fernando!" Miss Wilson will say, "it's your turn to read your poem!" And he'll walk up slowly, looking at everybody, and begin.

[*Here there is a blackout, and a voice comes over the speakers.*]

Voice: Fernando, it's your turn to do your poem!

[*A special light comes up on stage left, and standing there is Fernando. A Chicano, he looks over the audience and begins.*]

"MI PATRIA"
by

Ruben Sierra

Oyendo la voz del viento por la noche como una música triste
Que llena mi corazón de nuevas y brillantes alegrías,
Mi alma se estremece cuando oigo el llanto de mi patria suplicando
Mi atención sobre los problemas de este siglo.

Soy el hijo de mi patria,
Orgullosamente levanto la cabeza,
Suspirando, ansioso, exclamando,
Buscando la luz del día para dar una razón por todas
Las injusticias de la vida;

Sin desmayo con mi destino lucho,
Ante mis ojos pasan reflejos de las sombras de hombres que
     han muerto,
Uno por uno oigo los gritos de sus sufrimientos.
Valientes, sin pensamiento del brazo frío de la muerte
Que en un momento les puede quitar la vida,
Los ves, marchando, cantando, y hablando uno al otro.

¿Será inocencia? por parte de todo el mundo
Que en esta vida no conocemos lo que es la paz;
¿Será el hombre, brutal? pensando nomas en sí mismo;
¿Ha perdido la razón? el conocimiento profundo
De poder distinguir del bien y del mal.

¡O! patria mía, ilusión del hombre,
Tu belleza es más que todo el mundo para mí;
Tu eres luz sobre la luz,
Eres mi vida y mi ser,
Eres la voz de todo el bien,
Eres la roca del hombre;
Lloro sin consuelo cuando pienso que el hombre no ve la
Gracia de tu amor.

¿Cuál es mi patria?
¿Cuál es la patria en que debo mi vida?

Mi patria no está en Europa,
No está en la China,
No es la Asia,
Ni es ninguna nación sobre las tierras de este mundo;
Por mi patria muero,
Por mi patria sigo mi destino,
Y por mi patria vengo a la vida.

Extendiendo mi mano
Saludo a mi Dios,
Porque la única patria que tengo es mi patria celestial.

[*The special light fades out, and as the regular lights come up, we see Norma and Albert sitting there.*]

Norma: I'll bet that's just the way it'll be, too. [*Fernando enters.*]

Fernando: Hi guys!

Albert: Did you find a poem?

Fernando: Sure I did.

Norma: Will you help me with mine?

Albert: Yeah, mine too!

Fernando: Have no fear; naturally I'll help you. That is, of course, if you're willing to listen to mine?

Norma and Albert: Sure! What's it about?

Fernando: Basically it's a poem about a man's search for his true country. As he searches his mind he thinks about what his destiny will be, and at the end, after examining all the countries of the world, he declares that the only true country he has is the heavens.

Albert: Sounds kind of heavy.

Norma: Yeah.

Fernando: Would I have it any other way? [*Slow fade out.*]

Scene 14

[*There is another special light this time, somewhere in the middle of the audience. There a young man or a girl sitting on a stool with a guitar sings the following song (lyrics by Ruben Sierra).*]

"DON'T CALL OUT NAMES

When rage comes over your heart
And fear becomes your judge
Look into a mirror and see yourself
Don't call out names that bite and sting
Don't bring yourself to hate
Don't bring yourself to hate

Man's every enemy becomes his own
Together side by side

Down from his silver throne
No longer alone
Brother side by side
Each one free and proud
Each one free and proud

Abandon sides forget your rage
Come together . . . communicate
Then sing your songs and laugh out loud
Forget your fear forget your rage
Don't call out names that bite and sting
Don't bring yourself to hate
Don't bring yourself to hate

When rage comes over your heart
And fear becomes your judge
Look into a mirror and see yourself
Look into a mirror but wait . . .
Don't call out names that bite and sting
Don't bring yourself to hate
Don't bring yourself to hate

[*The special light fades out and the singer remains seated through the
following scene.*]

Scene 15

[*Lights come up on stage right, and in the front of stage center we are in a
bar room (need only to suggest bar room: two chairs with a board across
to represent a bar; a table down center with a couple of chairs). There is a
a bartender behind bar and a customer. At the table seated we find Jim,
an Anglo, and Carlos, a Chicano.*]

Jim: How about another beer, Carlos?

Carlos: Sounds great!

Jim: Okay. [*Starts to get up.*]

Carlos: Wait a minute, this is my round!

Jim: No, it's mine!

Carlos: Are you sure?

Jim: Well, let's see. You bought, then I bought, then you bought, then I bought, then you bought. It's my round!

Carlos: Sure, okay.

Jim: What kind do you want?

Carlos: Schlitz.

Jim: Out of state beer!

Carlos: What the hell, you're buying!

Jim: Yeah, I'm buying! [*Walks over to bar.*] Hey, bartender, let me have two Schlitz!

Bartender [*Giving him the beer*]:   That'll be eighty cents!

Jim: Have you got change for a twenty?

Bartender: No.

Bob [*Recognizing Jim*]:   Hey, Jim! How you doing, buddy?

Jim: Bob!

Bob: How ya been?

Jim: Okay, I guess. You?

Bob: Couldn't be better! Wanna sit down and join me?

Jim: I'm sitting with a friend; why don't you join us?

Bob: Sure, why not.

Bartender: Hey, you still owe me eighty cents!

Jim: You got change for a twenty?

Bartender: I said no! Now you got eighty cents or not?

Jim [*Digging into pocket*]:   Yeah, yeah, okay! [*Gives him the money.*]

Bob: Where you sitting?

Jim: Over there! [*They walk over to table; he hands Carlos the beer.*] Here you go, Carlos.

Carlos: Thanks, Jim.

Bob: Is *that* your friend?

Jim: Yes. Carlos meet Bob!

Carlos [*Extending hand*] :   Hi, Bob!

Bob [*Rejecting his hand and turning away*] :   Sure.

Jim: What's the matter with you?

Bob: I don't like spics!

[*Meanwhile a Black man has entered the bar and is asking bartender for a beer; at this point two conversations begin at the same time.*]

Black [*Astonished*] :   *Forty-five cents!*

Jim: Well, go to hell then!

Bob: Don't take me wrong!

Bartender: So pay up, or get out!

Jim: So what's the beef?

Black: I never paid *forty-five* cents for no beer!

Bob: Let's go over there! [*Moving away from table*]

Black: Boy! Boy!

Bartender: How old are you?

Black: You'd better have said Leroy!

Jim [*To Carlos, who is standing*] :   Stay here! I'll be right back!

Carlos: No!

Jim: I got to settle this by myself!

Carlos: Listen, Jim!

Jim [*Raising voice*] :   Sit down!

Carlos: Okay, okay. [*He sits down.*]

Jim [*Walks over to Bob*] :   Okay, so what gives?

Bob: Jim, you can't hang around with Messkins!

Jim: Says who?

Bartender: So go somewhere else!

Bob: They're bad for you, nothing but trouble!

Black: I've got my rights, the constitution says . . .

Jim: Look, goddamnit, go to hell!

Bartender: This is a bar, not a constitution!

Bob: Niggers are okay, but Messkins . . .

Black: Look, I don't want no trouble, just a beer. . . .

Jim: You know what you are? You're nothing but a damn whitey. . . .

Bartender: Okay, pay forty-five cents!

Bob: Spics are all bad. . . .

Black: You're crazy!

Carlos [*Who has walked over to the bar, to the Black*]: I'll buy you a beer!

Jim: You make me sick! [*Walks toward bar and leaves Bob.*]

Bartender: What kind?

Black: Miller!

Carlos [*Reaching for money*]: How much?

Bartender: Fifty cents!

Black [*Coming unglued*]: *FIFTY CENTS!*

Bartender: Pay up, or no beer!

Black: What is this, Blacks forty-five cents and Chicanos fifty cents!

Bartender: Yeah, fifty cents for Messkins, so what?

Carlos: Here's your fifty cents!

Black: Hell no!

Jim [*At bar*]: You bastard bigots are all crazy!

Carlos: Forget it!

Black: I'm leaving!

Jim: Come on, I know a bar down the road! [*The three of them exit.*]

Scene 16

[*Tri-colored girl; her face is painted in three sections; Brown, Black, and White. She goes in and out of the audience with a sunflower in the hand, singing and laughing and calling out names: "Nigger, honky, wetback, spic, browny, whitey, etc.," and then she exits.*]

Scene 17

[*As the lights fade on the Tri-colored girl, the lights cross, fade to center stage, and we are at the "ALL-PURPOSE AGENCY," with Agent I behind a desk.*]

Agent I: Let's see, now, what have we got: Grape jelly . . . "America is grape jelly!" No . . . uh, jam, "America is grape jam!" Nah, [*Pause.*] cobbler . . . apples . . . "America is apple preserves!" Negative on that one. How about [*Pause.*] pie. That's it! "AMERICA IS APPLE PIE!" That's wonderful; I'll use it. It's got a nice ring to it: "APPLE PIE AND MOTHERHOOD!"

[*Another agent enters.*]

Darcy: Hi ya, Chief! How's your slogan coming along?

Agent I: Darcy, just the one I wanted to see. Listen to this: "AMERICA IS APPLE PIE AND MOTHERHOOD!" [*Pause.*] Well, what you think?

Darcy: Chief, you're a genius. I couldn't have said it better myself.

Agent I: You're right, Darcy. After all, I didn't get to where I am today by sitting around on my tush. Now all I need is an image to go along with the slogan: a fall guy a patsy—you get my meaning.

Darcy: I got just the guy for you. There's a shnook outside that says he wants to become father of the country. He'd be perfect.

Agent I: Father of the country?

Darcy: Yeah, says he wants us to groom him and stuff.

Agent I: What's his name?

Darcy: Irving Muckaby.

Agent I: Irving Muckaby! With a name like that he couldn't sell Tootsie Rolls.

Darcy: We could change his name to something catchy like Einstein or Berlin.

Agent I: No, they've been used before. Besides, whoever heard of the father of a country with a name like Irving Einstein.

Darcy: I see what you mean, chief. We need something smooth and long lasting.

Agent I: What was your father's name, Darcy?

Darcy: Edgar.

Agent I: Negative. [*Pause*] Well, bring him in and let's see what we can come come up with. [*Darcy exits.*] Irving Muckaby, yuck!

Darcy: Right this way, Mr. Muckaby! [*Muckaby enters.*] Chief, this is Irving Muckaby.

Agent I: Mr. Muckaby, a pleasure, a real pleasure. Say, do you mind if I drop the formalities and call you Irving.

Irving: No, not at all, Mr. uh . . .

Agent I: Just call me Chief.

Irving: Mr. Chief.

Agent I: No, just Chief, without the mister.

Irving: Oh, are you an Indian?

Agent I: No, but that's besides the point. Let's get down to business. Darcy here tells me you'd like to become father of the country.

Irving: That's correct. I feel it is my patriotic duty.

Agent I: To each his own, huh, Irving?

Irving: To each his own, Mr. Chief.

Agent I: No, that's Chief without the mister. We got to do something about your name.

Irving: What do you mean?

Darcy: What the chief means is that your name is wrong for the image.

Irving: Image?

Darcy: Sure, if you're going to be father of the country, you got to have a name that sells.

Irving: What's wrong with Irving Muckaby?

Agent I [*Patting him on the shoulder*] :   Nothing, Irving, nothing, except we need something that everyone can identify with, and Irving Muckaby ain't the one.

Irving: Well, then, what is?

Darcy: Have you got another name besides Irving?

Irving: My middle name is Clarence.

Darcy: I don't think that'll cut it, do you, Chief?

Agent I: Negative. What was your father's name?

Irving: Muckaby.

Agent I: I know that; I mean his first name.

Irving: Percy.

Agent I: Percy. [*Pause.*] It figures. Okay. Well, we got to come up with a name.

Darcy: How about if we name him after a river like maybe the Delaware.

Agent I: Irving Delaware, the Father of our Country! [*Thinks about it.*] Nah, it sounds too much like a fruit drink.

Darcy: How about the capitol of our country?

Agent I [*Confused*]: Irving D.C.?

Darcy: No, Irving Washington!

Agent I: I like Washington, but Irving is definitely out.

Irving: How about Percy like my father?

Agent I: PERCY WASHINGTON! Naw, that sounds plain fruity.

Darcy: I got it Chief! D. C. WASHINGTON, THE FATHER OF OUR COUNTRY!

Agent I: Sounds too much like a light bulb. You got any other ideas, Darcy?

Darcy: Sure, Chief, lots!

Agent I: Well, just keep them to yourself. Now where was I?

Irving: I've always liked the name George.

Agent I: THAT'S IT! GEORGE WASHINGTON, THE FATHER OF OUR COUNTRY! I like it.

Irving: That's a wonderful name.

Darcy: Chief, that name sounds familiar.

Agent I: Shut up!

Darcy: But Chief . . .

Agent I: Nobody will ever know the difference.

Irving: When do I get started, Chief?

Agent I: Darcy here will take care of all those details; just go along with him.

Irving: Thanks, Chief.

Agent I: Not at all, my pleasure. [*Darcy and Irving exit.*] Boy, all that thinking made me tired. I think I'll take a nap. [*Sits in desk and starts to nap.*]

[*Enter Stanley Martínez, timid, shy, sloppy. There is fear in every step he takes; he looks around him and approaches Agent I slowly and with great caution until he gets about arm's length from him.*]

Martínez [*Clearing his throat*]: Uh . . . hum. [*Agent I is still asleep, so Stanley gets closer.*] Uh . . . hum! [*Agent I doesn't move; Stanley gets right up to his ear.*] Uh . . . hum!

Agent I [*Startled, looks at Martínez*]: Yes, sir, can I help you?

Martínez [*Cautiously*]: I've . . . I've . . . I've come to become . . . uh . . . anglocized.

Agent I [*Gleaming*] :   Oh, you mean you want to change your name! I see! Well, Mr. . . . ah . . .

Martínez [*In a whisper*] :   Mar-tín-ez.

Agent I [*Loudly*] :   MARTINEZ!

Martínez: Shh, please, not so loud. I don't want people to know that I'm . . . well, you know.

Agent I [*Condescendingly*] :   Yes, I know your problem well, Mr. Martínez.

Martínez: Please, call me Stanley.

Agent I: Stanley . . . Stanley . . . ! I once knew a man named Stanley. He was a good American; he died fighting for his country!

Martínez: Was he killed in Viet Nam?

Agent I: No, he died trying to kill three Niggers! [*Pause.*] I just can't understand why he had to die just because he was caught coming out the back door! I just can't understand! Can you give me a good reason why a thing like that had to happen? [*Pause.*] Well, can you?

Martínez [*Confused*] :   Ah, yes . . . I mean no . . . I can't give . . . you a reason . . . as to . . . why . . . or . . .

Agent I: That's what I thought and that's why you're here, and we're here to help you, Stanley! Now let's see, what good American name can we give you? [*Agent I begins looking through his "Change-a-Name Book."*] Spanish surnames . . . Spanish surnames . . . Ah! Here we are! Now let's see! Let's look for Stanley . . . Stanley . . . Stanley. . . .

Martínez [*Trying to break in*] :   Sir . . . sir, my surname is [*In a whisper.*] Martínez!

Agent I: Oh, yes, that's right, Martínez. [*Thumbing through book.*] Martínez . . . Martínez . . . Martínez . . . M. . . M . . . for Martínez. Let's see, how many letters in that Stanley?

Martínez [*Counting on fingers*] :   That's eight, sir!

Agent I: Yes, eight. Very good, Stanley! I can see you're going to make an excellent *Anglo*! [*Looking through book.*] Ah, yes, here we are, Stanley. According to my "Change-a-Name" book, we can change your name from Martínez to Martin. Stanley Martin! How does that sound to you, MR. MARTIN?

Martínez: Sounds Great!

Agent I [*Coming on strong*] :   Yeah, it does, doesn't it? That's a good American apple-pie type name! [*Looking up as though a vision has appeared.*]

STANLEY MARTIN! Just look! Everytime you say that name you can see Old Glory just a flowing in the breeze! Look at the American Eagle just a flying in the sky with all his pride and majesty! All the symbols of America come alive when you say—STANLEY MARTIN! [*He grabs Martínez by the shoulder and waves with his free hand to the sky, and at this point a strobe comes on and a bad rendition of "Stars and Stripes" begins over loud speakers and at the same time three or four girls dressed in red, white, and blue, holding small flags in each hand come marching out. They circle them twice and exit, the strobe goes out, and we go back to our regular lighting.*]

Agent I [*On the verge of tears*] :   I don't know why but all of a sudden I feel patriotic! I could almost sing a few lines of "God Bless America!" [*He regains his composure and turns to Stanley who is in a trance with one hand over his heart.*] Well, Mr. Martin . . . Mr. Martin . . . [*Agent I shakes him, and Stanley comes to.*] There's only one more thing you have to do in order to become a full-fledged Anglo! Like all good Americans, you have to take an oath! [*Picking up something from his desk.*] So would you please raise your right hand and place your left hand on the Constitution of the United States and repeat after me! I, Stanley Martin,

Martínez: I, Stanley Martin,

Agent I: do hereby solemnly swear

Martínez: do hereby solemnly swear

Agent I: to never renounce, denounce, or pounce

Martínez: to never renounce, denounce, or pounce

Agent I: the aforesaid which lies within the therefore

Martínez: the aforesaid which lies within the therefore

Agent I: or the latter of the former which never constitutes a right.

Martínez: or the latter of the former which never constitutes a right.

Agent I: Furthermore,

Martínez: Furthermore,

Agent I: I solemnly swear,

Martínez: I solemnly swear,

Agent I: to never let the witness sign below the dotted line

Martínez: to never let the witness sign below the dotted line

Agent I: which would make *you* the *stucco* and *me* the *stuckie,*

Martínez: which would make *you* the *stucco* and *me* the *stuckie,*

Agent I: so help me George Washington.

Martĩnez: so help me George Washington.

Agent I: Congratulations, [*Shaking his hand.*] Mr. Martin! You now have the power and authority to call [*Stanley repeats each name.*] Messkins—Messkins, Niggers—Niggers, Commies—Commies . . . and so forth. You're also entitled to make out an application to the Ku Klux Klan! [*Taking out a card from desk.*] Here's your Anglo Identification Card and number. You just can't tell who's who nowadays. These are just a few of the many advantages of your being a bona fide Anglo!

Martĩnez: Oh, I'm so Happy! Now I can walk the streets without feeling inferior!

Agent I: When you belong to the SUPERIOR, you never feel INFERIOR!

Martĩnez [*Elated*] :   Just think of it! Now I can walk anywhere, and people will know that I'm an Anglo! [*He has gone completely out of his mind with happiness and starts running around stage, shouting to the audience:*] MY NAME IS STANLEY MARTIN, AND I'M AN ANGLO! [*He repeats it a couple of times, and another man enters as if walking down a street. Stanley rushes to him with extended hand.*] Hi! My name is Stanley Martin and I'm an . . .

Man: Hi,there Messkin, how ya doing pal? How's the little fat wife? Is she still making tortillas and enchilidas and all that crap? Say listen, fella, I need somebody to cut my yard! [*Here Stanley hangs his head and begins to walk dejectedly out.*] Are you interested? [*Following Stanley off stage.*] I'll pay ya eighty cents an hour. . . .

[*The lights slowly fade out.*]

[*Note: When Stanley goes down to audience, the lights at the Agent's office should go out and Agent I should exit, leaving just Stanley and the other man on stage.*]

Scene 18

[*Lights up on stage right. We are in what could be a locker room; Felipe is standing there looking through a locker and Juan enters as if passing thru. Felipe and Juan are friends of Jorge.*]

Felipe [*Seeing Juan*] :   ¡Oye, Juan, ven pa acá! I want to tell you something!

Juan: ¿Que tal Felipe? ¿Qué paso?

Felipe: Have you heard about Jorge? He wants to get married con la Jenny!

Juan: Hombre, ¿cómo? She's a gringa!

Felipe: ¡Sí! Pero he wants to marry her!

Juan: ¡Pero no Puede! ¡El hefito de la Jenny lo mata!

Felipe: ¡Por eso mismo te digo! ¡Pobre vato!

Juan: We've got to help him out somehow!

Felipe: I know! ¿Pero cómo?

Juan: ¡Hablamos con él y haber que dice!

Felipe: ¡Allá viene! [*Jorge enters.*] Act like you don't care! [*Jorge walks up to them.*] Hey, Jorge, ¿qué paso?

Juan: Jorge, how you doing, compadre?

Jorge: ¿Felipe, Juan, qué tal?

Felipe: Not bad, not bad at all.

Juan: Yeah, not bad. You?

Jorge: Okay, I guess.

Felipe: That's good.

Juan: Yeah, that's good.

Jorge: Sure.

   [*Silence.*]

Juan and Felipe: Say, Jorge. . . .

Juan: Go ahead!

Felipe: You first!

Juan: No, I insist!

Felipe: Gracias. [*Pause.*] So where you been, Jorge?

Jorge: I just came from seeing Jenny.

Felipe: Oh.

Juan [*Excited*]:   Oye, ¿is puro nel que te casas con la Jenny, eh?

Felipe: Sh-h! Shut up!

Juan: ¡Oh, sí!

Jorge: That's okay; I don't mind. If everything turns out the way we plan, yes, we're going to get married.

Juan: But she's a gringa, man!

Jorge: So, why can't we get married?

Juan: Well . . . don't you like Chicanas?

Jorge [*Laughing*] :   Of course I do! But I'm in love with Jenny.

Juan: Ah, chihuahua, this is serious!

Felipe: You love her, de veras?

Jorge: What's so strange about that?

Juan: But . . . but.. . . . you're a, you're a Mexican!

Jorge: Not a Mexican, a Chicano! I was born here, remember? Besides, what's so wrong in falling for a girl with a Swedish background?

Juan: Nada, I guess. I just don't think of it like that, but even so people are going to talk about it like if it was a disaster!

Jorge: Let them talk; it won't make me feel any different about Jenny!

Felipe: We don't want to stand in your way, Jorge, pero es que no va trabajar, and we don't want anyone to make a fool of you!

Jorge: Felipe, I appreciate what you're trying to save me from, but it's not like that at all! It's different with Jenny! She's special and she understands and cares! You have to give people a chance before you turn them away. Otherwise you defeat your whole purpose! Eventually everyone shows his true colors if you give them enough time!

Juan: You're right Jorge, and we see all the possibilities. The thing is people don't always give us a chance: they make fun of our culture, and they laugh at us if we have an accent. They don't judge us as men or individuals, and it's just not right!

Jorge: All you have to do is hold up that chin and be damn proud that you are a Chicano and you can speak two languages. You have something that not everybody can have or even attempt to attain! [*Pause.*] Have you ever heard an Anglo speak Spanish? [*They chuckle.*] No matter how good he knows it, he always has an accent! Just don't let yourself come down to somebody's level because he envys the fact that you have a definite advantage over him!

Felipe: Fine and dandy, but it doesn't work like that all the time. It might for you but not for me! I just can't share the same attitude that you do; I can't!

Jorge: Man, it gets rough for me too, but I don't quit no matter what! If I did, then I wouldn't be the same; I couldn't!

Juan: Jorge, it's guys like you that can make it, because you've got brains and determination, but when you're a little "tonto" como yo, you don't make it!

Jorge: Sure you can; just keep trying and don't give up!

Felipe: You almost sound like you're trying to convince yourself of that. Aren't you sure?

Jorge: I'm never really sure of anything except the fact that I want to become what I make of myself, and not something that I would be ashamed of. Can't you see that I'm just like everyone else and I make mistakes too, but at least they're my mistakes and not someone else's.

Juan: I'm willing to try, mano, and maybe you can help me?

Jorge: Sure, Juan!

Felipe: If you make it, Jorge, let me know, but until then, mi vida es lo que es y nada más.

Jorge: Let's go get a beer. ¡Mañana será otro día!

Juan: Yeah, sure!

[*They exit laughing as the lights fade out.*]

Scene 19

[*This is a film sequence lasting about four minutes, possibly longer, which can be one of the nicest pieces of film in the play. The music to be used can be a piece like "It's May," "Enter the Young," or something. You need three couples and an open field which leads to some small hills with trees and possibly a brook with running water and a small bridge. The couples are mixed: Chicano boy–Anglo girl, Anglo boy– Black girl, Chicano girl Black boy. They should be running through the field and entering the trees, with individual shots of the couples climbing the hill and ending in an embrace. Last shot should consist of the three couples hands in a straight line coming up and holding hands as the music fades away.*]

Scene 20

[*Lights come up in front of center stage; there are two stools side by side. From stage left enters a young Chicano boy with a fishing pole and from stage right a Black boy with a pole. They exchange hellos and sit on stools and go into the motions of fishing. After a moment one of them speaks.*]

Rudy: Enrique, what's a melting pot?

Enrique: A what?

Rudy: A melting pot!

Enrique: ¿Quién sabe? Where'd you hear it?

Rudy: My dad told my mom that if I kept hanging around with you, we'd just become part of the old melting pot. And whatever it is, he doesn't seem to like the idea.

Enrique: Maybe it means we'll all just get to be alike, every color and group with every other color and group, like if it didn't matter.

Rudy: That'll never happen! I mean people just stay together . . . with their own kind. They just don't give the others a chance.

Enrique: Yeah, Blacks with Blacks, Mexicans with Mexicans, Honkies with Honkies . . .

Rudy: 'Specially *Honkies* with *Honkies.* The old melting pot hasn't got a chance as long as the white man's got any say!

Enrique: Yeah, I don't know what to do. My parents keep telling not to hang around with anybody but Mexicans.

Rudy: My parents keep telling me not to hang around with anybody but Blacks, but how can I help it? You're my friend, Enrique.

Enrique: Hell, just look how the government forces everyone to integrate. How can we help it?

Rudy: It's funny the government forces people to do things, and our parents keep telling us we're not supposed to mix with other cultures. But that's because the white man owns everything!

Enrique: I wonder sometimes how we got so screwed up? But most gringos are funny bastards! They'll work your butts off for a dollar an hour and you get things done for 'em, like roads, and bridges, harvesting crops, and crap like that. But who gets the credit? Some dumb architect who sits up on a tall stool and makes a bunch of lines.

Rudy: It's a funny thing about democracy. It's a wonderful thing as long as you don't try to define it.

Enrique: It's because the gringo has all the money and controls everything, just because he's a majority.

Rudy: Wouldn't it be something if we minorities got together and then we'd be the majority!

Enrique: That's a damn good idea! [*Smiling.*] Only thing is people ain't got guts enough to stand up and fight for what's really theirs.

Rudy: I bet if we did get together, though, we'd make the Watts Riot look like a birthday party.

Enrique: Sometimes I get so damn mad at the gringo, because of the rut I'm in, I feel like striking back!

Rudy: Hell, even animals fight when they're cornered and they ain't got no intelligence!

[*Silence*.]

Enrique: Oh, well, what the hell.

[*Silence*.]

Rudy: Enrique! I still don't know what a melting pot is?

Enrique: Yeah. Well, I gotta go, Rudy, See you later.

Rudy: Me too. So long, Enrique.

[*As they exit, the lights fade slowly out.*]

Scene 21

[*The lights come up on stage right. We see Jorge sitting on the park bench; he is waiting for Jenny.*]

Jorge: Why can't things be a little different? Why does life have to be so tough? [*Pause.*] I wish I knew the answers. I really wish I knew. I guess I'll just have to learn to live with things the way they are. But I don't have to sit still and not do anything about it. [*Jenny enters.*]

Jenny: Hi, Jorge.

Jorge: Jenny, for a minute I thought you hadn't gotten my message.

Jenny: As soon as my sister told me you wanted to see me about something very important, I rushed right over. What is it? Is something the matter?

Jorge: It's nothing drastic; it's about my Uncle Frank.

Jenny: Your Uncle Frank?

Jorge: Remember I once told you about an uncle of mine who was an alcoholic, and whose family left him because of it?

Jenny: I seem to remember something about it. Isn't he the one whose actually a very intelligent man and who tried to make amends for his going astray?

Jorge: Yes, that's him. Anyway, I ran into him yesterday on the way home from school, and I told him about us, and I asked for advice. He wants us to go by and see him.

Jenny: Do you think he can help us?

Jorge: I hope so. He's very wise, even though he has had a bad drinking problem most of his life. He's been through a lot of hell and he's seen a great

deal of things, some good, some bad, and he looks at life differently than
most people. Maybe he'll help us see something different or at least in a
new light. It's worth a try!

Jenny: If you really think so, then let's go see him!

Jorge: I was hoping you'd say that!

Jenny: You really like him, don't you?

Jorge: I love him like a father. [*Pause*] Jenny!

Jenny: Yes!

Jorge: I love you.

Jenny: And I love you, you big nut! Come on, let's go!

[*They exit and the stage goes to black.*]

Scene 22

[*This is the last of the film sequences in the play. For this you need to go
into a slum area of a ghetto, barrio, etc., shooting footage of everything
you see, with an emphasis on old people. It is best to find one individual
man or woman in their sixties or seventies and follow them about as
they go from one place to another. They should not be aware of the fact
that they are being followed; their actions should be as natural as possible. A good piece of music would be "Good Morning Mr. Blue."*]

Scene 23

[*Lights up on stage right, Frank Gómez' apartment, uncle of Jorge. He is
about fifty years old, tired looking, but yet he has a certain air of dignity
which is very much a part of him. He is intelligent and has his own philosophy of life. He is thumbing through a book as the doorbell rings; he
gets up to answer. Enter Jenny and Jorge.*]

Frank: Jorge, I'm glad you came!

Jorge: Hello, Tío, ¿cómo estas?

Frank: ¡Bien, bien! This must be the young lady of which I've heard so
much about?

Jorge: Yes, this is Jenny. Tío! Jenny this is my uncle, Frank Gómez, man for
all seasons!

Jenny: It's a pleasure meeting you!

Frank: The pleasure is all mine! Well, come on in and sit down. Make your-self at home! Can I get you something to drink?

Jorge: None for me. How about you, Jenny?

Jenny: No, thank you.

Frank: Jorge tells me you have somewhat of a problem on your hands.

Jenny: Yes, but actually I think it's more of a misunderstanding. However, when it comes to parents, how do you get them to understand?

Frank: I'm afraid that's one problem we've all had to cope with at one time or another.

Jorge: Yes, but if Jenny and I want to get married, then why can't we?

Frank: Who says you can't?

Jenny: I have to think about my parents, and they don't like the idea.

Frank: Do you always have to think of them? Where's the turning off point? The point where you break away and become your own?

Jorge: Life is full of breaking points!

Jenny: Sure, but when it comes to parents, what are you supposed to do?

Frank: Well, you tell them you love them, you thank them for the life they've given you, and then you try to lead your own life. Not forgetting them; just making your own way.

Jenny: But if we run off and get married, what will it do to our parents?

Frank: Don't worry; they'll soon learn to understand.

Jorge: Of course they will!

Frank: But if they don't, be ready to face life for what it will become.

Jorge: Nothing can stop us so long as we have each other.

Frank: Just remember to keep your chin ready for all the hard blows that life will throw at you!

Jorge: I'm ready!

Frank: Are you sure?

Jorge: Sure I am!

Frank: I hope so.

Jorge: What do you mean?

Frank: Well, there are times in one's life when one can't distinguish the good from the bad, and it seems that you're caught in a web that you can't break loose from.

Jenny: That's the kind of positions we're in.

Frank: Yes, sort of, but you've also got to know when you're licked.

Jorge: Are you saying we're beaten and shouldn't get married?

Frank: No, I'm not saying that. What I'm saying is if you feel that you're any way in the wrong, then don't continue, because you'll only suffer for it later. But if you know you're right, then follow through, get married, have a big family, and love them and each other as you love nothing else in the world. Just remember that in order to live life to the fullest you've got to learn what it is to be defeated, for defeat helps you to learn that life isn't always pretty, so when joy comes along, you can really appreciate it.

Jenny: Oh, Mr. Gómez, what a beautiful thought.

Frank: Well, Jenny, I'll tell you something: if I didn't have that to fall back on, I would be dead by now.

Jorge: I know what I want and I want Jenny, because I love her.

Frank: Love is many things, and everyone has his or her own way of expressing it, so if you love each other, then you should share it without being afraid of the consequences.

Jorge: In other words, we should make a life for each other, a life we can be proud of and happy in. But exactly how do we do it? You know more about life than anyone I know, and yet just what is the mystery of it all. To finding happiness without hurting others? What is it, Tío? What is life?

Frank: You want me to tell you about life? You want me to tell you what it is? [*Pause and slowly a light special comes up on Frank as if he were the only one in the room.*] What is life? Life is a mystery, full of truth. I think about life and what do I feel? I feel bewildered, I feel confronted by it, obsessed by it, but yet I'm controlled by life. I'm overcome by it. In the morning when I wake I feel it smiling down upon me. As I look into a mirror to see myself, I see life. Yet I feel only what I allow myself to feel, what I want to feel, what I want to know. Life can be beautiful; it can be like an instrument of joy which produces a peaceful tranquility for my soul. And yet life can be like a thorn which produces pain, and hate, and sorrow, and pity that tears into me and rips away all truth. When life comes to be like this, it overcomes you, it slips into the very essence of what you are, and it leaves you empty, and shallow, and you wonder if life is all it has to be. [*Pause.*] You walk out into a street and you feel lonely, even though a multitude of people surround you. You can't shake the feeling, the thought, that nothing pleases you. So you cast it aside, and you feel sorry for yourself! You can't breathe the same air as everyone else, and you find yourself dormant, unable to move because you're trapped by those around you.

[*Pause*] You're caught in a world where you're subject to man's hopes, his desires, and his most vivid imagination, but you find you cannot escape. And that which is you, what begins each day as a flickering light, will soon cease to exist. [*Pause*] What is life? I really wish I knew! [*The special light fades to regular lighting.*]

Jorge [*Crossing to Frank*]:   Tío, I don't know what to say, except thanks for what you've just shared with us. I'll try to always remember it, and I know it'll help me to see things through.

Jenny: Jorge, if you're willing to give it a try, so am I, and let whatever happens, happen. But let's be happy!

Frank: That's the important thing, Jenny, happiness! You can never be completely happy in this world, but you can give it a damn good try!

Jorge: Tío, do you think we have a chance if we get married?

Frank: You have something beautiful; nobody can take it away unless you let them. If that's what you want, then do it! Elope Go to the next town and get married! When you have something good, you must never let it go! I let something go, and now I live a life trying but never being able to fully correct my mistake.

Jenny: You have so much to offer; someday you will be completely happy.

Frank: Just knowing that you and Jorge have found what you want makes me happy.

Jorge [*Taking Jenny's hand*]:   Jenny, shall we elope?

Jenny: Yes, Jorge, yes!

Jorge: Tío, I think I'll have that drink now, and then we can talk over our plans.

Jenny: Yes, I'll have one also, please!

Frank: Good! We can toast to your love and happiness! But I'll make mine buttermilk.

[*They laugh and the lights fade out slowly.*]

Scene 24

[*Lights on center stage ALL PURPOSE RACIAL AGENCY, Employment Department. Agent II is in charge; he is Black and a slick sort of a character.*]

Agent II: Will Miss Ruby Bagoonya please come in. [*A Black sister comes in.*] How's it going, sister?

Ruby: Fine, honey, fine!

Agent II: How you been?

Ruby: Fine, honey, fine!

Agent II: Looking good!

Ruby: Fine, honey, fine!

Agent II [*Looking her over*] :   I know you fine, honey! [*Looking through her records*] Now I see here you're looking for a bookkeeping job?

Ruby: That's right honey: I'm looking for a bookkeeping job!

Agent II: Are you sure you don't want to be a model, honey?

Ruby: No, honey, no!

Agent II: *Ebony* could *sure use you!*

Ruby: I know honey!

Agent II: Now I see here you graduated from Howard Black University.

Ruby: Yes, honey, yes!

Agent II: Is that a good Black University?

Ruby: Yes, honey, yes!

Agent II: Yes?

Ruby: Yes!

Agent II: Yes?

Ruby: Yes!

Agent II: AW, RIGHT! Now I see here where you got an A, a C, a D, an F, and a J.

Ruby: No, honey, no! That F was an F+!

Agent II: What's the "J" stand for?

Ruby: Just right!

Agent II [*He chuckles*] :   Now I have a job here at the Electro-Electric Company, and they just need a Negro to sit there and look pretty. Do you want the job?

Ruby: Yes, honey, yes!

Agent II: Now you won't be doing no bookkeeping!

Ruby: How much does it pay?

Agent II: I'm sorry, honey, but the salary range is only $1.00 an hour.

Ruby: No, honey, that ain't right.

Agent II: Well, let me see what I can do here? We got a job for you working in a kitchen!

Ruby: No, honey . . .

Agent II: That pays $25 an . . .

Ruby: I'll take it!

Agent II: Sign right here! [*She signs and exits.*] Miss Garcia! Miss Garcia! [*A Mexican girl dressed in Mexican skirt and blouse enters; she nods.*] Oh, yeah! Fine little Mexican girl, fine little Mexican girl! Like your haircut, honey.

Miss Garcia [*Very shyly*]: Thank you.

Agent II: Now what do you want to do?

Miss Garcia: Well, I can't do too much.

Agent II: I see here I have you down for a bookkeeping job. What kind of books do you keep, honey?

Miss Garcia: Well, I once kept comic books.

Agent II [*Changing subject*]: Can you make a serrappi?

Miss Garcia: No.

Agent II: Can you make an inchillida?

Miss Garcia: With a recipe.

Agent II: How about a baco? I mean a taco?

Miss Garcia: With a recipe.

Agent II: With a recipe?

Miss Garcia: Yes.

Agent II: Are you sure you can't make a serrappi?

Miss Garcia: No.

Agent II: Well, I got a job for you working in a soul kitchen! Do you want the job?

Miss Garcia: Can I make enchilladas?

Agent II: Honey, you can make anything you want!

Miss Garcia: Okay, I'll take it!

Agent II: Sign right here and have a swinging time. [*She signs and exits.*] Will Miss Gypsy Belle please come in! [*An Anglo girl enters.*] Miss Bell?

Gypsy [*Very spirited, smiling broadly*]: Yes, sir!

Agent II: Well, Miss Belle, I see here you want to be a bookkeeper?

Gypsy: Yes, sir!

Agent II [*Looking her over*] :   Well, what kind of experiences have you had?

Gypsy [*About to fall for it, she suddenly stops smiling and looks at Agent II; he grins.*] Well, ugh . . . I worked for a CPA and two department stores.

Agent II: You seem to be very well off, [*Looking her over again.*] very well off! There's a slight problem, however.

Gypsy: What do you mean?

Agent II   This job I have open is at the NAACP!

Gypsy [*Smiling broadly*] :   Oh, goody!

Agent II [*Startled*] :   You mean you like the idea?

Gypsy: Sure!

Agent II: Have you ever worked with Blacks before?

Gypsy: No, but some of my best friends are Blacks.

Agent II [*Laughing*] :   Oh, my God!

Gypsy: What's so funny?

Agent II [*Still laughing*] :   Nothing, honey, you wouldn't understand!

Gypsy: Why?

Agent II: Because you're white, that's why!

Gypsy: So?

Agent II: Because when you're white you can't be black, so don't try to understand!

Gypsy: Can I still have the job?

Agent II [*Teasing*] :   The what?

Gypsy: The job!

Agent II: It's not going to bother you being surrounded by all those Blacks?

Gypsy: No!

Agent II: You got guts, fox!

Gypsy: Can I have the job?

Agent II: Sure, sure! Sign right here, and have a black old time! [*Laughing.*]

[*She signs paper and exits as the lights fade slowly out and Agent II is still laughing.*]

Scene 25

[The house is in total darkness and remains so during this entire scene.
Taped dialogue comes through all the loud speakers; it should be spoken
clearly and honestly.]

Tape: Is there such a thing as a pure race? Is it found in the past, the present,
or the future? Why are people different from one another? Perhaps purity
is in the mind of the beholder? Or maybe in the color of everyone's blood?

The Chicanos are a proud people whose heritage is beauty and harmony.
Look around and see the architecture, the names on street signs and buildings, the names of cities, and you will find names which exemplify what is
their past. That which is today and will always be, Chicano. They are not
a pretentious people, and are not afraid to be themselves. Today the Chicano people have emerged to find their place in this world, in this society.
They no longer are afraid to advance beyond the point which has limited
them in the past. They breathe, and eat, and live, just the same as anyone
else. So why is there such a difference among those who do not understand
them or their culture?

The Chicano finds joy in the closeness of a family gathered around the
table, saying grace over an evening meal, in a mother tending her garden, in
coming to the aid of a sick neighbor, in giving time of himself so as to bring
a little joy to one who is less fortunate. The Chicano finds beauty on the
smile of an old man's face whose life, though not blessed with the fruits
of materialism, has yet found beauty in the simplicity of life.

The Chicano is sensitive, aware, concerned, dedicated, meaningful, proud,
sincere, and loving. They are no different than anyone else except that they
have a culture which is unique and beautiful.

The Chicano is happy because he doesn't care what your color is or your
background or even if you hate him. He is an emotion, and an idea. He is
life itself. He is a person, a place, a substance, and that will never change.

Do you really think he was made different so that there could be turmoil
among others different than himself? I don't!

A Chicano is an Americano, is an Americano, is an Americano . . . .

[This phrase is repeated slowly, fading away as lights focused on the audience
begin to come up gradually until they reach full intensity. This is the last
scene, and the final scene is the audience!]

Dawn

ALURISTA

Poet, playwright, essayist, and writer, Alurista is one of the most versatile and outstanding figures in the Chicano literary world today. Known mainly for his beautiful poetic work, he nevertheless has cultivated the other literary genres with equal finesse and artistry.

His drama, like all his creative works, reflects a transcedental human consciousness as well as Chicano pride, love, compassion, strength, and unity as a race.

His numerous works include *Nationchild Plumaroja* (a collection of poems), *Floricanto* (collection of poems), and *El Ombligo de Aztla.*

Alurista is currently an assistant professor of Chicano literature at the University of Texas-Austin in the Department of Chicano Studies.

Dawn is a symbolic play which brings forth the social message of human exploitation by the Anglo-American people. "Manifest Destiny" as perpetrated by the Anglo-American people nearly destroyed the existence of the Indian, Mexican-American, and other culturally different people in this country. The playwright expertly employs symbolic mythical Aztec and fictitious characters to convey his message.

Characters

Council of Elders
Huehueteotl
Quetzalcoatl
Cihuacoatl
Huitzilopochtli
Tezcatlipoca
Coatlicue

Pepsicoatl
Cocacoatl
Mexican
Chicano
Chimalma
Mixcoatl

ACT I: THE HUNT

[Tree of life with huichol god's eyes hanging from its branches dominates stage. Cactus and rocks are the only other scenery. Correographed to the "deer dance" of the Yaqui. Council of Elders open in chorus.]

Council of Elders:

> we are the Council of Elders
> we gather
> and tell time to live again
> before us
> in our space
> and memories burn
> in the flames of the old fire
> Huehueteotl
> old firelord

Huehueteotl:

> lava blood and flesh
> Huehueteotl

105

rock bone of ages
bygone
the story of the bird in flight
and the flower in blossom
bygone
the cruelty of the hunter in chase
and the hunted in agony
bygone
the drums and flutes
the beat and song
bygone
but all the same
today
Huitzilopochtli, lord of war,
devours flesh and bone
with napalm
all the same
today
his mother Coatlicue
welcomes to her bosom
the dead, dying,
lost children
in the darkness of bombs
and fear of Tezcatlipoca
smoking mirror
dark reflection
of the warlord of earth
Pepsicoatl, Cocacoatl
magicians of colored
sugar water
and idiot box addiction
of our day
in age
the hunt goes on
Pepsicoatl, Cocacoatl
lord of imperial racism
lady of blood money
Pepsicoatl, Cocacoatl
hunts today
bronze land, rivers, and sky
choke in its smoking
agony of hot coals
flames of mine, Huehueteotl
have brought you wisdom
i've dispelled smoke
and light brightens

our faces, Huehueteotl
our hearts
know well the old ones
the master builders
toltecas, Huehueteotl
carvers of melodies
and dancers of colors
weavers of flowers
painters of songs
singers of morning dew
even today, Huehueteotl
the sun rises in fire
painting dawn

[*Enter Quetzalcoatl.*]

Quetzalcoatl:

i bring light to the darkness
mestizaje of bloods pounds
in my veins
i am the morning star
and the navel of earth
feathers and scales
color my face, Quetzalcoatl
i am Meshicano Mazateca
Meshicano Zapoteca
Chicano, Chicano
cheekbone to ankle
bronze
is
my
skin
and my heart
moves in balance to the stars
in the north
the Huelga thunderbird
in the south
the Chilean condor
Kukulcán cracks
dawn open
i wake through
la raza every morning
la raza wakes
through my star
every dew

[*Enter Cihuacoatl.*]

Cihuacoatl:

> ı bring fragrance to the day
> Cihuacoatl
> my arms tree houses
> for birds nests
> and my flowers
> honey to the bee
> Cihuacoatl Meshicana
> Chicana, Chicana
> my womb bore maize
> to Quetzalcoatl
> in our concern
> for man and woman
> my breasts bore
> fruits
> to the thirsty
> on earth
> for knowledge
> of me

Quetzalcoatl and Cihuacoatl:

> the tree of life
> in brotherhood
> in sisterhood
> the children
> round the trunk
> the tree of life
> bore fruit
> ce acatl
> topiltzin
> Quetzalcoatl, Cihuacoatl
> on the dawn
> of thirteen heavens
> the dawn
> of decreasing choice
> the dawn
> of thirteen cycles
> of fifty-two years
> each
> the sacred twins
> children of earth
> children of clouds
> two lord Quetzalcoatl
> two lady Cihuacoatl
> Salavi our mother
> Mixcoatl our father

our lord
our lady
one reed
feathered serpent
round the tree of life
we have flourished
well aware
of the sundown
of nine hells
of increasing doom
to be carved
by the Christian sword
and the tree of thorns
will bring suffering
war
confusion
and decadence
we will wither
till again
the tree of life
will bloom
in the dawn
of
ce acatl
august 16, 1987
from the dead
of april 21, 1519
we shall rise
to the cycle
of the thirteen
heavens of choice
past the nine
hells of doom
the Pepsicoatl
and Cocacoatl
will rule

[*Enter Huitzilopochtli.*]

Huitzilopochtli:

blood, blood
it is i thirst for
flesh, flesh
it is i hunger for
war is my name
hunting my game

son of Coatlicue
brother of darkness
brother of fear
blood, flesh and bones
Huitzilopochtli's soup
boiled human soup
and roasted heart
but come oh brother!
bring your smoke
onto our mirror
come oh brother
to the hunt!

[*Enter Tezcatlipoca.*]

Tezcatlipoca:

war is my name
hunting my game
son of Coatlicue
brother of death
planter of fear
breeder of darkness
ignorance and confusion
i bring
firewater to our heads
dark caverns to our hearts
smoke, Tezcatlipoca
smog
smoke, Tezcatlipoca
smog
where is the man
the woman
not yet my prey
addicts
to my way of death?
mother!
come join our feast
to hunt we go
to kill and maim
to rape and wound
to tear
destroy, dehumanize
deodorize
homogenize
sterilize
to paralyze the flow

of moving life
come, mother!
Coatlicue
come feast with us!
the prey
is running wild
open your womb
the live
return again
to you
in bones

[*Enter Coatlicue.*]

Coatlicue:

Huitzilopochtli, southern son
of mine
Tezcatlipoca, northern son
of mine
i bring your brother
and your sister
from the west
i, Coatlicue
bear two other
beasts of prey
hunters to be sure
i bore them
for the hunt
today
for the hunt
here, on Anahuac
Land Surrounded
by waters
circulating its body
cross mountains of iguanas
into lakes of serpents
jaguars purr to my call
and caverns open
where i slept the night before
i bore them
to be warlord and warlady
of all time
in all space
beloved sons
welcome your brother
welcome your sister
feast and kill with them

they've no scrupples
in their cruel games
nourishment from my breasts
and flesh of my flesh
make of your brother and sister
two of us
blood money
baptized their heads
our lord below
performed the rite
children of murder
genocide and biocide
aborted imperial racism
destroyers of hearts
colonizers of land
Pepsicoatl, Cocacoatl!
meet your old brothers
twister of tongues
blinder of eyes
join the hunt!

[*Enter Pepsicoatl and Cocacoatl.*]

Pepsicoatl and Cocacoatl:

look at us
lord of imperial racism
lady of blood money
war is our name
hunting our game
where are the bastards
niggers, spics
greasers, and japs
where is the son of whores
Quetzalcoatl
the China men and skwas
where is the daughter of lepers
Cihuacoatl
the Mezkins and gooks
where is our prey
our fangs are dry
and our pockets empty
coins and blood
coins and blood
where is our tribute
coins and blood
coins and blood
we see them nowhere

come out! come out!
our bullets throb for flesh
and our bombs for land
come out! come out!
and face your bones
in flames
[*Council of Elders closes as dance of death begins.*]

Council of Elders:

zipping through concrete spider webs
metallic ants turn to centipedes
and bright lights darken the eyes
with neon flashes and
towers of smoking oil refineries
of los angeles dying
dying in an august afternoon
the maize was trampled by dogs
and many birds took flight
in the maze, the crying
cursing winds
of northern icelands
in august twenty-nine
walk again on earth
and sing of peace
of brotherhood and sisterhood
of terrestrial roots
born of fertile womb
man and woman
stand and walk again
on earth
to listen with bare feet
to the murmuring caress
of mother earth's heart beat
she gave us birth
in blood
and for the sun
we have sacrificed
even roasted bones
in the deserts of our father sun
we have marched
migrated
walked the distance of our lives
in lonely stroll
below the moongloom of the night
as cherry headed
armored ants
wail

in the night of fire and smoke
splashing mud
on sidewalk and walls
rushing to the hunt
belly clubbed
gas masked
panting breaths
spit the joy of death
spit the death of joy
retiring at dawn
to the beer canned existence
of idiot box stares
waiting, waiting
for another
asphalt spider web ride
riding over brotherhood
riding over sisterhood
danza
riding over justice
danza
riding over peace
danza
danza of bare feet
danza of people
danza of day
danza of spirit
danza of bronze
danza, danza
danza, danza. . . .

ACT II: THE TRIBUNAL

[*Round table dominates stage. Screen for slides is directly above. Slides
of protesting raza and rioting police are shown throughout. Witnesses
(Mexicanos, Chicanos, and Chimalma) face Pepsicoatl and Cocacoatl.
Huehueteotl presides as judge facing audience. Audience is jury. Huehueteotl opens with indictment.*]

[*Enter Huehueteotl.*]

Huehueteotl:

huelga
red and black
huelga

justice will be done
Pepsicoatl, Cocacoatl
on two counts
before you [*to audience*]
our jury, today
crimes committed
against bronze people
and bronze land
genocide
genocide
killer of children
biocide
biocide
polluter of earth
waters and sky
Pepsicoatl, Cocacoatl
lord of imperial racism
lady of blood monies
Pepsicoatl, Cocacoatl
your poison is brought
to test, to trial
master of destruction
mistress of detergent
answer
to the charges
in Chicano tribunal
tribunal of bronze tribes
indigenous
rooted in Anahuac
our bronze
mestizo continent
of indian heart
indicts
you
as
a
world criminal
whose only justice is gunfire
whose only liberty is bought
a pusher of war
a pusher of fear
a pusher of money and checks
a paper pusher
a b-52's and napalm
a pusher of deception,
corruption, emptiness

and idleness
a pusher all the same
of gadgets and soaps
a pusher of pollutants
and insecticides
and herbicides
a pusher all the same
of death
the sun stone
awaits your shoulders
patiently
thirsting for your sacrifice
i, Huehueteotl
will burn copal
and cremate
the muscles of your hearts
i, Huehueteotl
have waited long to see
your hearts
before
the sun
stand
Pepsicoatl, Cocacoatl,
stand!

[*Enter Pepsicoatl and Cocacoatl.*]

Pepsicoatl:

now looke here
my woman and i
didn't mean no harm
you understand
orders are orders
war's our name
hunting our game
a little fun, no more
what's Quetzalcoatl
to you, anyhow
plumed worm
he nigger lover, anyhow
what's a spic to you
anyhow
world better off
without colored
stinking japs

they after my woman
i know
they after my money
i know
a man's gotta protect
his property

[*Enter Mexican.*]

Mexican:

what of your killings and hangings
what of the land you stole from us
our children starve while you fatten

Pepsicoatl:

now looke here
i'm a hard working
man
can't help it if money
comes my way

Cocacoatl:

just 'cause you
lazy
you think
we ought to live
dirty
like you never
take baths
and your woman
keeps a filthy house
i know
i got me a meskin maid
no good for what
my pay is worth
no good for nothing
that's why we took
the land
you stood on
my man and i
wanting to civilize
your kind . . .
i told you Pepsi [*Speaking to Pepsicoatl now.*]
we'd better

wipe 'em off
like them indians
these meskins
are dumb
no matter how kind
you treat them
they gonna
spit back at you

Mexican:

money comes your way
as we sweat on our land
you call it profitable investment
i call it yanki colonization
your foreign aid
chains our independence
with your guns
at our heads
with the one hand
you give one
with the other
you steal one
hundred-fold
as to your woman
keep her
no one wants her
you've killed [*Speaking to Pepsicoatl and Cocacoatl.*]
too many
bronze people
you've spoiled
too much bronze land
your manifest destiny
gave you holiness
your big stick
gave you control
holy control
of bronze people
and bronze land
enough
of your holiness
enough
of your control
enough of you
my verdict
is guilty as charged

my sentence
is death

[*Mexican pulls gun to shoot Pepsicoatl. Cocacoatl cuts him down with
her m-16. Pepsicoatl roars with laughter.*]

Pepsicoatl:

you see him [*To jury.*]
pull out his gun
to kill me
my woman
just
had a faster draw

[*Enter Chicano.*]

Chicano:

you are a murderer
and a thief esse
you too essa
colonized
our minds
wanting us
to be like you
telling us
we'd fare off well
forgetting
our mexican blood
you tried to rinse
our skins
with spain
while we worked
in your factories
slaved
in your mines
and died
in your pesticide fields
we fought your wars
and came back
to the yankee occupation
of our barrios

Cocacoatl:

now, now
you don't want to be

like the meskins
you in amerikkka now
now you just
pay attention to me
and everything
gonna be alright
uptight
and outta sight
now you just
get here
close to mama
and let mama
give you
what no
white woman
ever gave
no meskin
i'm gonna
give you
me white
rosy breasts
and embrace me
your dark waist
with me white
mama thighs
you gonna
be my boy
and we won't
let papa
know nothing
'bout our pretty
little
colored
affair
'cause papa
get mad
and mama
loves her
brown
amerikkkan
boy

Chicano:

look at this ruca now
alright then

let's get it on

> [*Chicano and Cocacoatl go under
> the round table. Moaning and love
> sounds are heard. Chicano stands
> tightening pants.*]

orale essa
ya estufas
enough honey
for today
now
all i got time for
is getting
Pepsicoatl
off his
master
hung up

Pepsicoatl:

you in amerikkka now
boy
you just gotta
settle your mind
as to who's boss
around these parts

Chicano:

you know what esse
you just never bothered
to look around
and see
what your amerikkkan dream
was building
you just never
realized
it was us
in aztlán
that taught you
everything you know
about our land
and our ways
you just never
realized
that your towers
of money and pollution
are built

on us
you know what esse
ya estufas
now it is time
to do time
and from the looks
of your own laws
you got
two chances
you killed
first degree
with premeditation
definite intent
and
unfair advantage
you got
death out here
or life in prisión
you
are
guilty
esse
no way
of poking holes
into this one
no way to plead
self defense
we ain't got the guns
no way to plead
insanity
you got all your marbles
you done it
knowingly
willfully
and even
spiritually
in the name
of Christianity
and
your teutonic origins
ya estufas esse
dig your own jail esse
you built it
dig your own chair esse
you electrified it

Pepsicoatl:

why
you dirty meskin
you all alike

> [*Runs to strangle Chicano. Chicano
> pulls knife. Cocacoatl cuts him
> down with her m-16.*]

Cocacoatl:

you seen him
pulling a knife
on daddy
like that
you heard him
before
talking
dirty
to
mama
them meskins
all
alike
treacherous
and
nasty

[*Enter Chimalma.*]

Chimalma:

fork-tongued white woman
tell of the times
when you dreamt
you could kiss
the wounds whipped
by your white master
on my brothers
my black brothers
my yellow brothers
my red brothers
tell of the times
when you dreamt
you could own
my bronze brothers
you called them

half-breeds then
white woman
speak of the many
things you own
and dream to own
speak of your position
of your property status
of your marriage
contract to a man of war
speak of the empire
your man has built
with
colored
people's
blood
little sun
touched
your
hearts
white people
of the caverns
look at our sun
and like moles
you are blinded
before the neon lighting
of your asphalt gardens
you are accomplice
to Pepsicoatl's genocide
you are accomplice
to Pepsicoatl's biocide
you are victim
to Pepsicoatl's suicide
Cocacoatl!
look at yourself
daughter of thorns
dawn does not
brighten your vision
darkness reigns
in your heart
possessed by your property
possessed by your dependence
Pepsicoatl has used you
as bait on a hook
to protect you
to keep you
to chain

and to fence you
Pepsicoatl
has brought
all
his
tree
of
thorns
hear Chimalma's truth

Pepsicoatl:

now look ye here
Coca
this here squaw
putting thoughts
in your head
cut her down
like you done in
all others
it ain't use
no sense
talking to half-breeds
or colored
they stupid
they born
to be slaves
you's a mistress
and Pepsi's
your master

Cocacoatl:

let her speak
never look
at myself
in them waters
you ain't master
of no one
no how
let her speak

Chimalma:

look yourself
in river waters
flowing from
mountain to sea

from the clouds
to the valleys
flowing still
unbound
unchained
you are not
Pepsicoatl's
property
you are not
Pepsicoatl's
maid
you are earthchild
and a servant
to the tree of life
we
have
care
for
the tree
you
have
eaten
the fruit
of our labor
come
labor with us
you are pregnant
with twins
your nine hells
of doom
are bursting
with mestizo
children
let them grow
on the mountains
drinking
spring
water
the autumn of your slavery
sheds the last leaf
it will be a cold winter
'till you bear
the children
come
and bear them
alone

i will see you
through labor
under
our
tree of life

Pepsicoatl:

looke here, woman
you just sit still
while i kill me
a squaw

Cocacoatl:

you just
put down
that gun
Pepsi

Pepsicoatl:

shut up, woman
you ain't got
nothing to say
you got
lot to explain

Cocacoatl:

i ain't shutting up
i am pregnant
and i want to
labor by
the tree of life

Pepsicoatl:

get on home
'fore i lose
my temper
and whip
you ass
till you
can't
sit down
in a month

[*Pepsicoatl aims his m-16 at Chimalma. Cocacoatl cuts him down with
hers, throws m-16 down and rushes to his fallen body.*]

Cocacoatl:

> Pepsi!
> i done
> gone
> killed
> you

Chimalma:

> you've done well
> now
> your children
> will live

Cocacoatl:

> i'm afraid
> never bore
> but a gun . . .
> i'm afraid

Chimalma:

> straighten your back
> bear your load
> walk steady
> beside me
> we
> shall
> live
> through
> winter
> without hunger
> nor cold
> Mixcoatl
> keeps
> a
> good fire

> [*Cocacoatl takes boots off and
> walks away to mountain where
> she is to bear the twins.*]

ACT III: THE LABOR

[*Stage is dominated by the tree of life with hanging Huichol god's eyes
and a fire. The fire is towards the stage on the left of the audience
and the tree farther back towards the right. Scattered cactus and rock.
Mixcoatl is guarding the fire. Huehueteotl speaks at the fire. It is dark,
the sun rises.*]

Huehueteotl:

> thirteen circles
> round the sun
> four seasons
> each
> prepare to see
> the light
> dawn is near
> and the twins
> kick the womb
> of Cocacoatl
> announcing
> their arrival
> out the mist
> into the dew
> morning
> breaks open
> the world
> as darkness
> passes on
> and brightness
> bursts forth
> round
> the tree of life

[*Cocacoatl enters mounting and calls for help; her labor has arrived.*]

Cocacoatl:

> Chimalma, Chimalma!
> my belly bursts
> my body aches
> help me
> i'm afraid
> Chimalma
> Chimalma

[*Enter Chimalma with dancing children around her.*]

Chimalma:

> lets walk
> under the tree
> now
> face the sun
> the branches
> to the East
> are low
> grab hold
> of one
> and squat
> do not fight
> your children
> in their birth
> they will seek
> the light
> alone
> let them be
> born
> you
> bear
> the
> pain
> of dawn

[*Cocacoatl bites her lower lip in pain, moaning. Children dance around her and Chimalma helps Cocacoatl in her labor. Cocacoatl screams. Her scream is followed by the birth-cry of two children. The dancing stops as the children dance off stage.*]

Cocacoatl:

> my breath
> Chimalma
> my wind
> it is [*Gasping*]
> gone

Chimalma:

> the dawn
> has come
> and you
> have lived
> to see it
> be brave
> now

Cocacoatl:

i will not
live
i lay here
dying

Chimalma:

under
this tree
peace is
with you
and death
holds
no darkness
in your
path
walk on
return
to earth
earth
welcomes
you
your flesh
to be
her flesh
again
around
the
sun
another
cycle
'till flesh
and bone
and blood
give
form
to
you
again, be gone

[*Chimalma covers Cocacoatl's body and children enter to dance again
around the tree of life and Cocacoatl. Cocacoatl brings newborn twins
to Huehueteotl and Mixcoatl.*]

Mixcoatl:

nine hells
of fifty-two
years
since april
1519
nine hells
of increasing
genocide
of increasing
doom
of increasing
biocide
of increasing
doom
with the dawn
the tree of life
blooms
and
the tree of thorns
withers
thirteen heavens
begin
august 1987
the birth
the new man
the birth
the new woman
the birth
the new world
the blooming of Anahuac
the rise of the red sun
the labor of red people
the blooming of humanity
of brotherhood
of sisterhood
of justice
of beauty
of labor
and of peace
the blooming of the human face
the cultivation of the moving heart
the birth
of the new man
the death of Pepsicoatl
the birth

the birth
of the new woman
the death of Cocacoatl
the struggle
on dark earth
the struggle
on bright sun
the twins
the dawn of life
and dusk of death
the morning star

Council of Elders:

let the young boy
be the lord of dawn
and the young girl
be the lady of dawn
let the morning star
guide them
to be servants
of the tree of life
to traverse
the red path
all throughout
looking
about
breathlessly
walking
the path
with a heart

Mixcoatl:

in the heart
of the children
the sun dawns
shadows hiding
from its light
lost the wind
in the fire
of our births
earth gives flowers
to our dawn
flowers in the heart
sing for the nation
walking down
many paths

without thinking
these steps
seek the path
of justice
finding thorns
in the darkness
we walk
alone
returning
to the sun of old
quetzal feathers
the return to our
beginning
walk on earth
again
forge our nation
carve it
with our Toltec heart
on earth
below the sun
the children
shall rise
in justice . . .
it
is
dawn
good
morning
fathersun
your fire
still
burns
and
motherearth's
copal
still
perfumes
our
heart

[*Music breaks into singing several songs, children dance.*]

The Ultimate Pendejada

YSIDRO R. MACIAS

Ysidro R. Macias, professor in the Department of Comparative Culture at the University of California (Irvine), is one of the most promising Chicano playwrights on the scene today. Unlike most other Chicano dramatists, who are primarily concerned with dramatizing the Chicano "experience," Macias goes beyond this dimension. His drama is characterized by the constant search for answers to questions pertinent to "el pensamiento Chicano." His work reflects a penetrating insight and introspective view of issues, ideas, and concepts which have and will influence the future of our Chicano people.

Mártir Montezuma and *The Ultimate Pendejada* are included in this anthology as samples of his promising works.

In *Mártir Montezuma* the playwright skillfully and artistically deals with Cesar Chavez's philosophy of non-violence in an earlier historic setting. The setting being during the times of the Aztec empire. *Mártir Montezuma* like the contemporary figure of Cesar Chavez endeavored to achieve the same human rights for his people, but failed in the end.

The Ultimate Pendejada is a provoking contemporary play treating the topic of "Chicanismo." In an attempt to rid themselves of a hypocritical state of existence in what is commonly referred to as the "American-way-of life," a young Mexican-American couple turns to and joins the Chicano move-

135

ment to find true meaning to their identity and existence. To their surprise, the Chicano experience turns out to be as equally absurd as their Anglo-American experience.

Characters

Mary
Robert
Jack
Jill
Cuahtemoc
Pancho Zapata
Flor
Margarita
Chuey

ACT I

Scene 1

[*A young Mexican-American couple (Robert and Mary Gomes) at home in a comfortable apartment. There are a table, four chairs, an American flag draped directly behind them, and "modest" posters on the wall. They are discussing pot, drugs, world politics, the domestic scene (including the educational system and the college they go to), the Chicano movement. They are very agringado in speech, behavior, customs, etc. They are finishing dinner.*]

Robert: That was a wonderful dinner, darling. You make the best roast beef and sauerkraut in town.

Mary [*Blushing*] : Ooh Robert, you're so . . . ooh sweet. And say the most darling things; oh my, I was so lucky to marry you and be blessed with all the virtues of a pleasant home.

Robert [*He puts on glasses and picks up newspaper*] : Here's a story in the paper about a checano [CHi-ka-no] from the bear-eo who was caught smoking mary-juana, Mary.

137

Mary [*Exclaiming disgust*] :   Those nasty people! When will they ever learn? I just don't understand why those bear-eo people do those things. Look at us; we're of Spanish descent and we made it. Why can't they?

Robert [*Putting on airs of academia*] :   According to my uncle taco, it is because of their refusal to accept assimilation into the stratification of our accelerated society.

Mary [*Very proudly and also picking up portion of newspaper*] :   You're so . . . oo smart, Robert. Oh! Look here! It's something about some communist rebels trying to overthorw the respectable government in Nicaragua.

Robert [*Putting down his copy and taking Mary's portion of paper*] :   I just can't understand why those peasants want to join those dirty reds. It's all a conspiracy, Mary, that Fidel Castro is public enemy number one of the United States. We should send the marines right down there to stop the people, cops, the reds, from doing what they're doing.

[*Robert puts down paper.*]

Mary: Toucheé, Robert. Those pinkos are everywhere. Did you know that they sat in in President Hiyawatha's office yesterday?

Robert [*In disbelief*] :   At our beloved aluma ma . . . aa . . ter!?

Mary [*Very angry*] :   Yes! Mr. Hiyawatha tried to talk them out of his office, but the pinkos couldn't understand what he was saying. The medics finally came and found him blabbering away [*Mary imitates a blabbering idiot.*] and took him to rest. Poor Mr. Hiyawatha.

Robert [*Furious*] :   Those dirty militants! [*Hand reaches out to touch flag.*] By the spangle of my stars, I swear it, I swear it [*He assumes patriotic pose.*] ; I pledge allegiance, to the flag, of the Un . . . I mean, I pledge to forever fight those who would desecrate the sanctity of my homeland.

[*Mary rises from table, picks up dishes and cups, goes to makeshift sink where she goes through motion of pouring soap and water on dishes. Entire conversation that follows is while they do dishes.*]

Mary: Robert, dear, its time to wash the dishes.

Robert: Yes, sweetheart. [*He puts on apron and stands next to Mary and assumes position to dry and put away dishes.*]

Mary: You know, Robert, our country is the most wonderful in the world. We have a specialized educational system that produces very disciplined minds and leaders. Why would anyone want to change it?

Robert: Both these "minority people" and the white hippies don't want to work. For them, it's all gimme. We've got to stop that. Either they accept things as they are or they can go back where they came from.

Mary: But don't those minority people know that all you have to do is work hard to make it? If those bear-eo people would just learn to speak English.

Robert: They're so stubborn; they want to hold on to their old ancestral ways instead of joining the modern generation. For them, its eat sleep, and fff . . . fornicate.

[*Robert stops and thinks about what he said; a sly grin comes to his face, and he quietly moves in back of Mary and attempts to arouse her.*]

[*Mary pushes him away and looks disgusted.*]

Mary: Oh Robert, you know we never do those things until 10:15 at night. Anyway, we did it two days ago and can't do it again until tomorrow.

[*Robert meekly assumes his position to dry dishes again; he is hurt by her refusal but bravely continues the conversation.*]

Robert: I'm sorry, honey, I guess you're right. Anyway, Amerika for Amerikans. I'm going to join the Support your Local Law Enforcement League.

Mary [*Thrilled*]:   That's wonderful, Robert. I'm going to ask my Delta Omega Phi sisters to hold a benefit dinner for our peace officers. [*She assumes a self-righteous position.*] Participation in our democracy is the key to all.

[*The scene ends as they finish the dishes. In the background can be heard cuts from "My Country, Tis of Thee" and "God Bless America."*]

Scene 2

[*A knock on the door. Robert rises and opens the door. The Gomes' are in their living room. A young gringolofico college couple enters. They are Jack and Jill Washington. There are the initial greetings as all four sit down.*]

Mary: Ooh, Jill, it's so good to see you. Won't you sit down, Jack?

Jack: I believe that would be appropriate, Mary.

Jill: You have such a wonderful apartment, Mary. The decor is absolutely marvelous. Everything is so chic, soo . . . oo groo . . . ovy!

Robert: Yes, we think so. I'm glad you two were able to drop by to chit and chat. We were discussing earlier the terrible outrages of these militants nowadays.

Jack: I wouldn't be so harsh on those . . . uh . . . misfits, Robert. After all, there's probably a reason why they're doing those things.

Jill: Maybe so, Jack, but I just can't understand the violence in their actions. Why can't they do things peacefully? Don't they understand the way things are done in this country?

Mary: I think you're being too easy on them, Jill. If those people don't act right, they should be arrested. We should all be able to get along in this great country of ours.

Jack: I agree with Mary. Look at Jill and myself, we get along with all kinds of people. Why, we have good acquaintances who are Negro and Oriental and . . . uh . . . Spanish.

[*A look of uneasiness comes over the four. All four shift nervously in their seats as Jack looks at the floor and Jill stares ashamedly at Mary.*]

[*Robert attempts to crack the silence. He clears his throat, which has a gargajo in it, by muffling the sound.*]

Robert [*Smiling bravely*] : Aaahem. A slight tonsillitis problem. [*He gets up to prepare some mixed drinks, goes over to a bar, and starts mixing some drinks.*]

Robert: What would you care for, Jack and Jill? And you, Mary?

Jack: I'll have an Agnew rinser. [*He grins sheepishly.*] It's a new drink. Mix red wine with white soda and add a blue cherry.

Jill: You're so debonair and groo . . . ovy, Jack! Just give me an ordinary manhattan on the rocks, please.

Mary: Oh, Robert, do mix me a double-upside down martini with scotch as a chaser. [*She looks at Jack and Jill.*] It's my favorite constitution.

Robert: By the way, Jack, how is the stock market coming along? [*He hands drinks to Jack and Jill, then to Mary and sits down with his own drink. Crossing his legs, he sits with his glass somewhat extended and offers a toast.*] Cheers everyone!

All four: Cheers! [*They sip from glasses.*]

Mary: Jill, before these men get started on their man talk, let's go into the kitchen. I want you to see my new electric osterizer, automatic garbage disposal, and self-cleaning, atomic-powered oven.

Jill: How marvelous that you *finally* got them, Mary. Mine are so old. Yes, let's go.

[*Mary and Jill get up and jointly depart from the room.*]

Mary and Jill: Bye, fellows!

Jack [*He sinks a little lower in his seat, with legs crossed, and attempts to make himself a little more comfortable*] :   Aaahh! Well, you know Robert, this has been a good year for me in the stocks. The recent bull market in Consolidated Napalm brought me a huge profit. Lately I've bought into Mace Incorporated and that's doing real well also. What about you?

Robert: So so with me. Red-white-and-blue Enterprises is up and United Lettuce went up 3/4. But my Bank of Amerika stocks have gone down recently. Do you have any tips for me?

Jack: Chemicals is the thing this day, my boy. Look into United Tear Gas and Associated Pesticides. You can't lose. They're selling very good at home and abroad. Not to say that I agree with everything our country is doing in Vietnam, you understand.

Robert: Nothing to it, my man. Personally I feel that we should do every thing we can to win over there and then get out. We've got to stop coddling the commies!

Jack: I agree with you, but what about the talk recently about some civilians being mistakenly caught in a crossfire at My Lai and other places?

Robert: Just hogwash in my opinion! There are some communists trying to discredit the heroic efforts of our GI's. We would *never* do anything like that! Our country would never stand for something like that to happen. . . . It would be totally un-Amerikan!

Jack: Yes, I guess you're right. [*He has a fierce look on his face.*] I just wish I could go over there and show those gooks how an Amerikan fights! [*He calms down and now has apologetic look on his face.*] Unfortunately, my country's priorities requires me to stay in college. How about you, Robert?

Robert [*He is also calmer and has an apologetic look*] :   Yeh, damn it, I've got a student deferment also. My . . . uh . . . knee isn't too good either. You know, athletics and all.

Jack [*Sympathetically*] :   I understand. You know, there should be a way to serve our country at home. [*He gets excited as an idea comes into his head.*] Yeah, that's it! A Freedom Youth League here in the United States, to fight the internal commies and the niggers and redskins and spics. . . .

Robert [*A little self-conscious but also excited*] :   Bravo, Jack. I could go for that. We would have our own uniforms and be deputized to keep the peace, especially on the campuses.

Jack: Yeah! We would write a proposal to be funded by the government. [*He then looks questionably at Robert.*] By the way, I didn't mean that about the spics. . . .

Robert [*Trying to put on airs of indifference*] :   Why shouldn't you mean it? You're not hurting my feelings; we're Spanish.

Jack: I'm glad to hear that.

Robert: Don't think that we Spanish have any feelings for the Mexicans or Puerto Ricans or Checanos. Me and Mary were talking about them before you got here and we feel that the whole Checano movement is a dirty commie plot by some people who just don't want to work!

Jack: Yeah, me and Jill were watching a picture on TV about Mexico and they sure are dirty. You would think that they would take a bath once in a while. I guess the Checanos in this country have inherited the slothiness and laziness of the Mexicans, don't you think?

Robert: Undoubtedly! Look at how dirty those people following Caesar Shaavez are. The nerve of them, trying to destroy our honorable tradition of free agricultural enterprise. [*Looks serious.*] Do you know that the agricultural worker in this country gets paid more than anywhere else in the world!

Jack: Yes. Why, if Caesar Shaavez and his cutthroats were living anywhere else they would be middle-class. They don't know how lucky they are!

[*Mary and Jill reappear onto the scene. They both sit down.*]

Mary: What's this I hear about Caesar Shaavez? That awful man! [*She clenches her fist and grits her teeth in an angry and anguished pose.*] Every time I hear about them wellgistas and the Brown Ber-ets and Tigerina and the rest of those stupied Checanos, my blood boils over! [*She assumes pose of self-pity.*] You don't know how difficult it is sometimes, Jill, being mistaken for a Mexican or Checano.

Jill [*Looking sympathetic*] :   It must be terrible. I understand you've already changed the spelling of your name once. Perhaps you could change it again, to Gometti or Gomeson or something.

Robert: We might be forced to do it. [*He looks uncomfortable and hurries to change the subject.*] Uh . . . what do you feel about the ecology issue, Jack?

Mary [*Taking cue from Robert to end the conversation*] :   Oooh Robert, let's not talk anymore. Why don't we all put on a record and dance some. Okay?

Jill: A grand idea, Mary; I feel like dancing so much.

Jack [*In a faggot voice*] :   To exercise one's libido is to emphasize the inner thoughts and creativity of the personality. [*He gets up and does some faggot-like ballet movements.*]

[*Mary gets up, goes to imaginary record player, returns, and takes Robert's arm. Jill takes Jack's arm.*]

[*The scene ends as a country style square dance record plays in the background. All four are thoroughly enjoying themselves. The actors are free at this time to give exclamations of their joy at dancing the square dance. The name of the record is "Oh Johnny, Oh Johnny."*]

[*Curtain falls on Scene 2.*]

ACT II

Scene 1

[*The curtain rises with a new background. A suggested background is an outline of the Berkeley campus of UC with the campanile viewed in the background. Robert Gomes is lazily walking on campus when he meets Cuahtemoc "Porfirito" Díaz, the "radical" Chicano campus group leader and spokesman.*]

[*Cuahtemoc is standing around, checking out the action, as Robert comes walking by. He motions to Robert to stop. Cuahtemoc speaks a la pachucaso.*]

Cuahtemoc: Hey, ése, are you a Chicano?

Robert: I beg your pardon. Are you speaking to me?

Cuahtemoc: Sure, ése. ¿Te pregunte, ares Chicano? I asked you, are you a Chicano, a Mexican, or a Mexican-American, lo que sayas, whatever you want to be called?

Robert: Aahem. . . . [*Looking a little bit scared.*] Well, I do happen to be of a Spanish-speaking background, if that's what you mean.

Cuahtemoc: Good . . . what's your name, ése?

Robert: My name is Robert . . . Robert Gómes. If I may inquire, what's yours?

Cuahtemoc: Me dicen Porfirito. My name is Cuahtemoc "Porfirito" Díaz. My nickname comes from a Mexican hero.

Robert: Very interesting. That's very quaint.

Cuahtemoc: That's very qué?

Robert: Very quaint. That means it's very romantic, to be named after a hero.

Cuahtemoc [*Chest puffs out, looks very macho*] :   Yeah, ése, I think que ésta de aquéllas. It's out of sight. Anyway, the reason I stopped to talk to you is if you've heard of our group here on campus.

Robert: I . . . I don't know. What's the name of your group?

Cuahtemoc [*Very proud*] :   M.A.F.I.A. It stands for Mexican-American for Important Action. We're very militant.

Robert [*Looking very scared now*] :   Noo . . . oo, I haven't. Could I go now?

Cuahtemoc [*Sensing that Robert is scared and wanting to talk to him some more*] :   Wait a minute, ése. I was just kidding about being militant. [*He leans over closely to Robert and whispers.*] We just say that to scare off the putos. You're not scared, are you?

Robert [*His machismo challenged*] :   Of course, I'm not scared. What sort of important action does your group do?

Cuahtemoc: Well, let's see. We write proposals to fund some projects. . . . We support the community. . . . We're for Chicano academic freedom. . . . We write proposals . . . uhhh. . . . Anyway, ése, we're for Chicanos. Have you ever heard of Chicano Power?

Robert: Well, I've heard something like that on the news. What sort of power is this Checano Power?

Cuahtemoc: I don't know exactly, ése, but it's for Chicanos. That means we do everything ourselves. [*He assumes militant pose and raises a clenched fist as he shouts.*] Chicano! Power! Chicano! Power!

[*Cuahtemoc is overtaken with his militant pose and emotions; he stops and sort of freezes for a while and then relaxes.*]

Cuahtemoc: Well, what do you think, ése, you want to come to one of our meetings?

Robert: I don't know, I've got to study tonight and I'm real kind of busy . . . you know, studying and all.

Cuahtemoc [*Sympathetic*] :   Yeah, we gotta study. [*He reassumes determined pose.*] Com-on, ése, come to one of our meetings. Or won't your gringa girlfriend let you come? [*He kids Robert to appeal to his machismo again.*]

Robert [*Angry as he forgets the militancy of Cuahtemoc*] :   What do you mean my gringa girlfriend? I don't have a gringa girlfriend. I'm married to my wife, a . . . aa . . . a Checana!

Cuahtemoc [*Happy*] :   That's the spirit, ése. I didn't know that you were married to a Chicana. Why didn't you say so.

Robert [*Surprised that he admitted the truth and feeling a little guilty*]:
Well . . . I . a . . . what I meant was that she is of a Spanish-speaking background herself.

Cuahtemoc [*Feeling he is winning and pushing to consolidate his gain*]:   I
understand, ése, I understand. So you're married to a Spanish-descented
wife, right?

Robert: Yes.

Cuahtemoc: Well, won't this Spanish-speaking descented wife of yours let
you come to a meeting?

Robert [*Exasperated and giving up*]:   Of course she will! I mean, I don't
have to ask her if she'll let me. [*He assumes macho pose.*] I'm the man of
my house!

Cuahtemoc: ¡Aai oo dioo, ése, con huevos! You got it, carnal, now you know
what you want.

Robert [*By now he has given up and is resigned to coming to the meeting*]:
I guess so. When is your next meeting?

Cuahtemoc: This coming Wednesday. We meet at Benito Juárez Hall at
7:30. Of course that's Chicano time.

Robert: Benito Juárez Hall?

Cuahtemoc: Yeah. [*He leans over to whisper softly.*] It's really Richard
Nixon Hall but we call it Benito Juárez Hall. Do you dig it, ése?

Robert: I understand. What's this about Checano time?

Cuahtemoc: Chicano, ése, Chicano, not Checano. Chicano time means we
show up a little bit later than we really mean, if you know what I mean.
You do, don't you, ése?

Robert [*Confused*]:   I guess so. What is going to be discussed at the meeting,
if I may ask?

Cuahtemoc: Sure you may, ése. A ver, que vamos a talk about at the meeting. [*He assumes a pose of thinking very hard.*] Let's see, bueno, we're
going to set up a tutorial program, we are going to get together to discuss
the issues, we are going to write a proposal. . . .

Robert: Well . . . [*Trying to get out of coming to the meeting.*] . . . I don't
know if I can come this Wednesday night, but maybe next week.

Cuahtemoc [*Pissed off that Robert is trying to get away again*]:   What's
wrong, ése, aren't you a macho or what?

Robert: What's a match-o?

Cuahtemoc [*Surprised*] :   You don't know what a macho is!? [*He puts his arm around Robert and sympathizes with him.*] No wonder, ése, why didn't you tell me? [*Whispers to him.*] A macho tiene huevos. Balls.

Robert: A matcho tener whae-balls? Whae-balls? What do you mean?

Cuahtemoc [*Puts his hand to his forehead as he looks up at the sky, disbelieving Robert*] :   ¡Madre de dios, qué pendejo! [*Puts his arm around Robert again.*] Look ése, a macho is a man! [*He struts around and speaks strongly.*] A man who decides for himself! Are you a man?

Robert [*A little bit angry but surprised to be questioned*] :   Of course I am!

Cuahtemoc [*Following up*] :   Good, ése, good. Now are you going to come to the meeting or are you going to let your old lady decide? ¿ ¡Eres macho! ?

Robert [*Excited and strutting himself*] :   Yes, I'm a match-o!

Cuahtemoc: That's it, ése, that's it.

[*Scene ends as they put their arms around each other's shoulders and walk away, strutting as they go, especially Robert. They both look happy.*]

[*Curtain falls.*]

Scene 2

[*The curtain rises with the scene being at the Gomes' apartment. Mary is dusting the furniture as Robert walks in. Robert struts in; Mary looks at him; Robert sees Mary looking at him and doesn't strut anymore. He goes up to her and kisses her on the cheek.*]

Robert: Good evening, dear. How are you?

Mary: Fine, darling. How did everything go for you at school today?

Robert [*Sheepishly*] :   Uhhh . . . okay. [*He sits down.*]

Mary: What's wrong, sweetie. Somethings troubling you, right. [*She walks up to him and pets his head.*]

Robert [*Scared to ask Mary*] :   Mary, dear, there's something I want to talk to you about. Please sit down.

[*Mary sits down.*]

Robert: Uhh . . . Mary dear, I met somebody at the school today.

Mary [*Wondering what Robert is trying to say*] :   Yes, dumpling, go on.

Robert: Well . . . I met this guy today. His name is Cooachtemoc Di-as.

Mary: Oh. That sounds Spanish. Is he some foreign exchange student from Spain or South America?

Robert: No . . . not exactly. He's from this country.

Mary [Starting to get worried] : From this country? Then you mean that he's a . . . a. . . .

Robert: Yes, that's right. He's a Mexican . . . a Checano.

Mary: Oh Robert, what happened?

Robert: Well, he started talking to me, introduced himself, and invited me and you to come to a meeting.

Mary [Really getting scared now] : A meeting! What kind of meeting?

Robert: A Checano meeting . . . I mean, a meeting of the Checano group.

Mary [A little relieved] · Well, that's nothing. You told him, of course, that we wouldn't come . . . didn't you?

Robert: Not exactly.

Mary [Angry] : What do you mean, not exactly? We're not going to no Checano meeting! . . . The idea!!

[*Mary gets up from her seat and resumes dusting the furniture. Robert looks questioningly at her.*]

Robert: Oh, come on, Mary, we can admit to ourselves that we're really Mexicans. Anyway, nobody's going to hear.

Mary [Angry] : No . . . don't say that word. We're Spanish . . . Spanish . . . do you hear . . . Spanish!!

[*Robert lowers his head and looks at the floor. He has failed. Suddenly he remembers Cuahtemoc's admonitions about who is boss and who decides. He realizes that they must go to the meeting if he is ever to face Cuahtemoc again. . . . He must prove his machismo!*]

[*Robert gets up, has a determined look on his face. He hooks his thumbs under his belt, throws out his chest, and assumes a look of severity.*]

Robert: Mary, we're going to the meeting.

Mary [Looks at him as if he is crazy] : What did you say?

Robert [Loses his composure for a second but regains it] : I said we're going to the meeting. It's this Wednesday night.

Mary [Still can't believe what he is saying but she challenges him anyway] : That's what you think. You're crazy if you think I'm going to be seen at Checano meeting. What would our friends say?

Robert [*Puzzled because he hasn't thought about their "friends' " reaction*] :
Well . . . let them say what they want. If they ask, we'll tell them that we
went to try and talk some sense to the Checanos.

Mary: But . . . what about if they talk Spanish at the meeting? We won't
know what they're saying. Maybe they'll be talking about us and we won't
know it.

Robert: They won't talk Spanish. I heard Di-as speaking English today.

Mary: But you have to study for a test on Friday.

Robert: I know all the material for that test. I don't need to study. Anyway,
we'll just go for an hour or so and come right back. It'll be dark and nobody'll see us.

[*Mary sees that she is losing and can't understand it. She has never seen
Robert on a "macho trip" before. She resorts to the last time-honored
tradition of throwing a fit and crying.*]

Mary [*Sobbing*] :   I don't have anything to wear.

Robert [*Not knowing what to do but surprised that Mary is giving in to his
"macho trip"*] :   Don't cry . . . you don't have to wear anything special.
I don't think those Checanos will look to see what you're wearing.

Mary [*Crying hard now and looking desperately for sympathy*] :   You don't
love me anymore. If you did you wouldn't make me go to any Checano
meeting.

Robert: That's not true and you know it, Mary. Now, let's not have anymore
of this crying. Do you hear me? . . . we're going to the meeting!

[*Mary sees that it is hopeless and quietly sits down in her chair. She is sobbing softly as the scene closes. Robert, with a happy and surprised look
on his face, struts around the room, smiling . . . smiling.*]

[*Curtain closes. In the background can be heard cuts from "Juan Charras-
queado."*]

Scene 3

[*The curtain rises on Scene 3. The scene is a room at the University, with
a poster of Emiliano Zapata on the wall. Cuahtemoc "Porfirito" Díaz is
at the podium as Robert and Mary Gomes walk in. Already seated are
Pancho Zapata and Flor Hermosa, along with Emilio Villa and Margarita
Mota. They greet Robert and Mary Gomes. Mary looks scared and so
does Robert but he struts in anyway.*]

Cuahtemoc [*Smiling and happy*] :   Buenas tardes, Robert. Happy to see that you could come. [*He comes over to shake Robert's hand.*]

Robert [*Shaking hands with Cuahtemoc*] :   Good evening, Cooachtemoc. May I introduce you to my wife, Mary.

Cuahtemoc [*Extending his hand*] :   Mucho gusto, señora. Glad to meet you. Meet the rest of our group.

[*Robert and Mary sheepishly exchange greetings with the other four people. Everybody introduces themselves to the Gomes'.*]

[*Cuahtemoc goes to the podium and shuffles his papers as he gets ready to begin the meeting. Everyone is seated.*]

Cuahtemoc: Well, ésos, let's begin the meeting. Again, I would like to welcome the two new people to the meeting. Let's all take turns standing up now and say our names and where we're from.

"Me llamo Emiliano Villa and I come from East L.A. I'm a junior majoring in criminology."

"Me llamo Flor Hermosa and I'm from San Diego. Sophomore in psychology."

"Me llamo Pancho Zapata y soy del chuco, Tejas. Soy senior in business administration."

"Me llamo Margarita Mota and I'm from Salinas, California. I'm an environmental design major with a minor in clinical psychology. Oh, yes, I'm a freshman."

"My name is Robert Gomes . . . uhh . . . I mean Gómez. [*Robert looks around and when he sees that he is not questioned goes on.*] My hometown is Santa Monica. I'm a senior with a pre-law major.

[*Mary looks scared and takes a while to answer.*] "My name is Mary Gomes . . . Gómez. My husband is Robert Gomes . . . Gómez. I used to live in Venice, California. I'm a junior in sociology but I'm not attending school this term."

"Me llamo Cuahtemoc 'Porfirito' Díaz y vengo de Sacra. Mi estación es sophomor-e and mi vocación es revolucionario. [*He grins sheepishly.*] Just kidding, ésos; I'm really majoring in English."

Cuahtemoc: Bueno, ésos, vamos a comenzar. Let's begin. Is there any old business?

Pancho Zapata: We were supposed to approve the allocation of $20 to Delano, jefe.

Cuahtemoc [*Assuming role of strongman and jefe*] :   Approved! Is there any more old business?

[*No answer. Cuahtemoc assumes it is okay to move on.*]

Cuahtemoc: Bueno. Is there any new business?

Flor Hermosa: What about the new proposal we're going to write, jefe?

Cuahtemoc: Don't worry about that, chica, I'll get it together and present it at the next meeting.

Emiliano Villa: What about the tutorial program, vato, let's talk about. . . .

Cuahtemoc [*Cutting off Emiliano*] :   Next time, ése, I've . . . I mean we've got too much to talk about tonight. Anything else?

[*The group senses that Cuahtemoc is on one of his many ego trips tonight. Cuahtemoc does not really want to discuss anything but rather he wants them to listen to what he has to say. They let him have his way, in order to end the meeting that much sooner.*]

[*Cuahtemoc begins his monologue*] :

"First of all, carnales y carnalas, let me welcome you to this meeting tonight. Let's begin by discussing the Chicano movement. Is there a Chicano movement? I propose that there is no real Chicano movement.
That is, there is no movement in a sense that viable gains can be seen
by our communities. I propose that in order for there to be a real movement we must first organize under one organization and I further propose that that organization be M.A.F.I.A. Yes, M.A.F.I.A. Why
M.A.F.I.A.? First of all, due to the overall diffusion of organizations
now in the movement . . . oops, I said there is no movement . . . all of
the organizations must come together . . . that is, be coordinated from a
central organization. The logical conclusion is M.A.F.I.A., since we are
a new and energetic organization. The rational approach, therefore is to
write proposals to initiate projects, getting the money from government
sources . . . incidentally, this is called exploiting the system . . . and co-
ordinating activities all around us. Let's hear a little bit of support from
the crowd . . . all together now, let's hear it . . . M.A.F.I.A. . . . .

[*The group is starting to respond to Cuahtemoc's heavy rap and are caught
up in his rhetoric . . . they start shouting M.A.F.I.A. . . . M.A.F.I.A.*]

[*Flashes of Hitler and John Kennedy now appear, alternating each other.*]

[*Cuahtemoc is in seventh heaven now; he has captured the emotions of his
audience; now he forgets them as he closes his eyes briefly, envisioning
himself speaking before a huge crowd . . . at an auditorium . . . in a
stadium . . . calling forth to millions over the radio and on TV.*]

[*Cauhtemoc has his hands and arms raised towards the ceiling, thinking it is the sky; he opens his eyes, slowly lowers his arms, silencing his listeners; he continues . . .*]

Yes, gente, we shall lead the movement. And this new movement must be made pure. Yes, pure. There shall be only Chicanos in this movement. There is no room for half-breed Latinos. If Mexican blood does not run in their veins, they shall not be allowed to join this movement. After all, we've been oppressed longer than they have . . . haven't we? . . .

[*His group responds in unison "Yes, we have been oppressed longer than they have been oppressed."*]

Cuahtemoc continues: and we shall decide who are Chicanos and who aren't. . . . In order to be Chicano, you must be Mexican and be a first generation Mexican in this country. . . . The only exception shall be if you are half-first generation on one side and half-second generation on the other side. . . . And the gringos, we shall exploit their system . . . yes, we shall exploit their government and not go to Vietnam anymore . . . unless they make us. . . . You can't have everything, you know. . . .

Pancho Zapata [*Interrupting his jefe*] :   Jefe, what about the commies and Cuba?

[*Cuahtemoc looks at him scornfully for interrupting him while he is speaking. He continues*] :

. . . don't speak to me of Cuba! Why should we concern ourselves of Cuba? Cuba is a communist country and does not represent anything to us! . . . I don't want to hear anything about Che or Fidel Castro either. . . . They represent the opposite of everything we believe in. . . . We must exploit this system. . . . Get into it and sabotage it from within. . . . That is why we are writing proposals, pendejo . . . We must break away from everything in Latin America except Mexico. . . . Look at Mexico; the people are happy; Mexico is becoming an industrial power. . . . There is progress there; yes, progress, and that must become our most important product. . . . In the name of the product . . . progress is our most important product. . . . In the name of the father, the son, the product . . . the product . . . the product . . . the product. . . .

[*The scene ends as the curtain falls. In the background the audience can still hear Cuahtemoc rapping. The product . . . the product. . . .*]

[*End of Act II*]

ACT III

Scene 1

[*The scene opens as Robert and Mary are back in their apartment. They are engaged in putting up new posters now, Chicano posters, to replace the "modest" posters that they had before. The American flag, however, still remains on the wall in the middle of the room. They are experiencing a cultural rebirth, now call themselves Roberto and María Gómez, and are very excited about their new cultural nationalist trip.*]

Roberto: Essa María, what are we having for sena tonight?

María: Well Robert-o, I thought it would be good to have some tortillas and beans. Also, I'll make some chili con carni. How does that sound, om-brae?

Roberto: That's really . . . uh . . . together, essa. Are you glad now we went to the Checano meeting?

María: Claro que yes! I'm so happy. The Washingtons . . . those gringos! . . . were so surprised when we told them to get lost . . . ha . . . ha . . . ha.

Roberto: Yeah, those stupid gringoloficos. . . . How did we ever speak to them in the first place? Wow, being a Checano sure makes everything easier, huh baby?

María: A la braba . . . My, that Cooactemoc Di-as sure is a good speaker, isn't he? Everything he said sure made sense.

Roberto: Sí. With guys like him around, we'll take over soon. You know something, I'm going to be just like Cooactemoc and be a heavy speaker. What do you think?

María: I'm sure you can do it, honey. After all, you do have more education then he has. I better check the dinner now. . . . Remember that our carnalees are coming over here to eat tonight.

Roberto: Yeah. Let's surprise them and speak Spanish tonight, okay? Let's practice right now and just talk Spanish to each other in order to surprise them.

María: Okay . . . oops . . . Sí, mi ombrae.

[*María rises and goes over to imaginary stove to check the dinner.*]

Roberto: Dónde you get recipe for sena, kerida?

María: Flor darme recipe, kerido. Ella decir recipe para chili es de Guadalahara.

Roberto: Que bu-a-no. Esper-o estar good.

María: Do you want to hear some Mexican music, kerido?

Roberto: Claro que yes!

[*María disappears temporarily and returns. In the background you can hear the sounds of "Granada."*]

Roberto: Aaah . . . that sure es Mexican music, kerida.

María: Yes . . . que pensar we do to become more Mexican, kerido?

Roberto: Bu-a-no, voy a comprar a brown ber-et for me and one for you, too. Then we'll get some buttons . . . the kind that say Mexican-American Liberation.

María: Good . . . but do you think we need to be liberated?

Roberto: I don't know. But Cooactemoc said those are good buttons to show yo're a Checano. We've already got some posters up. I think we should also buy some records . . . Mexican music, you know . . . like Edie Gorme and the Trío los pan-chos. . . .

María: Yeah, we could also pick up Trini López . . . Herby Alpert and the Tijauna Brass. . . .

Roberto: And Doris Day . . . you know, she sings that song "Ka Sera, Scra" [*He sings it for a while*] . . . That's a nice song.

Mariá: Aaah . . . it sure feels wonderful to feel Checano, doesn't it? Think of all the beautiful people we'll get to meet now!

Roberto: Yeah . . . we can invite some foreign exchange students to come eat. . . . Say! . . . We can take a trip to Mexico this summer!

María: Oh Robert-o, you really think so?

Roberto: Of course. Why don't we plan our trip right now? Let's see, what will we need?

María: Well . . . we'll need some smallpox shots . . .

Roberto: . . . and some Tums for the tummy. . . .

María: I like Alka-seltzer.

Roberto: . . . and some constipation pills . . .

María: . . . and a hat because of the sun . . .

Roberto: . . . and some Coppertone to tan us . . .

María: . . . and a camera to take pictures . . .

Roberto: . . . and some insurance in case the camera gets stolen . . .

María: . . . and get our car tuned up . . .

Roberto: . . . and more insurance. . . .

María: Where shall we go?

Roberto: Where we can see the people, of course! . . . We'll go to Mexico City!

María: How charming. When we get there we'll hire a guide to show us around. . . .

Roberto: Yeah . . . we don't want to miss anything!

María: How wonderful. When we get back, we'll show our slides to everyone to show them where we've been.

María: What about doing something for the Checanos here, kerido?

Roberto: Well . . . we could join M.A.P.P.A. . . . They're a very militant group.

María: M.A.P.P.A.? What does that stand for?

Roberto: I think it stands for Mexican-American Political Participation Association. They're for the community. Last year I heard they gave a convention in Sacramento and in order to help the community, they charged admission into the conference. . . . They sure are helpful.

María: Oh yes! Now I know who you're talking about. Aren't they the ones who met at the Hilton Hotel recently? . . . What a smart way to exploit the system!

Roberto: Or we could get to the Nuevas Vistas conference. They always invite celebrities like Blue Max Rafferty and Ronnie Rerun to talk and explain the problems of Checanos. . . . Someone we can listen to!

María: Oh my! Being a Checano sure makes you feel good, doesn't it? Sometimes I wonder, however, if that word isn't a little bit vulgar.

Roberto: Don't worry about that. We're really Mexican-Americans but we use the word Checano in order to exploit the system.

María: How does using the word Checano make us exploit the system?

Roberto: Well, we write proposals . . . get jobs at the top . . . with a nice salary, of course . . . and then we help other Checanos to exploit the system until everyone becomes a good capitalist. . . . That's how we exploit the system!

María: You're so smart, Robert-o.

[*A knock is heard at the door.*]

Maria: Oh. Oh. Our carnalees are here. I hope the chili con carni came out good. This is our big test.

[*End of Scene 1.*]

Scene 2

[*Roberto and María have invited their new Chicano friends, Pancho Zapata, and his girlfriend Flor Hermosa, and Emilio Villa and his ruca Margarita Mota, over for a cultural dinner. The setting is a table, six chairs, and the background is the same as before (in their apartment). The Gómez' are a bit uneasy with their newfound Chicano talk and mannerisms and continue to create pendejadas.*]

María: Bu-a-nas tardees, siniores y sinioritas. Oh, carnalees mios, pa-sen a mi casa!

The four guests: Buenas tardes, señora. Orale, Roberto, ¿qué tal?

Roberto: Oh, Ka tall! . . . Paa-scn, paa-sen. . . .

[*Pancho Zapata extends his hand in the traditional Chicano Style. Roberto extends his hand in the conventional Anglo way. There is a mass of confusion that follows as Pancho attempts to give the Chicano handshake and Roberto does not know how to react to Pancho's hand twisting in his.*]

Pancho: Aliviánate, Roberto! I'm only trying to give you the Chicano handshake.

Roberto: Oh! . . . mi error. . . . I thought you were practicing your karate on me. Teach me how to do it, Emilio.

Emilio: Órale. . . . There's nothing to it. . . .

[*Emilio attempts to shake Roberto's hand Chicano style and it goes off pretty well until Emilio unconsciously hits Roberto's shoulder a little bit too hard and Roberto's shoulder sags as his face has a look of pain on it.*]

Emilio: I'm sorry, ése, I didn't mean to hurt you.

Roberto [*Smiling bravely*] :   That's all right. I don't think I'm ready for the Checano handshake yet.

[*María senses that she must pick up the slack for Roberto and take him "off the hook."*]

María: Oh . . . Flor! Tu bestido estar tanto bo-nito . . . Margarita . . . ka you have to decir?

[*Flor and Margarita start jabbering and jibbering (hablando como siempre) away and the three girls lose themselves from thinking of the guys and sit down to gossip a while. They continue and can be heard faintly in the background as the conversation of the men dominate.*]

Pancho: Bueno, Roberto . . . how did you like the meeting the other night?

Roberto: El junta estar muy buano, carnalee . . . como lae gusta ustedd mi es-pañ-ol?

Pancho [*Chuckling a bit to himself*] :   Está de aquellas, ése. I didn't know you could speak Spanish. Where di you learn?

Roberto: Yoe apren-derr hablarr es-pañ-ol en Méjico. [*He breaks out in a grin.*] Not really. Spanish was my foreign language. I'll never forget my last Spanish teacher . . . Mr. Supertaco . . . he was from Valencia, you know . . . he taught me a lot. . . .

Emilio: Yes, we sure are lucky to have good teachers here at the University, ése. Last quarter I had this teacher in economics; he knew economics like he knew his own barrio . . . they call him Aggie. . . .

Roberto: Aggie? That's a funny name . . . what does that stand for?

Emilio: Uhhh . . . I think it stands for agringado. Now there's an honor-able name . . . Agringado Cortez de Vendido . . . that's real class, ése.

Roberto: I can dig it, esse, I can dig it. Let's join the girls and see what they're doing, okay?

Pancho and Emilio: Orale.

[*The men move over to where the girls are sitting and sit down.*]

Roberto: Kerida, when is the cena going to be done?

[*The girls stop gossiping.*]

María: Let me check it. It should be done by now.

[*María goes over to the imaginary stove and checks the cena.*]

María: It's done. I hope you carnalees like my chile con carne. Will you girls help me serve?

Flor and Margarita: Sure.

[*Flor and Margarita get up and go over to stove. Flor goes over to get imag-inary dishes, Margarita imaginary cups, and Maria serves chile con carne on plates. Flor carries plates to table, etc. until everyone is served. The girls sit down again and everyone starts eating.*]

Roberto: María, Kerida, can we have some tor-till-ias?

María: Of course.

[*She gets up and goes over to imaginary stove where she picks up tortillas.*]

María: Oh, my! The tor-till-ias are a little bit burned. [*If possible, some round cut-up pieces of paper depicting tortillas with huge black sections should be available for the audience to see.*] I hope you carnalees won't mind too much.

Pancho: Aahh . . . I'm really hungry. Chili con carne is my favorite.

[*Pancho goes through motions of scooping chili con carne up and places it in his mouth. His reaction is one of being burned up alive.*]

Pancho: Ay . . . Ay . . . Ay . . . yi . . . yi. I-jue-la . . . ¡this cosa es puro lumbre!

[*Pancho reaches for his glass and takes a huge drink. He then manages a brave smile.*]

Pancho: It's not really that hot, María.

María [*With a look of concern on her face*]: I hope not. How are the fri-jol-es, Margarita?

[*Margarita takes a gulp of frijoles and a lump comes to her throat. She bravely swallows them.*]

Margarita [*Gagging somewhat*]: They're real good, María . . . real good.

[*The characters continue to eat the cena in the best way they can. The food is terrible but in order not to make María and Roberto feel bad no complaints are made. Throughout the meal the characters make faces and struggle to complete the dinner.*] [*Live Theatre*]

* * * * * * * * *

[*The characters have now finished the cena. They are kicking back (relaxing) and a conversation follows.*]

Roberto: Well . . . essos . . . what is everyone going to do for the movement?

Emilio: I plan to be a parole officer. That's why I'm majoring in criminology. By being a parole officer, I feel that I can help a lot of young Chicanos who go wrong, ése.

Margarita: I don't know yet. Maybe I'll be a psychiatrist so I can solve our problems.

Flor: Yeah, that's what I want to be. I figure that we are suffering from a family schizophrenia complex that is limiting our effectiveness within this society.

Roberto: But are you going to work for the movement now or when you get out?

Pancho: When we get our degree, ése. That's the only way we can do anything for the movement. Look at me . . . what could I do now as a student? But when I get my degree, I'll be able to go *down* to the barrio and help.

Roberto: What will you be doing?

Pancho: Well . . . I'm in business administration, ése. I figure I'll be in some corporation or something. But I'll be able to work weekends in the barrio. . . . You know, little league or something. . . .

Emilio: What about you and María, Roberto?

[*Roberto and María see hypocracy of Chicanos.*]

María: I'll go into social work. Be a welfare worker or something.

Roberto: Well, I don't know yet. I'd like to be a judge some day. But I've been thinking lately about joining some group . . . you know . . . doing some work . . . like maybe the whale-ga in Delano. . . .

Emilio: That's not too exciting, ése. Who wants to picket Safeway every Saturday? I want some action!

Pancho: Yeah! Anyway, who wants to join an outside gorup? Right here at school we have M.A.F.I.A. I think we should only concern ourselves with our own territory and not get involved with other Chicano groups.

Margarita: I'd like to get into Chicana Liberation. How about it, María . . . you want to join?

María: Chicana Liberation? What are they doing?

Flor: Liberating Chicanas, of course. We've got to demand our rights from these hombres! They don't let us participate in anything!

Emilio: ¡Women's Liberation no vale caca! ¡Es una pendejada! How can you liberate yourselves from us when we're not liberated ourselves?

Margarita: ¡Qué macho! If you guys don't let us participate, we're going to be against you, wait and see!

Pancho: What would you rucas do to us?

Flor: ¡Aver, a ver! How are you going to stay warm at night?

Emilio: Ahah! You're trying to apply a blockade, eh? Just wait, what do you think the gringas are good for?

Flor: ¡Hijo de tu chingada madre! Just let me catch you with a gringa! You'll see what we'll do! [*She threatens to hit him with her fist.*]

Margarita: ¡Sí, cabrón! ¡A ver si te agarro con una gringa!

Roberto [*Trying to calm the situation down*] : Easy, easy. There's no use fighting amongst ourselves.

Pancho: Yeah, you're right, ése. Say, why don't we smoke some yeska?

María: Yae-ska? What's yac-ska?

Flor: Oh, María, you mean you don't know what grifa is?

Roberto: Grifa? I'm afraid you have me confused also.

Emilio: It's marijuana, ése, marijuana. Let's roll some up and do a number. Do you have any papers, Pancho?

Pancho: Yeah, ése. Right here. Give me the grifa and I'll do the thing.

[*Emilio reaches into his pocket and takes out a lid of grass. He hands it to Pancho. Pancho takes the yeska and proceeds to go through the motions of rolling up a couple of joints.*]

María [*Very worried*] : Robert, dear. Do you think it's all right?

Roberto [*Hesitant*] : I don't know. You guys know it's against the law, right?

Pancho: Law y que law. ¡Que se chingen los marranos! How are they going to catch us?

Flor: Yeah, don't worry about it. You'll like it once you smoke it. I didn't know you had never smoked it before.

Roberto: Well . . . we've tried to live by the law, you know. . . . We wouldn't want to do anything undemocratic.

María: Yeah, I heard that Mary-juana is a communist plot. Do you think it's all right?

Emilio: I don't know about no communist plot but it sure is pot! It'll be all right, wait and see.

[*Pancho has finished rolling up the joints and hands one to Roberto and the other to Margarita. He lights up a match and lights the two numbers.*]

[*Margarita expertly inhales her joint while Roberto gags on his. She passes it on to Emilio.*]

Pancho: Don't bogart that joint, ése. Pass it on!

[*Roberto passes it on to María who chokes on it herself. The actors continue to pass the joints around and proceed to get high.*]

[*The rest of Scene 2 should be Live Theatre. It would be convenient to have a light show come on at this time with Santana's album softly heard in the background. Both Roberto and María should initially express surprise at being turned on and exclaim pendejadas such as "Wow!" "Geez!" etc.*]

[*The next three to five minutes are Live Theatre. The actors are free to act as they wish or say what they want as if they were really turned on.*]

[*End of Scene 2. Curtain falls.*]

Scene 3

[*Roberto and María are back in their own apartment.*]

Roberto: Let's see. What did Cuahtemoc say about following the example of Mexico?

María: He said that there is a lot of progress in Mexico. . . .

Roberto: According to what I've read, Mexico is a very poor country. In fact, according to my political science teacher, the PRI is the only real party in Mexico. That means that Mexico is a one-party state.

María: In other words . . .

Roberto: . . . there is no freedom in Mexico. Remember how the Mexican government killed all those students back in '68!

María: Yeah, I hear they still have hundreds of political prisoners in jail . . . and killed hundreds more. . . . That doesn't sound too democratic to me . . .

Roberto: . . . so if things don't look too good in Mexico, why should we follow Mexico? Is it because we're Mexican?

María: I guess so. He also said something about only Mexicans or Chicanos being in the movement.

Roberto: Oh, yeah! I thought that all Latin-Americans were part of La Raza. Why should only Chicanos be part of the movement?

María: Beats me. What's a Chicano, anyway?

Roberto: According to Cuahtemoc, it's a first-generation Mexican in this country. But what happens to those Mexicans who are second or third generation, or have just come to this country from Mexico?

María: Oh Roberto, this is all crazy! Everything was much easier when we were just two people alone!

Roberto: In a way, I guess you're right. But we can't go back the way we were. We were living in a dream-world.

María: I know what you're saying is right, but it seems to me that we're worse off now. What are we going to do?

Roberto: We've got to do something. At least we now know that everything Cuahtemoc or the rest of our carnales say isn't right.

María: You can say that again. I think they're as mixed-up as we are.

Roberto: Either that or they're worse off. I don't think they really know how how screwed up their way of thinking really is.

María: But whose way of thinking is right, Roberto? Who determines what is right and what is wrong?

Roberto: It seems to me that what is right is to practice what you preach. I know that's an old cliché, but I'm sure Cuahtemoc isn't right if he preaches being a Chicano but isn't really against the government when he knows that same government is screwing the Chicano people.

María: What are you saying? That we become communists or something?

Roberto: You don't have to be a communist in order to oppose the government! If the government is bad, it's bad, and we shouldn't work with it.

María: How do we work with it?

Roberto: Well, by fighting in Vietnam and other wars, I guess. Also, there's something about writing proposals that I don't like.

María: What about them?

Roberto: I don't know. I can't put my finger on it but there's something wrong.

María: That's the problem with us. We know something is wrong but we don't know what it is.

Roberto: Don't feel so bad, María. There's got to be some answers somewhere. There must be somebody we can talk to.

María: Who do you suggest?

Roberto: Well, we can rule out our carnales at the University. They're as mixed-up as we are.

María: I don't think the Mexican-American administrators can help us either, they don't seem to be too concerned with the Chicano movement.

Roberto: Yeah. All they seem to be concerned about is their salaries.

María: It's useless, Roberto. Let's give up and just don't see anybody anymore.

Roberto [*Very emphatic*] : NO! We just can't give up. We can't go back where we were before. Once you find out about the Chicanos it's like education. It's good but you never get enough and you can't be like you were before.

María: I don't know. I've seen a lot of kids at the University who have a lot of education and they come out the same four years later.

Roberto: Yeah, but that's not real education. That's an assembly line at the University. All those people come out like robots!

María: You're probably right, but that still doesn't help us. What are we going to do?

Roberto [*In despair he cups his head in his hands*] :   I don't know, María. . . . I just don't know.

Roberto: Everything is phony around us . . . everything . . . our apartment, our way of talking . . . our education . . . our clothes . . . everything! It's like it was made out of plastic for us.

María: It probably was. Roberto, let's not think about it for a while, okay?

Roberto: I suppose you're right. Maybe one of these days we can go down to the barrio and look around a bit.

María [*Very tired*] :   If you want. But let's go to sleep right now and maybe we'll feel better tomorrow morning.

Roberto [*Also very tired*] :   Yes . . . sleep . . . sleep. . . . I think we sleep our lives away.

[*The scene ends as Roberto and María walk hand in hand out of the room. Their heads are bowed and they are visibly tired and disappointed and sad. There is complete silence and they shuffle their feet slowly out of the room.*]

[*End of Scene 3. Curtain falls.*]

Scene 4

[*The scene opens with a background of the barrio and sounds of the barrio being heard. Standing around is a local vato loco, Chuey. Strolling down the street come Roberto and María Gómez. As they approach Chuey, Roberto decides he is going to ask directions to the M.A.P.P.A. office.*]

Roberto: Pardon me, could you tell me where the M.A.P.P.A. office is at?

Chuey [*Eying Roberto suspiciously*] :   They're down the street, ése.

Roberto: Could you tell me what their number is?

Chuey: Síʹ. Creo que es 1617. [*Diez y seis, deiz y siete.*]

Roberto: I'm sorry. I don't speak Spanish that well. No lo entiendo.

Chuey: 1617. [*Sixteen seventeen.*]

Roberto: Uhh . . . what do you think of M.A.P.P.A.?

Chuey [*Getting a little upset at Roberto's questioning*] :   How come you ask so many questions, ése? ¿Eres placa o que?

Roberto: I'm sorry. I didn't mean to bother you.

[*Roberto takes María's hand and starts to walk away. They take a couple of steps before Chuey calls out to him.*]

Chuey: ¡Ese! Ese vato, come here!

[*Roberto and María freeze, Roberto slowly turns his head around to look at Chuey. They are very much afraid that something is going to happen to them.*]

Chuey [*Motioning to Roberto*] :   Ven aquíʹ, ése, Come here.

[*Roberto lets go of María's hand and walks toward Chuey. María is frozen where she stands waiting to see what is going to happen.*]

Roberto [*In a meek voice*] :   Were you calling me?

Chuey [*Smiling in order to make Roberto relax a bit*] :   Sure, ése . . . I was calling you. Relax. Aliviánate. I thought you were a placa.

Roberto [*More relaxed now*] :   A placa? What's a placa?

Chuey [*Smiling openly now*] :   ¡Ay qué vato! . . . ¿no sabes que es un placa? A placa is a juda . . . I mean, a policeman.

Roberto [*Now relaxed that he understands Chuey's original uptightness*] . Ooh. . . . Now I understand why you were so cautious. No, I'm not a police . . . a placa. I'm a student down here from the University.

Chuey: Why do you say you're "*down* here from the University?"

Roberto: We are, aren't we?

Chuey: Nobody is "down" here from anywhere, ése, except in their heads. Do you think you're superior to us because you go to the university?

Roberto: I . . . I didn't mean to imply that. In fact, the reason we're here is to get some answers.

Chuey: What kind of answers, ése?

[*Roberto proceeds to tell his story of how he and María changed from thinking Spanish to Mexican-American to being doubting Chicanos. María is now next to him. Chuey listens with compassion.*]

Chuey: Sabes que, ése, we all go through changes like that. Es nuestra vida; it's our life. Tenemos que evolucionar. And that causes much pain, much heartache and hardship. Your ultimate pendejada was that you changed on the outside only, pero no en donde cuenta, not inside where it really counts. But that is coming. You're being here shows it.

Roberto: Do you really think we will find the answers now, now that we're here in the barrio?

Chuey: The answers are within yourselves, carnal. You are a Chicano. And wherever a Chicano is exists a barrio. It exists within yourself. Look within yourself for the answers. You will find them there for they always were there. Bueno, me tengo que largar, hay los wacho. Adiós.

[*Chuey shakes hands and starts walking away. Roberto and María look at each other, and their eyes reflect a growing inner peace. Suddenly Roberto realizes that he didn't even know Chuey's name. He calls out.*]

Roberto: Hey! I didn't even get your name!

Chuey [*Shouts back to him*] : ¡Chuey, ése, Chuey!

Roberto [*Calling back*] : Mine's Roberto! This is María! [*He remarks to María.*] You know what, María; his name in English mean Jesus!

[*Though Chuey is now over a block away, he silently, with a smile, remarks, "Mejor Quetzalcoatl, mejor Quetzalcoatl."*]

[*End of* The Ultimate Pendejada.]

Mártir Montezuma

YSIDRO R. MACIAS

Characters

Mártir Montezuma, non-violent jefe of the Aztlecas
Hernán Gimarra, Spanish owner of chile plantation
Juan Hantle, gachupín owner of corn plantation
Francisco Marrano, Gimarra's chile foreman
1st Aztleca, Montezuma's right-hand man
2nd Aztleca, Montezuma's left-hand woman
Roberto Quinadi, distingusihed young liberal senador
Viceroy Rigan, the Spanish viceroy in charge of Nueva España
Spanish policeman
2 Aztlecas
Mamacita
Quinadi's artist
Revolución, young Aztleca activist
Justicia, young Aztleca activist
Judge, a Spanish judge
Hay-tol Quinadi, widow of senador Roberto Quinadi
Padre Miguel Hidalgo, Father of Mexican independence
Revolución y Justicia, Hidalgo's lieutenant
Maya-Xochimil, the reincarnation of 2nd Aztleca

[*The background is a field of chiles. The indigenous natives (Aztlecas) are demonstrating against Hernán Gimarra, the Spanish owner of the chile plantation. They are standing with placards denoting the need for higher wages, a big banner with Tlaloc reverently and prominently displayed in the center of the demonstration, and another Aztleca holding the symbol of their movement, the United Aztleca Organizing Committee (UAOC), which is a bird. The actors may be dressed in regular fashion except for headbands and a sash around their waist (both colorful to depict the times). The year is approximately 1524 A.D.*]

[*The Aztleca signs read "Viva UAOC y Mártir Montezuma," "Aztleca Power," "Queremos Justicia," and "Huelga."*]

[*The Aztleca demonstrators are silently marching in a circle when two gachupínes arrive, one of them being Hernán Gimarra, the owner, the other Francisco Marrano, his foreman.*]

Marrano: There they are, jefe. They say they want better money and living conditions and a union.

Gimarra: Unión y que unión. If they don't start working again, I'll call Cortés. [*He calls out to the Aztlecas.*] Hey, you, which one of you is the leader?

1st Aztleca [*He comes with head bowed and very afraid*]:   Our leader is not here, patrón. He'll be coming soon though.

Marrano [*He grabs the 1st Aztleca by the hair and yanks him*] :   ¡Pinchi indio! You have no respect for the patrón. On your knees, indio. [*He forces Aztleca to his knees.*] What is this UAOC y Mártir Montezuma about?

1st Aztleca [*Terrified*] :   It stands for United Aztleca Organizing Committee . . . y Mártir Montezuma is our leader, jefe.

Gimarra: This Montezuma better be ready to answer for all this. [*He stops as Mártir Montezuma comes on stage, walking very slowly, patiently, with love on his face and in his motions.*]

Montezuma: Yo soy Mártir Montezuma, Señor Gimarra. Do you wish to speak to me?

Gimarra: Listen, you . . . Montezuma. What is this all about? Why aren't your people working?

Montezuma: They are not working, Señor Gimarra . . . because we are tired of working for nothing and living like dogs. . . . We want decent treatment . . . we want to be human beings.

Marrano: Silencio, you dog! How dare you speak to el patrón like that! On your knees

Gimarra: Hold it, Marrano. Look Montezuma, if your people don't like it here, why don't they go back where they came from?

Montezuma: Came from, Señor? We come from here!

Marrano: Silencio, you son of a jackass!

Gimarra: I'm going to be reasonable with you, Montezuma. If I fire all of you, where are you going to get jobs? How can you eat?

Montezuma: We'll find a way, Señor. We'll work somewhere else.

Gimarra [*Laughing*] :   Somewhere else, eh! Ha ha. Nobody will hire you; besides, you're my slaves. What I say goes!

Montezuma: Not anymore, Señor. We are prepared for a long struggle. We have pride, you know.

Gimarra: Pride! A la chingada with your pride. [*He motions to Marrano.*] Call the policía, Marrano. We'll see how long pride feeds your stomach, Montezuma.

[*Marrano goes offstage and promptly returns with a Spanish policeman, who starts dispersing the strikers.*]

Marrano and Policeman: ¡Vámonos! Away from here, you miserable dogs . . . animals . . . hijos de sus retechingadas madres.

[*Marrano and the policeman proceed to disperse and physically assault the strikers, beating up on them incessantly while none of them offers resistance.*]

Montezuma [*As he and everyone of the Aztlecas are being beat up*] : Don't hit them back, muchachos. Remember, our philosophy is non-violence. Our philosophy is non-violence. Our philosophy is non-violence.

[*The Aztlecas including Montezuma, slither away and offstage under the assault of Marrano and the policeman. These two come back to Gimarra who has been watching the spectacle with much humor and enjoyment.*]

Marrano: I guess that teaches them who's boss, patrón . . . ¡perros!

Gimarra: Good job, boys . . . Come on, I'm going to have a meeting with Viceroy Rigan about this.

[*Gimarra, Marrano, and the policeman leave the stage happily as the scene ends.*]

Scene 2

[*The same background as Scene 1. Mártir Montezuma is sitting, yoga fashion, with his two lieutenants, 1st Aztleca and 2nd Aztleca. 2nd Aztleca should be a woman. They are discussing strategy for the struggle against Gimarra. Mártir and 1st Aztleca are for non-violence strategy, 2nd Aztleca agrees but doesn't want to rule out violent confrontation tactics in order to win the struggle.*]

1st Aztleca: Well, Mártir . . . I guess we showed them. . . . They can't make us work, can they?

Mártir: I don't think so. Not if we don't let ourselves. . . . Yes, it was a great victory out there yesterday.

2nd Aztleca: I don't think so. Look what happened to all our people. Look what happened to you, Mártir. They kicked you . . . te pegarron . . . maltratarron . . . ¡oyeiiee que fee!

Mártir [*Very saintly*] : Don't worry about that, hermana. We must learn to accept that. . . . It will be a long struggle.

2nd Aztleca: Learn to accept that! That's nothing new! They've been doing that to us all our lives. I thought we were going to change our way of life. [*She is angry.*]

Mártir [*Hurt by her words*] : We are going to change it, manita. But it has to be done non-violently and through reforms. We must have faith in Tlaloc, in time He will change the gachupines' ways. He will make them see the light.

2nd Aztleca: But what happens to our people until the gachupín sees the light? Do we still live like dogs and accept the scraps from the master's table?

1st Aztleca: Tienes que tener esperanza, hermana. . . . Have faith; Mártir knows what he is doing, sister.

Mártir [Using his arms and hands as if extending benediction]:   Hermanos, I am going to reveal to you my ultimate strategy for winning this struggle. It is called the boycott!

[*Both 1st and 2nd Aztleca are very excited. They are leaning forward to hear Mártir.*]

1st Aztleca: A boyco . . . boycott. What is a boycott, Mártir. Tell us!

Mártir: A boycott, hermano, is when you appeal to the hearts and minds of men everywhere. [*He sweeps his arms in a grand circle.*] Gente everywhere are touched by our struggle . . . our conditions . . . the inhumanity of the gachupín growers!

2nd Aztleca: It sounds wonderful, Mártir; go on.

Mártir: Well, what happens is we ask them not to buy any more chiles. We pressure every mercado across the land not to stock chiles . . . until at last Gimarra is forced to meet our demands . . . in order to sell chiles again.

2nd Aztleca [Excited]:   Magnífico, Mártir, eres un genio. Oh boy, I'm going to enjoy pressuring those mercados not to stock chiles.

Mártir [Looking at her suspiciously]:   What do you mean, enjoy pressuring the mercados?

2nd Aztleca [Half-way stuttering]:   Wh . . . Why, of . . . of course, Mártir. We're going to have to get tough with the mercados in order to stop the chiles, no?

Mártir [Emphatically]:   No! Hermana, how many times do I have to tell you . . . no violence!

2nd Aztleca: But Mártir, how else are we going to make sure the gachupines honor our boycott? Our picket lines? What if they jail us and beat us up again?

Mártir: We will resist non-violently, hermana. That means they do anything they want to with us. In the end, Tlaloc and people's consciences will make the gachupines change.

1st Aztleca: We must have faith, hermana. Mártir knows what he is doing. We must follow him.

2nd Aztleca [*Confused*]:   Mártir, will you explain what this non-violence you talk so much about means? Do we all have to follow that?

Mártir: Non-violence, hermana, is a philosophy. I first learned it from reading the works of Gandi. We must all follow this philosophy if we are going to belong to the United Aztleca Organizing Committee and be truly in support of our struggle and boycott. It is our way of life.

2nd Aztleca: But how can we follow this philosophy when we don't know what it means!

Mártir: Pacienca, pacienca. Non-violence as a philosophy is an aggressive philosophy, hermana. It means to avoid physical violence as a means of getting what you want, but at the same time to appeal to the human-ness in people in order to get what you want. In other words, make the person who is giving you trouble look so bad, even to his own friends, that he finally gives in.

2nd Aztleca: That is a beautiful philosophy, Mártir. But even if you change one or two or three gachupines' minds, what about the rest? What about this system of slavery that España has put our people in; do you think non-violence will change that?

Mártir [*A little irked by her questions but answers softly*]:   Everything will change one day, hermana, everything. We are not interested in changing this system; we are interested in more money, more food, better living conditions, things that we need now.

2nd Aztleca: But we need other things besides money, food, and beds, Mártir. What about our minds, our pride, ¡nuestro corazón!

1st Aztleca [*Astonished that 2nd Aztleca is still challenging Mártir*]:   HERMANA! Why . . . why this is almost blasphemy. Mártir knows what he is doing!

Mártir: Don't be too hard on her, manito. She is still young, has much to learn. . . . She will see the way. [*He rises and gestures to them.*] Come. We must tell the people about our strategy. They will be happy . . . the Boycott!

[*Mártir and 1st Aztleca walk away, arms around each other's shoulders. They are very happy. 1st Aztleca is telling Mártir, "This non-violence of yours, jefe, puro genio."*]

[*Scene 2, Act 1 ends as 2nd Aztleca stops walking away, looks at the audience, and says to herself, "I'm sure Mártir knows what he is doing, but does that mean its the best thing for us?"*]

Scene 3

[*The background is the same (chile fields). Mártir Montezuma is seated, yoga fashion, and seems to be in deep meditation. 1st Aztleca rushes in excitedly to speak to Mártir. The picture of Tlaloc and UAOC's bird are in back of Montezuma.*]

1st Aztleca [*Excited*]:   Mar . . . Mártir! Guess who is coming? He's . . . He's here . . . he's here in Telano-xochimil!

Mártir [*Calm voice*]:   ¡Cálmate . . . cálmate, hermano! Tell me, who is here?

1st Aztleca: El senador Roberto Quinadi, that's who! He heard about our boycott and your fast and so he decided to come!

Mártir: Good! You see, hermano, I told you our boycott would reach the hearts of the gachupines. Imagine, el senador Roberto Quinadi coming to visit . . . me!

1st Aztleca [*He assumes an alert position*]:   I think . . . I think I hear horses, jefe. Maybe that's el senador now.

[*Sure enough, it is el senador Roberto Quinadi. He strides in very arrogantly, looks at 1st Aztleca, and forces a smile on his face as he addresses Mártir. 1st Aztleca leaves.*]

Quinadi [*Extending his hand*]:   Mártir Montezuma, I presume.

Mártir [*Very excited as he shakes hands and rises*]:   Mucho gusto, señor senador . . . mucho gusto. You honor our humble house by your presence here. Sit down, please.

Quinadi [*Clearing his throat*]:   Aahem . . . [*He proceeds to sit down.*] Yes, thank you. How are you, my dear man?

Mártir [*He is seated also*]:   Fine, thank you. I have been fasting for twenty days now. It gets kinda hard on your stomach when you don't eat that long, you know.

Quinadi [*Still feeling uncomfortable*]:   I don't know . . . I mean, yes, it must be awful. Tell me, how long do you people plan to continue this boycott?

Mártir: As long as it is necessary, honorable senador. Why do you ask?

Quinadi: Well . . . it seems to me that this boycott isn't doing you any good. Think about all the bad publicity.

Mártir: But, senador, we're not causing any violence. What sort of bad publicity are you talking about?

Quinadi: It isn't the violence, my good man. But think of all the consumers who would like to eat chiles but can't. Don't you feel that a customer should be able to make a choice whether he wants to eat chiles or not? It just seems un-español, that's all.

Mártir [*Hurrying to assure Quinadi*]:   Oh, we don't want to be un-español, honorable senador. No, we don't want that to happen. All we want is decent treatment from the gachupines; I mean, the españoles, señor senador.

Quinadi [*Eying Mártir suspiciously*]:   Well . . . I don't know. It seems there should be a better way of solving this. I am going to use the influence of my good offices to try and solve this problem. Do you mind?

Mártir [*Very excited*]:   No! Of course not, my honorable senador. Please do everything in your power to bring justice!

Quinadi [*Arrogantly*]:   I will, my good man, I will. Look at what my dead brother did for your people. Why, he made Cuba safe for españoles . . . and indios, too . . . even though there's not too many of them left. He committed our loyal troops to fight those dreadful Incas down there in Peru. They're lower-class indios, you know.

Mártir: Yes, our people are aware of your dead brother, senador Quinadi. We honor him highly.

Quinadi: You should! Yes sir, his dream of an Alianza for Progress is a beautiful plan to bring civilization to all those heathen indios . . . not you Aztlecas, of course.

Mártir: Yes, of course, my senador. I am concerned with Aztlecas, you know. Tell me, what else brings you here.

Quinadi [*Shyly*]:   Well, you know that the King of España is going to name a new Supreme Viceroy soon to govern here. And you know all the trouble with the natives . . . you Aztlecas . . . that we've been having. Well, the King wants someone who gets along with the natives, you see. . . .

Mártir: Ah, yes, I see. You mean you want us to support you and say good things about you.

Quinadi: Sure, that'll help. Of course, I have my own press agents who'll give me the image I want.

Mártir: Yes, you españoles are very brilliant. I sometimes wonder why we cannot be like you.

[*2nd Aztleca rushes into the meeting between Mártir and Quinadi very excited. Quinadi looks at her very arrogantly.*]

2nd Aztleca: Mártir! Mártir! The gachupines are attacking our people! Women, children, everyone; they are being beaten, jailed!

Mártir: Cálmate . . . cálmate hermana. Be sensible and talk quiety, do you not see el senador Roberto Quinadi is here?

2nd Aztleca [*Ignoring Quinadi*] :   But, Mártir! What are we to do? What about our people?

Mártir [*Getting mad*] :   What about our people? Tlaloc will take care of them. Control yourself! Our people have nothing to worry about, our philosophy will win.

2nd Aztleca: You mean we should let ourselves be kicked and beaten? ! ! Say it isn't true, Mártir! !

Mártir: It is true!! You know our philosophy is non-violence. We must resist in a non-violent fashion. In the end, we will win. Now go back and join your people!

[*2nd Aztleca looks at him incredulously and leaves, crying and sobbing loudly. Mártir looks at Quinadi with a look of "you have to forgive this" type.*]

Mártir: We're not all like that, you know. She just doesn't understand non-violence yet. [*Apologetically.*] She was born just before you españoles came, you know.

Quinadi [*Nose in the air*] :   I should hope there are not many like those around! Are you sure you can hold your people from reacting violently to the peaceful law-and-order tactics of our police?

Mártir: I promise you that, señor senador! My people will learn non-violence even if I have to teach them myself!

Quinadi: Well, I hope so . . . for yours and my sake as well. Otherwise I will not be able to help you. Violence cannot solve anything, you know. We must do it democratically.

Mártir: Our philosophies are the same, señor senador . . . remain assured of that. Violence doesn't do anything but change things and then what?

Quinadi: Well, Mister Montezuma, it was a pleasure meeting you. You reaffirmed my beliefs that our indios still believe in the español way of life.

Mártir: It was an honor for you to visit me, señor honorable senador. In honor of your visit, it would please me if you would join me in some food to break my fast and celebrate our non-violence agreement.

Quinadi [*Not very enthusiastic at first*] :   Well . . . yes, of course. I'll have my painter come in and make some drawings of us eating some food . . . for my image, you know.

Mártir: Of course. [*He claps his hands and shouts.*] Food! Mamacita, bring us some food!

[*Mamacita comes from backstage with two bowls (can be imaginary). She hands them to Mártir and Quinadi. Quinadi's artist appears and gets ready to make sketches.*]

Mártir: Eat . . . eat hombre. [*He dips into his own bowl and goes through a heavy scene as this is first food he has eaten in twenty days. He is in ecstasy.*]

Quinadi [*Picks up scoop from his bowl, makes brave smile at his artist, and stuffs food into his mouth. He grimaces.*] : . . . Beans . . . uggh . . . beans.

[*Scene 3 ends as Roberto Quinadi bravely continues to eat the beans and smiling for his artist while Mártir slowly and ecstatically eats his beans.*]

Scene 4

[*The background continues to be the field of chiles. However, there is a big sign saying "Support Your Peace-Enforcing Law-and-Order Agencies" propped against the field of chiles. Hernán Gimarra and Viceroy Rigan are seated in a couple of chairs, discussing the boycott and its effects. It is five years later, 1529 A.D.*]

Gimarra: Well, you know, Viceroy, it has been five years since those savages led by Montezuma refused to work. Thanks to that damn Quinadi, Montezuma received a lot of support . . . from some damn priests, too . . . god damn them!

Rigan: I can't figure those savages out, either. . . . What else are they good for, being built close to the ground and all?

Gimarra: That's what I figured too. . . . But that means they have smaller stomachs, too. All they need is beans to keep them going.

Rigan: I've tried legislation . . . cut off any aid from my office. What else can we do, Hernán? The courts won't let them picket.

Gimarra: I know you've tried your best to do your duty, Viceroy. Don't feel bad. It's just that goddamn boycott! If that savage indio Montezuma wasn't an indio, I would almost have to respect him, you know. That was a smart move on his part.

Rigan: Yeh, curse his idol-worshipping soul. But it could've been worse.

Gimarra: What do you mean?

Rigan: Well, the whole strength of his boycott was in them being non-violent. Right?

Gimarra: Right.

Rigan: We tried all we could to try and break their boycott . . . took them to court. . . . That didn't work. Then we tried to change the public's mind about how bad the indios were. That didn't work. . . .

Gimarra: We even beat them up and threw them in jail all the time for the last five years. That didn't work also.

Rigan: Right! Remember, we were trying to get them to react to us violently, but they wouldn't.

Gimarra: So if nothing worked, what's so good about it? Why did you say it could've been worse?

Rigan: Don't you see? We made them do things the español way. They played our game. We should let them "win" now.

Gimarra: Are you crazy, hombre? Let them win! Sign a contract with them?

Rigan: Rrright. Look, what if they had decided to fight back instead of taking everything we gave them. Hey, there might have been some serious trouble. We might not be here, right now, talking like we are.

Gimarra [*Rigan's line of thinking is beginning to sink in now*]:   So . . . I'll sign a contract with them . . . which really won't be a big thing. In fact, compared to our workers back in España, it'll by nothing. [*His face lights up; he slaps his knee and is very happy and smiling.*] Hey . . . hey . . . ha ha ha ha ha yippeee. . . .

Rigan [*Smiling also*]:   You finally caught on, huh . . . ha, ha, ha . . . We'll let Montezuma become a big hero . . . but people will also know he did it the español way . . . which means our way of life is right. We still control . . . and we still have the indios eating beans . . . ha, ha, ha [*He starts laughing hysterically.*] ha, ha etc.

Gimarra [*Also laughing hysterically*]:   You are some coyote, Viceroy Rigan . . . some coyote . . . beautiful . . . ha, ha, ha . . . and if Montezuma decides to boycott something else. . . .

Rigan [*Still laughing*]   . . . after a while we'll let him "win" there too, as long as he does it the español way . . . ha, ha, ha . . . no violence . . . ha, ha, ha. . . .

Gimarra [*Still laughing*]:   . . . I can just see the headlines . . . ha, ha, ha . . . Aztlecas win Chile Boycott. . . . Everyone will be eating chiles even if they like them or not . . . ha, ha, ha . . . and we'll make more money . . . ha, ha, ha. . . .

Rigan [*Laughing*]:   . . . make more money, and the indios will be convinced that Montezuma was right . . . ha, ha, ha . . . We can destroy the indios who want change now . . . ha, ha, ha . . . ha, ha, ha, ha, ha, ha, ha, ha, [*He is laughing hysterically now, bending over from the pleasure of laughing so hard.*] . . . ha, ha, ha, ha.

[*Scene 4 ends as both Gimarra and Rigan are rolling back and forth with laughter.* . . . *Ha, ha, ha, ha, ha, ha, ha, ha, etc.*]

Scene 5

[*The background is still the field of chiles. The audience can hear the sounds of celebrating Aztlecas offstage; gradually the Aztlecas come on stage, still celebrating and congratulating each other. They carry Tlaloc and the UAOC bird with them. They are Mártir, 1st Aztleca, 2nd Aztleca, and another Aztleca or two.*]

1st Aztleca [*Slapping Mártir on the back*] :   We did it, jefe, we did it!!! . . . we won!!!

Mártir: We sure did . . . whoopeee. . . !

[*They continue to congratulate each other and celebrate. 2nd Aztleca separates herself from them and quietly sits near the front of the stage, As soon as she sits down, the celebrating Aztlecas can still be seen celebrating, but they should make no sound. 2nd Aztleca porceeds to talk to herself (out loud).*]

2nd Aztleca: I wonder whether we really won. Somehow something is missing. It's been five years now and something is still missing. Maybe its the way the gachupines smiled and shook hands when we signed the contract. I just don't know . . . Oh well . . . like Mártir says, time will tell. . . .

[*She rises, goes back to the celebrating Aztlecas, who are now audible (being heard) again, and proceeds to celebrate with them. Act 1 ends.*]

ACT II

[*The background is the same as before, a field of chiles. The mood in Nueva España is changing. Other Aztlecas are on the move; they want to challenge the gachupines physically and violently if necessary. They want changes, not reforms. Mártir Montezuma rejects them and renounces violence. He has been acclaimed by the gachupines as being "the" Aztleca leader. Older Aztlecas find his non-violence comforting; younger Aztlecas flock to his side because he has shown dedication and has won. While other Aztlecas are seeking to create a nation of their own, Mártir leads his people towards better treatment from the gachupines.*]

Scene 1

[*Mártir and 1st Aztleca are seated, discussing their recent victory over Gimarra, when 2nd Aztleca bursts into the scene to announce the arrival of Revolución and Justicia, two young Aztleca activists who are seeking to liberate the Aztleca people from Spanish domination and establish an Aztleca nation.*]

2nd Aztleca: Con permiso, jefe, but two young people are here to see you.

Mártir: Yes. Who are they?

2nd Aztleca: Revolución and Justicia, jefe. They are with the other groups who are trying to start a nation for our people, called Mexico.

1st Aztleca [*A little annoyed*]:   Dreamers! Why don't they help us out instead of going around talking all that talk about "we want to be free? "

Mártir: Be patient, hermano. [*He motions to 2nd Aztleca.*] Tell them to come in, hermana, let's hear what they have to say.

[*2nd Aztleca goes to call in Revolución and Justicia. They enter alone without 2nd Aztleca. All four greet each other and shake hands (Aztleca style).*]

Mártir: Be welcome here in our house, hermanos, what brings you here?

Revolución: Muchas gracias, hermano. We come hoping to talk to you about this nation we are trying to create . . . the nation of Mexico.

Mártir: Yes, I've heard about it. What about it?

Revolución: Well, you know that you are considered by our people to be one of our best and respected leaders. We want your support and cooperation.

1st Aztleca: What about all this violence you people have been advocating? How can you expect us to support you?

Justicia [*A little surprised*]:   Violence? . . . Support? . . . You know we have not reacted violently unless we have been attacked first. We have only acted in self-defense!

Mártir [*Trying to calm the situation before it becomes angrier*]:   Paciencia, hermanos. Look, hermanos, you know our philosophy here at UAOC is nonviolence. We have a responsibility towards our members not to get involved in something which could harm them.

Justicia [*Calmer*]:   We know that, señor Montezuma. We are not trying to harm our own people. But what good is it when our people are still little better than slaves?

Mártir: Our people may not be on top, but violence is not going to get them there. Here at UAOC we are concerned with food, better wages, health care, better living conditions . . .

Revolución: So are we. But our people need to be free also!

1st Aztleca [*Angry again*]:   Freedom! You people use that word to justify violence!

Revolución: I'm sorry you see it that way, hermano . . . but I can see why you would say that. The gachupines are very clever in turning things around.

1st Aztleca [*Very angry*]:   Do you call me a fool!

Mártir [*Calming things again*]:   Contrólate, hermano. Let's not fight amongst each other. Perhaps you brothers could explain a little bit more.

Revolución: Well, hermano . . . you know that our people are colonial subjects for the gachupines. We have no education . . . bad jobs . . . and the gachupines are trying to destroy our culture. . . .

Mártir: Yes, I know it is something like that for us. . . .

Revolución: Well, we also know that you have a commitment and responsibility towards the chile and other farm workers . . . but there are even more of our people living in Tenochtitlán and other cities. . . .

Mártir: I understand that. But don't you see, we are trying to make things better. . . .

Revolución: We know that, hermano. But we feel that our people need more than just a few reforms once in awhile. . . . We need to have our own nation!

Mártir: But do you feel that is possible? Don't you feel you are being destructive when you strike back at the gachupín? He can destroy us . . . they are so powerful!

Revolución: We don't want to be violent, hermano. But we feel we cannot let the gachupín step all over us either. We want changes, not reforms! We want our people to have educations.

Justicia: . . . better jobs . . . and houses too . . . but we are people too, not animals, and we want to determine for ourselves how we are going to live day after day. . . .

Mártir: Those are fine ideals, hermano . . . but we cannot accept violence if that is the means by which to attain them!

Revolución [Exasperated]:   We don't want violence either! But when nature changes things, she does it violently too. Are we to remain slave workers for the gachupines for the rest of our history?

Mártir [Resigned attitude]:   I am sorry, hermanos, but we cannot actively help you. We support your ideals in spirit but not in the way you hope to gain them. I hope we split here still brothers.

Revolución [Sees that Mártir cannot be swayed]:   I am sorry you see it that way too, hermano. We want you to know that we respect you deeply and are fully confident that you are a very sincere and dedicated Azteca.

Justicia: We love you, brother.

   [*All four rise, and all four exchange farewells. Revolución and Justicia leave with bowed heads. Mártir and 1st Azteca look at each other, wondering.*]

Mártir: They just didn't understand that we cannot condone violence. . . .

1st Azteca [Sympathetic]:   Do not worry, jefe, they will see in time.

   [*End of Scene 1.*]

Scene 2

   [*Mártir Montezuma leads his non-violent forces against Juan Hantle, corn plantation jefe. A trial ensues in which gross misjustice is present, and Mártir goes to jail. The background is a corn plantation, with a jail outlined in the center. For the courtroom scene, the judge is seated. Mártir is also seated, facing the judge at least fifteen feet apart. A Spanish policeman is also present, standing next to Mártir.*]

Judge: Well, Montezuma, you are charged with illegally leading a boycott against the corn plantation of Señor Juan Hantle. How do you plead?

Mártir: I plead not guilty, your honor!

Judge [Giving Mártir a cross look]:   Not guilty, you say . . . ummm . . . we'll see about this. Bring in Señor Hantle.

   [*The policeman goes and calls in Juan Hantle. Hantle comes in looking very haughty. He stops and waits for the policeman to swear him in.*]

Judge: Buenos días, señor Hantle. You are looking very good today, sir. [*He motions to the policeman.*] No need for that, policía; señor Hantle is a gentleman. He does not have to swear that he will tell the truth.

   [*The policeman goes back to his position while Hantle sits down, as in a witness stand. Hantle looks at the Judge with a knowing smile.*]

Hantle: Thank you, your honor.

Judge: Now then, señor Hantle, can you tell us the nature of your complaint?

Hantle [*Smiling*]: Be happy to, your honor. [*He looks savagely at Mártir and points at him.*] . . . this indio here, the one they call Mártir Montezuma, has called for a boycott against my corn plantation.

Judge: For what purpose?

Hantle [*Irritated*]: To organize my indios, that's what for!

Judge: But aren't your indios already organized by the Gachupiners' Union?

Hantle [*Smiling*]: Yes, they are. I told this indio I would have him jailed!

Judge [*Smiling also*]: All in good time, of course. Now there, Montezuma, you've heard the unimpeachable word of señor Hantle; what do you have to say?

Mártir: His contract with the Gachupiners' Union is not valid, your honor. It is a phony contract to cheat our people. . . . Why, the Gachupiners' Union almost owns part of señor Hantle's corn plantation. . . .

Hantle [*Very angry*]: That's a lie, you dirty indio! I only borrowed 500,000 pesos from them, that's all!

Judge: You better watch what you say, Montezuma. [*He looks at Mártir threateningly.*]

Mártir: Well, your honor . . . it is within our rights to call for a constitutional and peaceful boycott against the corn. . . .

Judge [*Angry*]: What rights! Where!

Mártir [*A little cowed*]: Your honor . . . does it not say that as long as a citizen is peaceful and orderly he may pursue non-violent protest. . . .

Judge: It does say that! For citizens! But you are an indio, Montezuma!

[*Hantle is smiling broadly.*]

Hantle: Your honor . . . we can be reasonable with an indio once in awhile. . . . [*He turns towards Montezuma.*]

Judge [*Surprised but eager to accommodate Hantle*]: Yes, distinguished señor Hantle? . . .

Hantle [*Turns towards Mártir angrily*]: Call off your boycott, indio . . . and we'll set you free!

Mártir: I cannot, señor Hantle, I cannot. We must sign a contract first. It is the español way of doing things.

Hantle [*Turns towards Judge angrily*] :   I cannot waste time with this miserable animal! Do your job, judge!

Judge [*Hurrying to please Hantle*] :   Yes . . . of course. Stand up, Montezuma!

[*The policeman does not wait for Mártir to stand up but grabs him by the neck and holds him up.*]

Judge: Mártir Montezuma . . . I sentence you to jail until your workers stop this illegal boycott . . . and if that doesn't work, we'll figure out a way to stop you for good. [*He motions towards policeman.*] Out with him, guard!

[*The policeman hustles Mártir out of the courtroom, still holding him by the neck.*]

Judge [*Looking at Hantle*] :   Did I do all right, señor Hantle?

Hantle: Well . . . I guess so. [*He hits his fist into his open hand.*] I want that indio beat in jail until he loosens up . . . understand?

Judge: Of course, señor Hantle. I will order it personally . . . be sure of that. My, my . . . I get tired sometimes of judging those indios. They're all guilty, you know.

[*End of Scene 2.*]

Scene 3

[*The background is the corn plantation with the jail in the center. Mártir Montezuma is seated, yoga fashion, in the center front of the background. He has been fasting again, to protest his incarceration, but more to attract widespread sympathy to the UAOC's corn boycott. The Spanish policeman comes to inform him of a visitor.*]

Policeman: Hey . . . indio! How were the beans I brought you, huh? [*He is teasing Mártir.*]

[*Mártir slowly lifts his head and looks sympathetically at the policeman.*]

Policeman [*Getting angry*] :   ¡Cabrón indio! You have a visitor . . . a very distinguished visitor . . . one of your liberal friends to visit you. Ha, ha, ha. . .!

[*The policeman turns away and leaves. Presently a woman arrives. She is Spanish, the widow of senador Roberto Quinadi. She is Hay-tol Quinadi. Mártir strives to get up to greet her, but he is too weak. She rushes to reassure him he does not have to rise.*]

Hay-tol: Please! Don't exert yourself, Mister Montezuma! [*She touches him gently on shoulder.*]

Mártir [*Talks very slowly due to weakness from lack of eating*] : I . . . am . . . very . . . honored . . . , Señora Hay-tol Quinadi.

Hay-tol: The pleasure is mine, Mister Montezuma. Tell me, how was your trial?

Mártir: There . . . was . . . no . . . misjustice. The judge . . . was . . . a . . . very honorable . . . and . . . decent . . . man.

Hay-tol: Yes, that's what I read you said in the *Tenochtitlán Evening Tabloid.* That caused quite a furor there, you know.

Mártir: W . . . h . . . y?

Hay-tol: Well . . . it seems most everyone knows you got a dirty deal, being sent to jail. Yet by your statement, you implied that everything was hunky-dory.

Mártir: We . . . must . . . not . . . do . . . or . . . say . . . anything . . . that . . . will . . . give . . . rise . . . to . . . violence.

Hay-tol: Yes, you're a very respected man, Mister Montezuma. Do you know that you're our favorite Aztleca leader? Why, we can relate to you!

Mártir [*Managing to smile*] : Why . . . thank . . . you. Thank . . . you . . . very . . . much.

Hay-tol: You are exactly the type of Aztleca leader we like. Not like those other rabble-rousers!

Mártir: Yes, I see . . . you agree . . . with . . . the philosophy of . . . your late and beloved husband.

Hay-tol: Of course I do!

Mártir: That . . . is . . . good . . . to . . . hear. Tell me, what is going on . . . out there?

Hay-tol: You mean out of jail? Your fast is receiving great national attention. People are beginning to buy only UAOC corn. Your people are maintaining a beautiful vigilance outside on the streets. . . .

Mártir: You mean . . . everything . . . that . . . we . . . did . . . before . . . is . . . working . . . again?

Hay-tol: Everything! Of course it'll probably take about three years. Things take time, you know. . . .

Mártir: I . . . know.

Hay-tol: I must leave now. [*She rises.*] You know, Mister Montezuma, you're almost a saint now. By the time this boycott is over, you will be a saint.

Mártir: Thank . . . you. My . . . belief . . . in . . . non-violence . . . shall . . .
remain . . . firm . . . and . . . dedicated . . . forever.

[*Hay-tol Quinadi is leaving the cell. On her way out she exclaims to herself, "Yes, well I've done my duty by coming here. Now to meet those
dreadful indios out there. This public-relations job of being a liberal
sure is tiring sometimes."*]

[*End of Scene 3.*]

Scene 4

[*The scene is the same as for Scene 3. Corn plantation, jail, Mártir seated
yoga fashion. Suddenly offstage a ruckus is heard. The policeman suddenly appears, half-dragging a resisting 2nd Aztleca with him. The policeman heaves 2nd Aztleca into the cell with Montezuma. 2nd Aztleca
rushes to the imaginary bars and curses at the police.*]

Policeman [*As he walks away laughing*]:   Here's another stable-mate for you,
indio.

2nd Aztleca [*Seething*]:   ¡ ¡ ¡Hijo de tu chingada madre, pinchi gachupín! ! !
¡ ¡ ¡El diable fue tu abuela, maricón! ! !

Mártir   [*Astonished to hear 2nd Aztleca talk and act this way*]:   ¡Hermana!
What is wrong with you! Have you taken leave of your senses? [*He rises
and attempts to comfort her.*]

2nd Aztleca [*She shrugs him off*]:   Do not touch me! I want to get out of
here! I want to be free!

Mártir: Hermana! Remember our philosophy of non-violence. Do you know
what you are saying?

2nd Aztleca: Do you know what you are saying? What makes you so right
all the time? ! I don't believe in your non-violence anymore, Mártir!

Mártir [*Confused*]:   Why not? What happened to you?

2nd Aztleca: What happened to me? What hasn't happened to me should be
your question! I was beaten up again, for the 10,000th time in my life.

Mártir: I am sorry to hear that, hermana. But we must learn to resist non-
violently.

2nd Aztleca: Why? Because you say so? What is right for you may not be
right for me!

Mártir: But hermana, I have been beaten and abused and starved many times.
You don't see me react violently, do you?

2nd Aztleca: Yes, I know that you have also been mistreated. Of course, you are an indio . . . like me. But your way is wrong, Mártir. When you are jailed for nothing and you say the judge was honest and there was no misjustice, you lie to the people. [*She shouts out through the bars.*] LET ME OUT; I WANT TO BE FREE!!

Mártir: How do I lie to the people?

2nd Aztleca: Our people love and respect you, Mártir. We know we are treated badly. When a person like you . . . a leader . . . maybe the top leader . . . says that a dishonest and corrupt judge was committing no misjustice . . . our people listen . . . you lead them to believe that we can get justice from the courts. . . .

Mártir: The courts may not be right all the time, hermana . . . but we must believe in non-violence!

2nd Aztleca: Don't you see?! Are you blind?! Your non-violence is a chain holding our people back from freedom. The gachupines are using you to continue to enslave our people!

Mártir: I cannot believe you are sane at this moment, hermana. I choose not to hear the words you say to me.

2nd Aztleca: They are not words hermano. [*She is pleading with him.*] They are cries. Cries of agony. Cries of sorrow. Cries of frustration. Do you not hear me? Do you not hear us? [*She shouts.*] WE WANT TO BE FREE!

[*The policeman comes. He yells at 2nd Aztleca "Shut up, you miserable whore!" He motions towards Mártir, "Okay, indio . . . your liberal friends got you out again . . . come on . . . you're going out of here."*]

Mártir: What about my hermana here? [*He motions towards 2nd Aztleca.*]

Policeman [*Wicked grin on his face*] :   Not her . . . uhh, nooo. Not her. She stays.

Mártir [*He turns towards 2nd Aztleca*] :   Do not worry, hermana. We will get you out. I have friends, you know. [*He starts to leave.*]

[*Mártir is let out of the cell and is about to walk away when 2nd Aztleca cries out to him.*

2nd Aztleca: Mártir! Mártir! Be good to our people, Mártir. They love you, do not let them down!

Mártir [*Smiling gently*] :   I will be good to them, hermana. I will not let them down. Have comfort in knowing that our non-violence will win.

2nd Aztleca [*In despair*] :   Non-violence after the revolution, hermano!!

[*Mártir smiles gently again and leaves muttering, "I will not let them down. I will not let them down."*]

[*The policeman has a club in his hand. He slyly approaches 2nd Aztleca.*]

Policeman: As for you, you bitch, you are about to experience an unfortunate accident. A suicide, they call it.

[*2nd Aztleca is aware that she is going to be killed by the policeman. She snarls at him and prepares to defend herself. They struggle until he hits her a couple of times and she is on the floor; he is getting ready to administer the death blow, club in the air, and she shouts out for the last time. . . .*]

2nd Aztleca: Ayyyy . . . GENTE MIA . . . I LOVE YOU, MY PEOPLE . . . VIVA MEXICO . . . VIVA MEXICO. ¡¡ PATRIA O MUERTE, VENCEREMOS! !

[*The policeman strikes the death blow on her neck. 2nd Aztleca slumps to the floor, dead. End of Act II.*]

ACT III

[*After the end of Act II, the lights are dimmed to maximum. A narrator from behind the background can be heard saying:*]

And so another martyr died in the fight for Aztleca freedom, in the fight to establish Mexico. And in time the gachupines even killed Montezuma, who went to his death like the gentle bird that he was. The people of Mexico lived in near-slavery and misery. Montezuma, despite his great wisdom and leadership, made a mistake when he accepted the Spaniards into his home. His people were to pay the price of accepting the Spaniards ways for 300 years, 300 long years of deprivation, 300 long years of cultural rape, 300 hungry years of empty bellies. The Spaniards ruled Mexico as a colony, exploiting it for their own benefit, and leaving the native tribes little good in return. One day however, in 1821 . . . there was a cry heard: ¡¡¡EL GRITO DE DOLORES . . . Aaayyyeeeeiiiiiii! ! !

[*In the scene are Padre Hidalgo and Revolución y Justicia seated, on chairs. They are discussing the recent victory against the Spaniards and are hunched over, working out details on an imaginary map on an imaginary table. In the background is seen the flag of Mexico in the center, dominating, and in the far background are seen old buildings, some on fire. The year is 1821, A.D. Revolución y Justicia wears a sword.*]

Revolución y Justicia [*Pointing towards spot on map*]:   . . . and here, Padre, is where we shall engage the Spaniards tomorrow. . . .

Hidalgo: Well done . . . excellent, hijo. The people are ready to fight!

Revolución y Justicia: They are not only ready, Padre . . . but willing . . . we are struggling to keep them from attacking every gachupin they see.

Hidalgo: Yes. It is quite different now . . . from the days of our long departed hermano . . . Montezuma.

Revolución y Justicia: And we are better for it, Padre!

Hidalgo [*Sympathetically*]:   We must not be harsh on him, comandante. He was a sincere and very dedicated man. He loved our people.

Revolucion y Justicia: Yes . . . he was good. But teaching our people to wait for the gachupines to change . . . Whew! That was loving our people to death!

Hidalgo [*Softly and wistfully*]:   Yes . . . he was wrong . . . but a good man nevertheless. I sometimes wonder, however, how our land might be today if only he had not let the gachupines enslave us. . . .

Revolución y Justicia: Mexico would have existed 300 years ago. That's how our land would be today! We would not be having to fight for our freedom as we are now.

Hidalgo: You're right, of course. It is about time our people established their own system of government . . . of living. . . .

Revolución y Justicia: Yes. Well, Padre, I must leave to arrange some matters . . . Con su permiso. . . .

Hidalgo [*Still wondering*]:   Yes, of course. Vaya con Dios, comandante.

> [*Revolución y Justicia gets up, adjusts his hat and sword, and leaves. Padre Hidalgo stares out a window and spots a woman crossing in front of him. It is Maya-Xochimil, the reincarnation of 2nd Azteca, who is walking towards the front of the stage slowly, carrying a rifle in one hand and a basket in the other. Hidalgo calls out to her.*]

Hidalgo: You . . . there . . . hermana. Have you anything to eat?

Maya-Xochimil [*She turns around, looks at him, and walks towards him. Hidalgo remains seated, Maya-Xochimil standing*]:   I have some tortillas, Padre . . . and frijoles. Would you care for some?

Hidalgo [*As he reaches out for the tortillas and the bowl of beans*]:   Muchas gracias, hermana. I am famished!!

> [*Hidalgo gulps down the tortillas and beans quickly as Maya-Xochimil*

lovingly and patiently watches him. Suddenly, he looks at her, stares very hard, and exclaims.]

Hidalgo: You . . . you . . . remind me of a painting I have seen somewhere before. . . .

Maya-Xochimil: Was it of Maya-Xochimil, the Aztleca follower of Montezuma, Padre Hidalgo?

Hidalgo: Yes!! Why you look exactly like her. How did you know my name? You cannot be!!

Maya-Xochimil: Do not be frightened, Padre Hidalgo. Yes, I am she you call Maya-Xochimil. I have waited 300 years for this event, Padre . . . 300 long years. . . .

Hidalgo [*Astonished*]:   But how is this possible!!!!!

Maya-Xochimil: Tlaloc gave me the power to reincarnate myself until the day that Mexico would exist . . . until the day that my people would be free. . . .

Hidalgo: But things have changed much since the gachupines first came and you fought with Montezuma!

Maya-Xochimil [*Nodding her head*]:   Yes . . . things have changed. . . . There is no longer Tenochtitlán. . . . Now there is Mexico City. . . . Now we are a nation of mestizos. . . . Nauhautl is no longer spoken everywhere. . . . Instead the gachupín has everyone speaking español. . . .

Hidalgo [*Astonished*]:   You know all this??!!

Maya-Xochimil: Tlaloc has given me the power to see what is in the past and in the future.

Hidalgo [*Worried with a hand supporting his chin*]:   Ahh . . . yes . . . the future. We have started to rid ourselves of the gachupín today . . . but tomorrow . . . mañana. . . . [*He sweeps the air with his hands.*] What will Mexico be mañana? ?

Maya-Xochimil: Mexico, my good Padre, will see a wise and respected Zapotec truly create a Republic. It will suffer under the cruel dictatorship of a despot named Díaz. It will suffer ten years of civil war to rid the land of parasites only to see that honorable struggle sold out by a traitor named Carranza. Oohhhhhh, the people will still suffer, my good Padre!!!

Hidalgo: But why shall they still suffer that long, Maya-Xochimil??

Maya-Xochimil [*Heartbroken*]:   Because of greed . . . corruption . . . because our people will throw out the españoles . . . but their system will stay and cause much suffering. Only until that day when our people return to the ways of true brotherhood. . . .

Hidalgo [*Depressed*] :   The future does not seem too bright.

Maya-Xochimil [*Sweeping the air with her hands*] :   The future is bright, Padre. . . . It is bright. Generations from now, a lost tribe of Mexicanos . . . calling themselves Chicanos . . . in the lands to the north called Aztlán . . . they will rise, one day . . . and all of Mexico will also rise . . . and the days OF THIS MONSTROUS SYSTEM SHALL BE NUMBERED! ! ! ! !

Maya-Xochimil [*Calls out to the audience*] :   OH CHICANOS OF AZTLAN . . . HEAR ME . . . WITH YOU RIDES THE SALVATION OF MEXICO. DO NOT MAKE THE MISTAKES OF YOUR FATHERS!!! ¡ ¡ ¡PATRIA O MUERTE! ! !

No Nos Venceremos

ROBERTO J. GARZA

Roberto J. Garza was born and reared in Edinburg, Texas. For the last four-teen years, he has been a teacher and professor of Spanish at both the secondary and college levels. As a recipient of several fellowships, which include an NDEA award, a John Hay Whitney Foundation Grant, and a National Endowment for the Humanities post-doctoral research grant at the University of Notre Dame, he has done extensive work in the Chicano creative arts.

While teaching at Sul Ross State University, he founded and directed the Spanish Experimental Theatre (SET). Composed of Chicano college students, this theatre toured and performed to audiences in both Mexico and Texas.

His plays are characterized by the experimental treatment of historical, social, and psychological issues pertinent to the Chicano in a contemporary setting. His plays are written entirely in Spanish. While other Chicano play-wrights use archetype characters to depict mainly Chicanos in the *barrios* or in the fields, this playwright concentrates on character development to reflect the Chicano "experience." *No Nos Venceremos* is an example.

No Nos Venceremos is a one-act Spanish tragicomedy. Its plot centers around the human agony and tribulations of seven individuals imprisoned for taking part in the "Revolution." Due to the appearance (dress) of the charac-ters and physical setting of the play, it will be assumed that the human drama takes place immediately following the Mexican Revolution of 1910. But it

could very well be that the seven protagonists in the play are in reality proto-
types of individuals who have and will always fight in order to remain free as
human beings. They are very much symbolic of those who struggle against
the social and human forces that physically and mentally enslave mankind.

Characters

El General
El Estudiante Universitario
El Teco
La Soldadera
El Guardia
El Gordo
El Güero

Lector,

Quizás este acontecimiento que está por leer nunca sucedió. Pero supongamos que se hubiera prestado la ocasión, la oportunidad, el tiempo o la circunstancia, entonces tal vez. Es así pues, basándonos en esta suposición el Teatro Experimental desarrolla argumentos o temas que tengan algún parentesco a los de la lucha de nuestra 'Raza'. Entonces, ¡experimentemos!

Primera Escena

[Un par de años después de la Revolución, en la celda de una carcel en un país Hispanoamericano. Por todas partes hay heno desparramado en el piso. A ambos lados de la celda está un catre de campaña, que serán los únicos muebles de casa que darán decoro a la pieza. Hay una sola puerta, y ésta está al fondo de la celda. Tanto la celda como los personajes que van casi todos harapientos dan un aspecto sucio y bastante triste.
Al abrirse el telón, El Teco está reclinado en uno de los catres, acompañando con su guitarra a la Soldadera quien canta una canción de la Revolución. Esta está de pie, cerca de la cabecera del Teco. En el otro catre está El Estudiante acostado de espaldas, leyendo un periódico todo amarillento y casi deshecho. El Gordo y el Güero están en el centro del foro, frente a los otros personajes, sentados en dos pacas de heno, jugando a la baraja. Al terminarse la canción entra el Guardia.]

El Guardia *[Un tipo malhumurado y bastante despota. Viste de pantalón y camisa 'khaki'. Lleva un 'kepis' y botas de montar. A la cintura lleva una pistola y también trae un garrote en las manos. Tanto como su vestido limpio su rostro afeitado y sus botas bien aseadas, hace que toda su persona tenga un aspecto de inmaculada limpieza]:* ¡Bueno, ya basta de cancion-

193

citas! [*Ademán con la mano.*] A ver si me le dan una limpiada a este chiquero de marranos, que ya mero llega su famoso 'General' a darles una visita. [*Sonrisa burlona.*] No quiero que va a creer que no los tratamos bien aquí ¡ja! ¡ja!

Todos [*Menós El Estudiante que permanece callado demuestran algún gesto o expresión de alegría y sorpresa a la vez*]:   ¡Nuestro General! ¡Aquí!

El Guardia [*Enfadado*]: Sí, hombre, sí. ¿Qué no me oyeron?

La Soldadera [*Con mucha alegría*]:   ¿Pero han oído muchachos? ¡Viene a visitarnos nuestro General!

El Estudiante [*Irritado y poniéndose de pie*]:   ¿Y quién le quiere ver la cara a ése . . . ese 'General'?

El Gordo: ¿Pos quién ha de ser? ¡Pos nosotros mero! [*Enojado viendo al Estudiante.*] ¡Pos éste!

El Estudiante [*Incrédulo, mirando a los otros personajes*]:   ¿Qué todavía no se dan cuenta ustedes? ¿Qué no compreden, que por la culpa de ése . . . ese 'General' estamos aquí . . . encerrados como luego dice éste [*Apuntando al Guardia.*] . . . como marranos?

El Güero: ¡Oyeme! ¡No fue culpa de nadie que nosotros estemos aquí metidos! Es que a nosotros ya nos tocaba, ¿y qué? Ahora ni llorar es bueno.

El Estudiante [*Ignorando lo que El Güero acaba de decir, camina hacia al frente del foro, y meditando en voz alta y grave, se dirige a la audiencia y a la vez también a los otros personajes*]:   ¿Quién había de pensar que la Revolución acabaría en esto? [*Ademán con la mano.*] Yo como todos mis otros colegas, creí que los motivos de ese 'general' y éstos [*Apuntando a los otros personajes.*] eran nobles y sinceros. Que la 'causa' por la cual peleábamos era justa y verdadera, porque nuestra gente se merecía mejor vida que la que llevaban. Pero que equivocado estaba. ¡Qué decepción! ¡Qué desilusión fue la nuestra!

El Guardia [*Con sarcasmo*]:   ¡Ay amiguito! ¡A uste' si que deveras me lo embobó la Revolución! ¡Cómo será uste' bruto! ¿De qué le sirvió tanta escuela? ¿Qué no le enseñaron nada de la vida en la escuela? ¿No le 'dijieron' que en la vida, el más vivo vive del más pendejo? ¡Pero bien merecido se lo tiene uste' por meterse a donde no le importa! ¡Ja! ¡Ja!

El Estudiante [*Dirigiéndose al Guardia*]:   Quizás tenga usted razón. Desgraciadamente fue muy tarde cuando me di cuenta que ese mentado 'general' y todos aquellos [*Apuntando a los otros personajes.*] quienes le seguian eran 'oportunistas'. La unica 'causa' por la cual peleaban era para sacar beneficio propio. ¡Miserables!

El Teco [*Quien ha permanecido sentado todo este tiempo escuchando al Estudiante, se levanta enfurecido, poniéndose cara a cara con éste*]:
¡Cuidado, amiguito! ¡Mida sus palabras! ¡Uste' es un miserable estudiante universitario que no sabe de cosas de hombres! ¡Sí, señor, porque una Revolución es cosa de hombres y no cuestión de pantomina o de juego como ustedes los estudiantes se lo pensaban! ¡Cuando uste' sepa y sienta lo que es el dolor de ser pobre, vivir abusado por un gobierno que nos ha tenido aplastados toda la vida . . . entonces háblenos de sus creencias, sus ilusiones y desilusiones!

El Estudiante: Bueno aunque nunca supe lo que fue ser pobre, sin embargo, me interé de las injusticias que se cometián contra el pobre. Me di cuenta por medio de mis estudios que nuestro gobierno siempre ha estafado al pobre de todos sus derechos humanos. Fue entonces cuando empecé a simpatizar, a . . .

El Teco: ¡No, amiguito! ¡No se aprende a vivir de los libros! Sufra las injusticias que hemos penado nosotros los pobres. ¡Sienta el yugo del mísero trabajo con el cual nos ha esclavizado este miserable gobierno . . . y entonces sabrá porque el pobre suda sangre para ganarse la vida! ¡No nos hable de simpatía, de lo que ha leído, o lo que le han contado de nosotros! ¡Viva como nosotros lo hemos hecho . . . y entonces sabrá porque la Revolución era la única salida que teníamos . . . de vengarnos contra quienes nos aplastaban! [*Vuelve a su sitio pero permanece de pie.*]

La Soldadera [*Se acerca al Teco y al Estudiante. Dirigiéndose a éste*]:   ¡Así es, Teco! ¡Qué sabe este mocoso de cosas de la vida!

El Estudiante: ¡No hablo de cosas de la vida! ¡Hablo de ese 'general', ese jefe de ustedes!

La Soldadera: ¿Pero cómo se puede hablar de nuestro 'jefe' sin hablar de la Revolución o la Vida del Pobre? ¿Qué no ves que la una es la otra? ¿Qué si no se nos hubiera tratado como esclavos . . . como animales, no hubiera habido Revolución, ni tampoco necesidad de nuestro 'jefe'?

El Estudiante: ¡De acuerdo! Pero no había motivo para que ese 'general' nos engañara . . . nos mintiera con sus promesas!

La Soldadera: ¡Miserable Catrín, eres tú quien miente con toda la boca! El nunca nos prometió ni más o menos. Siempre nos habló con la puritita verdad y si bien lo seguimos fue porque fue muy macho. ¿Me entiendes, criatura? [*Burlándose del Estudiante, trata de acariarle la cara.*] ¡Muy macho, y no como todos de tu clase que ni hombres son todavía! ¡Ja! ¡Ja!

[*El Estudiante con mucho desdén se quita la mano de La Soldadera y va a su catre donde se sienta.*]

El Gordo: ¿Y yo, mamacita? ¿Soy bastante macho pa' tí?

La Soldadera [*Indignada, acercándose a donde están El Gordo y El Güero.*
Dirigiéndose al Gordo] :   ¡Tu abuela! ¡Ya quisieras que me fijara en tí,
mantecoso!

El Gordo: ¡Vóytelas! ¡Pos que se cree esta vieja . . . !

El Güero: ¡Ya Gordo! [*Bastante ufano.*] ¡Ya sabes que esta morena es muy
mía. [*Trantándole de darle una nalgada a ésta.*]

La Soldadera: ¡Ahora sí, nomás eso me faltaba! ¿Pues qué se creen ustedes
costrosos? ¡Todavía no ha nacido el hombre que sea dueño mío? ¿Y por
lo visto aquí hay solamente un hombre! [*Dirigiéndose al Teco.*] ¡Los demás
son puros habladores y de muy pocos pantalones! ¡Ja! ¡Ja! [*Se da la*
vuelta y va y se para enseguida del Teco.]

El Güero: ¡Anda vieja rialera! ¡Yo no gasto mi parque en tórtolas!

[*Se ponen de pie El Güero y El Gordo. Caminan hacia al frente del foro.*]

El Gordo: ¡Véngase, compadre! [*Echándole el brazo al hombre.*] ¡No le
ponga caso a esa vieja [*Ademán con la mano.*] que a uste' le sobran las
viejas!

El Güero [*Más recobrado y ufano ahora*] :   Tienes razón, Gordo. ¡Pero quién
me manda ser tan simpático y enamorado!

El Gordo: ¡Pos que le vamos a hacer, compadre, cuando estas viejas no lo
dejan a uno en paz!

El Güero: ¡Pos ése ha sido mi destino! ¡Si sólo hubiera seguido adelante
con mi 'General' aquel día, en vez de quedarme enredado con unas 'naguas'
. . . pos no estuviera aquí eneste gallinero!

La Soldadera [*Gritándole al Güero*] :   ¡No seas hablador! [*Se va acercando*
poco a paco a donde están El Güero y El Gordo.] ¿Qué hembra se había de
fijar en tí, guerinche? ¡Si bien estás aquí, es por cobarde! ¡Te pescaron
cuando tratabas de huir en el último agarrón con los federales! ¡Ja! ¡Ja!

El Güero: ¡Mira que vieja lenga larga, que te reviento todo el hocico!
[*Ademán con la mano.*]

La Soldadera [*Desafiándolo, le pone la cara*] :   ¡Huy que miedo!

El Teco [*Gritándoles a estos*] :   ¡Basta ya! ¡Cállense!

El Guardia [*Cerca de la puerta, de donde ha estado de pie todo este tiempo,*
sonriendo y burlándose] :   ¡Mírenlos! ¡El mismo sainete de todos los días!
¡Engarruñeados como los animales! ¡Ja! ¡Ja!

La Soldadera [*Dirigiéndose al Guardia*]   ¡Mejor animales y no vendidos como
tú! ¡Miserable chaquetero!

El Guardia [*Acercándose a La Soldadera*] :   ¡Soy vendido, y ¿qué? ! ¿De qué
les sirvió a ustedes tanta lealtad a su mentado 'general'? [*Dirigiéndose a todos*.]
¿En qué acabaron aquellas compañas de batalla? [*Al Estudiante.*] ¡Y
aquellos sueños de libertad e igualdad humana para los pobres? [*Ahora al
Teco.*] ¿Y aquella revancha . . . aquella revancha contra los ricos? [*Retra-
sando hacia la puerta.*] ¿A ver dónde está ese mejoramiento . . . esa gloriosa
victoria de la Revolución? ¡Díganme! ¿Dónde están todos esos mara-
villosos resultados? ¡Hablen ahora atajo de mugrosos! ¡Ja! ¡Ja!

El Gordo [*Balbuciando*] :   Pero es que . . . !

El Guardia [*Con más fé en sí mismo y en lo que dice*] :   ¡No, señor! ¡Aquí
no hay pero que valgan! ¡Yo no fuí pendejo como ustedes! ¡No me deje
llevar por promesas o ideales. . . . ¡Eso es juego de niños o diversión para
los tontos! ¡En esta vida hay que existir a como de lugar! ¡Pescado que
se duerme se lo lleva la corriente!

El Estudiante: Pero no sólo es cuestión de existir! ¡Hay que. . . !

El Guardia: ¡Mire, Inocente de Dios, a mí no me venga con esas tonterías que
aprendió en la escuela! ¡Primero se guarda uno el pellejo a como de lugar!
¿Me entienden? ¡A como de lugar! Por eso, cuando vi que ese 'general' y
su gente la llevaban pérdida, pos luego lueguito me pinte pa'l lado con los
federales, ¡y aquí me tienen muy amo de ustedes!

El Gordo: ¡Mira que pelado sinvergüenza hijo de . . . !

El Guardia [*Amenazándole con el garrote*] :   ¡Cuidadito costroso! ¡Bueno, ya
basta de Líos y laberintos! Yo nomás vine a decirles que se pongan muy
'changuitos' para cuando llegue su famoso 'generalito' . . . ese 'Centauro del
Norte' ¡Ja! ¡Ja! [*Sale por la puerta.*]

Segunda Escena

[*En la misma celda de la carcel. Se vuelve a oír música de la Revolución, que
se desvanecerá lentamente al abrirse el telón por completo. Todos están
sentados, menos el Gordo y el Güero. Estos dos se asean y de vez en
cuando ven hacia a la puerta para ver la llegada del 'general'.*]

El Güero: ¡Oiga, compadre, tápeso esa panza! ¡No sea descarado! Ya mero
llega nuestro 'jefe' y no quiero que se lleve una mala impresión de nosotros.

El Gordo [*Rápidamente sigue abotonándose la camisa*] :   ¡Sí, tiene razón,
compadre!

[Entra el Guardia.]

El Guardia [*Viendo a todos. Se sonríe y con un tono burlón en en su voz*] :
¡Señores, aquí tienen a su 'generalito'! ¡Ese gran libertador, quien los hundió
en este atolladero! . . . ¡Pase por aquí, señor 'caudillo'! ¡Ja! ¡Ja!

[*Aparece el General. Es un hombre alto, robusto, fuerte de piel morena y de
bigote grueso enrizado. Aunque se ve que es una persona de recio carácter,
sin embargo se transluce un calor y candor humano para con los suyos
cuando habla. Viste todo de 'khaki', bota alta de cinta y lleva un sombrero de fieltro sentado bastante alto en la cabeza.*]

El General [*Al entrar se detiene y se dirige al Guardia*] :   ¡Oigame pelado
hocicón, no sea igualado y pendejo para hablar! ¡Lástima que con pelados
lambiscones como usted, yo no me enmugro las manos! [*Empujando al
Guardia bruscamente a un lado.*] ¡Hágase un lado! ¡Váyase que no necesito
monigotes para hablar con mis muchachos!

[*El Guardia se marcha de la celda asustado y sin decir una palabra.*]

El General [*Dirigiéndose a los de la celda*] :   ¿Qué tal, muchachos?

Todos [*Todos menos El Estudiante, muestran algún gesto o gesticulación de
alegría. Se van a encontrar al General*] :   ¡Mi General, que gusto!

[*El General va y abraza a cada uno menos al Estudiante que no se levantó
a saludarle.*]

El Gordo: ¡Caray mi general, no sabe el gusto que nos da volverlo a ver!

El General: ¡No tanto como yo a ustedes, muchachos! ¡Si parece que apenas
ayer nos andábamos dando pelotazos con esos pelones! ¡Ay que agarrones
nos dimos con esos desgraciados! ¿Se acuerdan?

El Güero: ¡Cómo que no, mi General! ¡Sí eso discutíamos antes que usted
llegara!

El Gordo [*Cambiando de conversación*] :   Pero usted no ha cambiado nada, mi
General! ¡Tan bueno y sano . . . tan lleno de vida como todo el tiempo!

La Soldadera: ¡Tan simpático y macho como siempre!

El Gordo: ¡A que vieja chiflada y resbalosa!

El Teco [*Echándole el brazo al hombro*] :   ¡No les haga caso a éstos, mi
General! ¡Véngase pa' 'ca que uste' y yo tenemos mucho de que hablar!
Dígame ¿cómo lo han tratado allá 'fuera?

El General: Pues te diré, Teco. [*Se detiene cuando ve al Estudiante.*] Oye,
¿y éste, quién es? [*Apuntando al Estudiante.*]

El Teco: Ese es El Estudiante. También tomó parte con nosotros en la Revocución.

El General [*Bromeando le da la mano para saludarle al Estudiante*] :   ¿Oiga a usted no le enseñaron como saludar?

El Estudiante [*Sin aceptar la mano del General y con desdén*] :   ¿Y por que tengo que saludarle? ¿Quién se cree que es, para que todo el mundo esté de pie cuando usted entra?

El Teco [*Iracundo, lanzándose contra el Estudiante*] :   ¡Mira, miserable esquincle, yo te enseñaré a tenerle más respeto a mi General!

El General [*Detiene al Teco*]:   ¡Déjalo, Teco! ¡A este curro algo le pica! [*Dirigiéndose al Estudiante.*] ¡A ver, amiguito, échelo 'fuera antes que le haga mal! ¡Hable!

El Estudiante: ¡Ya lo creo que hablaré! [*Con mucho desdén.*] ¡Usted señor 'guerrillero' ¿cómo puede ser tan poco hombre y tener tan Poco vergüenza de pararse aquí ante nosotros como persona a quien tenemos alabar? ¿Cree usted que es justo que mientras que usted anda libre, gozando de aquella gloria revolucionaria y disfrutando de los bienes que ésta le acomoda, gente como nosotros quienes le siguieron en batalla están pudriéndose en calabozos como éste? [*Ademán con la mano.*]: ¿Qué no tiene usted conciencia?

El General: ¿Libre dice usted, joven? Cómo se ve que usted no sabe de lo que son las trampas o manganas políticas. ¡Porque si ando libre, sólo lo han hecho para que mañana o pasado, algún vendido me pegue un tiro! ¡Me han soltado como perro rabioso para que todos hagan blanco conmigo! [*Viendo a los demás.*] ¿Creen ustedes que no se me hacen nudo las tripas verlos a ustedes encerrados como animales en bartolinas como ésta? [*Ahora dirigiéndose al Estudiante.*] ¡Pero usted es un inocente que deja que las apariencias lo engañen!

El Estudiante: ¡No señor! ¡No son apariencias lo que usted ve aquí! ¡Es una realidad tan viva que poco a poco nos ahoga, porque sabemos que nunca saldremos de aquí vivos! Por lo menos usted si podra gozar de esa libertad por la cual nosotros peleamos . . . no importa por breve que sea. ¡Y nosotros que creíamos que la Revolución cambiaría todo!

El General: ¿Pero quién le hizo creer que la Revolución era cosa de milagros? ¿Qué todo acabaría con bien? ¡No sea usted niño! Una Revolución es como un albur que los pobres nos jugamos contra aquellos que nos oprimen! ¡Es una jugada donde se juega el todo por el todo, a como nos toque . . . y a veces hasta el pellejo sale perdiendo uno!

El Estudiante: ¡Por lo visto usted no perdió nada!

El General: ¡Está usted muy equivocado amiguito! ¡Es una miseria tener que seguir viviendo cuando lo han derrotado uno . . . cuando le han quebrantado a uno la fuerza espiritual y la razón de seguir luchando!

El Estudiante: ¿Y entonces, General, para qué fue la Revolución? ¿Qué nos ganamos? [*Dirigiéndose a todos.*]¿Qué nuestro esfuerzo y el de aquéllos que perecieron fue solamente un sacrificio humano? ¿Qué todo fue en vano?

El Teco [*Emocionante, acercandose al Estudiante*]: ¡No, Señor, no fue en vano! ¡Pa 'l pobre como yo, la Revolución fue como una . . . una borrachera donde podía desahogarme del coraje, las penas, las injusticias y sufrimientos que llevaba por dentro! ¡La Revolución fue el único modo como podía recobrar mi dignida' de hombre, y de vengarme de 'aquéllos' que todo me lo habían quitado!

El Estudiante: ¡Pero no se inicia o se toma parte en una Revolución por motivos personales o cuestiones de venganza . . . y mucho menos por pasiones o emociones humanas!

El General: ¿Y entonces, por a cuáles razones amiguito? ¡Hombres como nosotros no tomamos parte en una Revolución por cuestiones de razonamiento, o porque ésta sea lo más conveniente! ¡Tampoco porque creemos que ésta es la solución que tiene más sentido común y a la vez se provee la victoria al tomar parte en ella! . . . ¡No, señor! ¡Lucha y se rebela el pobre cuando ya está cansado de pasar humillaciones y ya no puede aguantar más hambres! ¡El pobre tiene el derecho de alzar la voz y hasta levantarse en armas cuando su vida ya es intolerable como era la nuestra!

La Soldadera: ¡Así es, mi General! ¡Ya no le ponga atención a ese mocoso! [*Apuntando al Estudiante.*]

El General: ¡No Prieta, tengo que escucharle! ¡Este joven como todos aquéllos que anduvimos en la bola, tenemos el derecho de pedir explicaciones, de saber que fue de nuestra lucha! Desgraciadamente, a nosotros nos tocó la de perder . . . fuimos derrotados.

La Soldadera: Derrotados sí, mi General, pero no vencidos, ¡Nunca! ¡Ya habrá otros como nosotros que levantarán la bandera y seguirán adelante con el 'movimiento' que nosotros comenzamos!

El General [*Dirigiendose al Estudiante y a la vez, apuntando con la mano a La Soldadera*]: Allí tiene usted los motivos porque iniciamos la Revolución! ¡La Revolución fue la expresión de libertad humana que buscaba nuestra gente! ¡Fue el espíritu de Nuestra Raza que volvía a nacer para jamás ser oprimido por nuestros adversarios!

El Estudiante: ¿Y nosotros? ¿Qué va a hacer de nosotros?

El General: Nosotros, mi estimado amigo, como aquellos que también murieron por ésta u otras 'causas' anteriores, seremos . . . como usted lo

dijo, 'un sacrificio humano'. ¡Seremos aquella oferta espiritual que dará
aliento, fuerza y valor a la lucha eterna del pobre contra su adversario que
siempre tratará de desnudarlo de sus derechos humanos! ¡De nuestro
ejemplo, otros seguirán adelante y alcanzarán aquellos bienes con los cuales
nosotros soñabamos para Nuestra Raza!

La Soldadera [*Emocionada*]:   ¡Pero que bonito habla uste'! ¡Que lindo lo
bien nacido que ni trabajo cuesta de criar! ¡Pero ya véngase con nosotros
y deje a ése [*Ademán con la mano.*] que se la averigüe como pueda!
¡Uste' no vino aquí para que nadie le haga la vida pesada!

El General: ¡Claro, Prieta! ¡Tienes mucha razón! ¡Para qué amargarnos
la vida cuando es tan corta! [*Echándole el brazo a La Soldadera, luego
viendo a los demás.*] ¿Qué tal si nos echamos unas canciones de ésas como
cuando andábamos en campaña?

El Gordo: ¡Pos pa' luego es tarde! ¡A ver Teco tráete tu guitarra pa' ca!
¡Y uste', compadre Güero, arrímese aquí conmigo y la Prieta, pa' hacerle
segunda al General!

[*Todos menos El Estudiante, quien vuelve al catre para sentarse, cantan,
gritan y bailan. Después de la segunda canción entra el Guardia.*]

El Guardia: ¡Bueno, ya está bien de tanto laberinto! ¡A uste', General,
ya se le acabó la hora de su visita . . . así es que váyase! [*A los demás.*]
¡Y ustedes se me están muy quietecitos!

El General [*Levantándose muy despacio*]:   ¡Ya le dije antes amiguito, que
no se mande con mis muchachos! ¡Tenga en cuenta que no trata con
coyotes como usted, sino con hombres!

El Guardia [*Retrazando hacia la puerta y a la vez balbuciando*]:   ¡Bueno
General . . . nomás no se enoje!

[*Se despide el General de todos, menos del Estudiante. Todos están de pie
cuando se cierra el telón.*]

Tercera Escena

[*En la misma celda. El Estudiante está acostado leyendo su periódico. El
Teco, reclinado, toca su guitarra pero no canta. El Güero y El Gordo como
en la primera escena juegan a la baraja, mientras La Soldadera está de pie,
cerca de ellos, viéndolos jugar. Se nota que hay más alegría, más vida en
la celda.*]

El Güero [*Dirigiéndose al Gordo*]:   ¡Palabra, compadre, que me siento
retebien aquí 'dentro! ¡Sí hasta parece que tengo más ganas de vivir ahora!

El Gordo: ¡Pos yo también! ¡Siento que hasta es más facil resollar ahora! ¡Como si con la visita de nuestro General me hace sentir más hombre!

La Soldadera: ¡Pos claro, muchachos! ¡Es porque mi General siempre fue fina persona y sabe tratar a los suyos como se merecen, con mucho respeto y dignida'!

El Güero: ¡Asĩ es, Prieta, si parece que cuando está con nosotros, hasta nos sentimos con más valor para seguir viviendo, aunque ya estamos todos jodidos!

El Gordo: ¡Eso sí que no, compadre! ¡Yo nunca me voy a dar por rendido!

[*Entra el Guardia. Está bastante serio.*]

La Soldadera [*Viendo al Guardia, luego al Güero y al Gordo*]: ¿Y éste? Qué le pica?

El Guardia [*Desde la puerta*]: ¡Muchachos! ¡Les traigo malas noticias! Pero no sé como. . . .

El Gordo: ¡Mira vendido ya estamos hasta el copete de malas noticias! ¡Mejor píntate con ellas a otra parte!

El Guardia: ¡Bueno si no las quieren oĩr, a mĩ 'ni el mal de viejo me da!

El Teco: ¡Ya está bien! ¡No se haga tonto sólo! ¡Díganos lo que tiene que decirnos y lárguese!

El Guardia: Pos a General . . . hace . . . una como una hora . . . que . . .

La Soldadera: ¿Qué? ¡Habla baboso!

El Guardia: ¡Pos lo mataron . . . se lo tronaron cuando iba camino a su casa, después de visitarlos a ustedes!

Todos [*Estupefactos momentaneamente, luego recobrándose se lanzan contra el Guardia*]: ¿Qué dices desgraciado? ¿Habla? ¡Ahora si te lleva la . . . !

El Guardia [*Retranzando hacia la puerta a la vez amenazándoles con el garrote*]: ¡Cuidado indios apestosos! ¡No me hagan enojar, porque les parto la cabeza! ¡Ahora sĩ que tienen a nadie quien los defienda!

El Estudiante [*Interviene*]: ¡No, muchachos! [*Apuntando al Guardia.*] ¡Este no tiene la culpa de la muerte del General!

El Teco [*Se lanza contra el Guardia*]: ¡A poco no! ¡Todos los Vendidos son iguales! ¡Y éste pagará por todos!

El Estudiante [*Otra vez interviene*]: ¡No Teco! ¡Déjalo! [*Al Guardia.*] ¿Y usted dice la verdad!

El Guardia: ¡Pos claro que sĩ! ¿Qué esperaban pendejos? ¿Qué se los iban a dejar vivo? ¿Como serán brutos? [*Ademán con la mano.*] ¡Así como lo mataron a él, también barrerán con ustedes! ¡Ya verán como todo acabará en nada!

El Estudiante [*Enfuercido, dirigiéndose al Guardia*]:   ¡Cómo será usted, imbécil! ¿Cree usted que el movimiento Revolucionario se acabará porque ha caído uno de sus líderes? ¡Está muy equivocado! ¡Ahora más que nunca tendrá más fuerza ese movimiento!

El Guero: ¡No han hecho más, que moverle a la jicotera! ¡Ahora sí que se los va llevar la tiznada!

El Guardia [*Dirigiéndose a todos*]:   ¡Mire 'maistrito 'y todos ustedes guarachudos, a mí no me andan con pendejadas! ¡Aquí no hay ningún movimiento o lucha revolucionaria! ¡Eso ya es historia! ¡Ya no hay gente bruta como ustedes que quieran 'arraisgar' el pellejo como ustedes pa' cambiar las cosas del gobierno!

La Soldadera [*Dirigiéndose al Guardia*]:   ¿Y crees que todos son como tú o los tuyos?

El Guardia: ¡Pos a poco no! ¡Así es la vida! ¡Hay que sobrevivir . . . algo que ustedes no supieron hacer!

El Teco [*Dirigiéndose al Guardia*]:   ¡Pos ya que estamos perdidos, a lo menos voy a tener el gusto de darle en la chapa a este desgraciado! [*Se lanza contra el Guardia.*]

Todos [*Menos El Estudiante*]:   ¡Sí, mátalo! ¡Dale en la . . . !

El Estudiante [*Deteniendo al Teco*]:   ¡No, Teco, no se crea usted de este estúpido guardia! ¡Así como nosotros, habrá muchos más! [*Viendo al Guardia.*] ¡Con éste no vale la pena ensuciarse las manos uno! ¡Gente vendida como éste [*Al Guardia.*] son como las moscas! ¡Vive del despojo o fruto que nosotros dejamos! ¡Y allí donde lo ven [*Apuntando al Guardia.*] es más mugre y bajo que uno! ¡Nosotros seremos Indios, pero este pobre desgraciado nunca sabrá lo que es! ¡Será lo que otros que lo compren quieran que sea!

El Gordo [*Dirigiéndose al Estudiante*]:   ¡Así es mi cuate! [*A Todos.*] ¡El 'maistrito' sabe lo que dice! ¡Por qué nos habíamos de fijarnos en tan poquita cosa como éste! [*Apuntando al Guardia.*]

El Güero: ¡Claro! ¡Nosotros no somos pelados relajes como este vendido! [*Al Guardia.*] ¡Aquí donde nos ves, todavía nos sobra mucha vergüenza y valor! ¡Nos tumbará el hambre pero el orgullo nos levantará!

El Estudiante [*Dirigiéndose al Teco, Gordo, Güero y La Soldadera*]:   ¡Vénganse, amigos, vamos a platicar!

La Soldadera [*Al Estudiante*] :   ¡Si, vamos, pero . . . vamos lejos de éste [*Apuntando al Guardia.*] que a mí me dan mucho asco las moscas!

[*Todos, menos el Guardia que permanece cerca de la puerta caminan hacia el frente del foro. El Guardia, bastante serio se les queda mirando a éstos que ahora platican animadamente. Lentamente se va apagando la luz de la celda, mientras en la distancia se oye la música de la Revolución que se aumenta en intensidad, a la vez que la luz se apaga. Se Cierra el Telón.*]

The Day of the Swallows

ESTELA PORTILLO

Estela Portillo is a prolific and versatile writer whose literary works include a short novel, several plays, short stories, and poetry. Quinto Sol Publications Inc., which recently presented her with an award for her literary contribution to Chicano Literature, will publish a complete collection of her literary work entitled *Rain of Scorpions*.

Along with her literary accomplishments, Estela Portillo has been dynamic in promoting Chicano Cultural Arts programs in her native city of El Paso, Texas. She was instrumental in the founding of the first Bilingual Theatre in that city. She has been the hostess of a talk show over Radio Station KIZZ and has written, directed, and produced the television series *Cumbres* over KROD-TV in the same city.

She is employed in special services with the El Paso Public Schools at the present time.

Besides *The Day of the Swallows*, two other dramas—*Morality Play* and *Black Light*—have won high literary recognition.

Morality Play is an existential drama which depicts civilization by using the same technique employed in the old morality plays of the fifteenth century. The theme of the play concerns the struggle between Power and the Humanist over 5,000 years. The plot involves man's rescue of Faith, Hope, and Charity.

In short, the drama presents man as the Superhuman who has escaped and risen above the institutionalized values that have dehumanized him.

Black Light, a Chicano play with a "Prometheus-Bound" theme, is a tragedy of the displacement of a proud people of Mayan origin. Nacho, symbolic of the Chicano people, descendent of Mayan warriors, never finds new roots in the United States. The play has a dream sequence that involves music and symbolic Mayan dances.

The Day of the Swallows, which is included in this anthology, is one written in a more contemporary vein. Through the powerful character of Doña Josefa, a misanthropic lesbian, the dramatist lays bare the passions and frailities of human beings. Doña Josefa, considered to be the epitome of virtue by all the towns people including the village priest, prefers to die a martyr rather than to face her human weaknesses.

Characters

Alysea
Clemensia
Josefa
Tomás
Eduardo
Clara
Don Esquinas
Father Prado
1st Boy
2nd Boy

*[The tierra of Lago de San Lorenzo is within memory of mountain sweet
pine. Then the maguey thickens with the ferocity of chaotic existence.
Here the desert yawns. Here it drinks the sun in madness.*

*The village of Lago de San Lorenzo is a stepchild; it is a stepchild to the
Esquinas hacienda, for the hacienda has been a frugal mother and a
demanding father. Its name comes from the yearly ritual of the saint-
day of San Lorenzo when all the young women gather around the
lake to wash their hair and bathe in promise of a future husband. The
tempo of life, unbroken, conditioned, flavors its heartbeat with dreams
and myths. The hacienda is the fiber upon which existence hangs. The
church, the fluid rose, assures the future promise of Elysium fields.
No one dares ask for life.*

*What is this footfall beyond ritual, beyond livelihood? What is this faint
unknown ache in the heart? It's more than just the rasp of hope. . . .
The young know this, and they go the the spring with lyrical intimacy.
By the lake, eyes burn and feet dig the mud of the spring; someone
traces mountain against sky and gulf expands drowning, drowning.
The obligation is remembered back in the village; the toll of the church
bell offering sanctuary is a relief; the lake becomes too much for them.*

At daybreak the fiesta day is sanctified with a misa at sunrise; the choir rejoices the promise of day. A holy procession is led by the priest and an "honored member" of the church. Offerings to the patron saint are generous amidst frugality. The animals are blessed; the people are blessed; all is washed clean.

Perhaps secretly each villager senses the werewolf moon inside him; the bite into passions will be hard and fierce after sunset.

On the day of San Lorenzo, in the heat of July, everybody goes to the lake; this day the lake is invaded by village life. When the church bells toll eleven in the sun, the late morning is the sole witness to the bathing of the virgins. The lake becomes a sacred temple. The high priestesses talk of hopes, lovers, and promises. In earnest belief, they wash their hair in spring water to insure future marriages in heaven. It is true no one has seen a marriage made in heaven, but each girl hugs the private truth that hers will be the one.

Two hundred years before, the Esquinas family had settled in Lago de San Lorenzo on a Spanish grant of fifty thousand acres; the Indians were pushed out farther into the desert. This was the way of the bearded gachupín, with his hot grasp and his hot looks. Their greedy vitality was a wonder to the Indian. It was also death.

But now the barrio clustered itself around the hacienda. The conquered conquered the conquerors.

There is a house, the only house close to the edge of the lake. Here our story begins. . . .]

ACT I

Scene 1

[Josefa's sitting room; it is an unusually beautiful room, thoroughly feminine and in good taste; the profusion of lace everywhere gives the room a safe, homey look. The lace pieces are lovely, needlepoint, hairpin, limerick, the work of patience and love. Upstage left is a large French window; from it one can view a large tree. On the tree is a freshly painted tree house of unusual size and shape. It is an orb that accommodates a great number of birds. The room faces south, so it is flooded with light; the light, the lace, the open window all add to the beauty of the room, a storybook beauty of serenity. To the right is a door leading to the kitchen; there is another door leading to a bedroom; downstage left there is a door leading to the outside.

[*Alysea is sitting on the floor when the curtain rises. It is before dawn;
but a few minutes after the curtain rises, light begins to fill the room.
Alysea is cleaning the sitting room carpet, an unusual task for this hour.
Next to her is a pail; she uses a piece of cloth with quick frantic movements, rinses, and continues the scrubbing. After a while she looks at
the cloth in her hand intently, as in realization of what she is doing.
Suddenly she drops it, seemingly in horror. She looks helpless and lost.
Still sitting on the floor she leans her head against a chair and cries
silently staring up into the now streaming light from the window. There
is the sound of the milk bell. It is Clemencia delivering. When she hears
it, Alysea jumps up, wipes away traces of tears with her apron, then
opens the French window and looks out.*]

Alysea: She'll come right in if I'm not at the door to pay her.

[*She looks around the room. Her eyes fall on a small side table next to the
couch. She goes to the table and stares at a long kitchen knife with traces
of blood on it. Hurriedly, she picks up the cleaning cloth, and uses it to
pick up the knife gingerly. She wraps the cloth around the knife and
places it in a side table drawer. During this interval, Clemencia's noisy arrival is heard. The kitchen door is opened; there is a tug of milk can,
then a pouring of milk. Several sighs and ejaculations about hard work
are heard. Alysea looks around the room one last time as Clemencia
walks in.*]

Clemencia: ¡Josefa! ¡Alysea! My centavos for the week are not on the kitch-
en table. Hombre . . . do I have to beg for my money? ¿Oye . . . dónde están?

Alysea: Buenos días, Clemencia . . . early?

Clemencia [*Staring at Alysea*]:   Qué horror! What is the matter? You look
terrible. Have you been up all night?

Alysea [*Smooths her hair; looks at her hands guiltily*]:   Yes . . . I stayed up
late. A new pattern in lace.

Clemencia: You work hard to please Josefa, don't you? [*She notices Alysea
looking at her hands.*] What's the matter with your hands? Not rheumatism
. . . you're just a girl. . . . Look at mine! Life has eaten them up. I fell pain.
Ay! . . . It is my destiny to suffer. You owe me seven pesos.

Alysea: Yes, of course. [*She goes to the household money box, takes a set
of keys from her apron pocket and opens it. She counts out the money.*]
Cinco . . . seis . . . siete.

Clemencia: Gracias. . . . [*Looks at Alysea again and shakes her head.*] Rest
in the afternoon . . . you look all in. You can in this house. There is beautiful peace here.

Alysea: Yes . . . here it stretches itself out to breathe . . .

Clemencia: You begin to talk like Josefa now. You like her . . . eh? She doesn't want you to work yourself to death. She is too kind.

Alysea: The most considerate of persons . . . but there is so much to do.

Clemencia: Of course, San Lorenzo . . . mañana . . . Josefa will be so grand leading the procession with the Father to the church. A happy day for the barrio. We all share Josefa's honor like we have shared her goodness . . . a great lady.

Alysea: I had forgotten . . . the procession tomorrow.

Clemencia: What's the matter with you? Forgotten?

Alysea: Don't mind me . . . I'm not myself today . . . Clemencia.

Clemencia: Doña Josefa is an angel. All her life, she goes around . . . with that walking stick of hers . . . always she goes . . . like an avenging angel . . . helping . . . what a sight she must be . . . pounding with her stick on those evil people. One, two . . . that's for wickedness! [*She makes motions of one pounding away.*] She takes care of the devil all right . . . eh? Yes . . . she saved you from the sickness . . .

Alysea: Saved me . . . from the sickness . . . what is shadow? What is sickness?

Clemencia: Talk sense, child! You need rest. [*She looks at lace work on table.*] My . . . you are making lace as beautiful as Josefa's! You are lucky.

Alysea: Lucky? [*She goes to the window.*] This room is beautiful . . . isn't it? I'm lucky to be here . . . aren't I? [*Pause.*] Appearances . . . they are very funny! Tomorrow the church will honor Josefa . . . how very funny! [*She begins to laugh; then, the laugh is eventually lost in sobbing.*] Oh, God!

Clemencia: What is the matter? [*She looks around.*] Where is Josefa . . . Josefa! [*She goes to Alysea and feels her forehead.*] Are you feverish?

[*At this point, Josefa enters. She is a tall, regal woman about thirty-five. Her bones are Indian's; her coloring is Aryan. She wears her hair back severely. Her movements are graceful and quiet. The cuffs and collar of her dress are of exquisite lace. She walks up to Alysea and puts her arm around her.*]

Josefa: Alysea, quiet! [*She turns to Clemencia.*] She's not feeling well, I suppose.

Clemencia: She worked all night.

Josefa: Oh?

Clemencia: You must make her rest.

Josefa: You're right, of course. . . .

Clemencia: Well . . . I must be going. I'm late on my rounds. [*She sighs.*] I
  wish I could stay here. [*She looks around.*] What heavenly peace . . .

Josefa [*Smiling*]:   You are welcome . . . this is your home.

Clemencia: Doña Josefa . . . you are an angel!

Josefa: No . . . just happy! Did you get your money?

  [*Josefa escorts Clemencia to the door. Clemencia gives a last anxious look
  at Alysea.*]

Clemencia: She'll be all right in your hands, Josefa.

Josefa: I'll see that she rests.

  [*Clemencia leaves through the kitchen door. Josefa remains silent as the
  sounds of departure from the kitchen are heard.*]

Josefa: You should rest . . . Clemencia's right.

  [*Alysea shakes her head.*]

Josefa: Do you think it's wise . . .

Alysea: Wise! The way you word it . . . wise!

Josefa: Very well, I'll put it another way. Is this the time to break down?
  Beautiful days demand our strength. . . . We must be faithful to loveliness.

Alysea [*Incredulously*]:   You believe that? [*She walks up to Josefa almost
  menacingly.*] How can you justify in that way? You!

Josefa [*Softly*]:   There are things we must do . . . to keep a sanity . . . to
  make the moment clear. [*Pause.*] Any signs of the swallows? Isn't the tree
  lovely?

Alysea: Have you forgotten? How can you! Josefa, last night . . .

  [*Alysea is overwhelmed with the memory; she runs out of the room. Josefa
  looks for a moment after her; then she touches the lace curtains on the
  window.*]

Josefa: We pattern our lives for one beautiful moment . . . like this lace . . .
  little bits and pieces come together . . . to make all this . . . my world . . . a
  crystal thing of light; Alysea must understand . . . she must!

  [*There is a knock to the door leading outside. Josefa goes to the door; she
  opens it; it is Tomás, her shiftless uncle.*]

Tomás: Oh . . . it is you, Josefa! You're not at the hacienda this morning.

Josefa: What are you doing here?

Tomás: The pump . . .

Josefa: You fixed that already. I've told you not to come around here at this time of day . . .

Tomás: You do not appreciate . . . always suspicious. . . .

Josefa: I don't want you bothering Alysea . . . ever. . . .

Tomás: It is like you . . . to think the worse of me.

Josefa [With resignation] :   How are the children? Your wife Anita?

Tomás: They manage better than me. Thanks to you. . . . There is little steady work. . . . I need a few centavos. Josefa . . . you're rich!

Josefa: What for . . . Tequila?

Tomás: Just a little money. Look, my hands . . . they shake. I need it, Josefa . . . please!

Josefa: Don't beg!

Tomás: You let Clara have all she wants. . . .

Josefa: That is none of your business.

Tomás [Noticing the pail] :   Eh . . . what's this? Looks like blood!

Josefa: Go to the kitchen. Help yourself to meal and beans . . . for the family.

[*Tomás is still staring at the pail.*]

Josefa: Did you hear me?

Tomás: Yes . . . yes, Doña Perfecta . . . doña Perfecta . . . so charitable . . . ha! ha!

Josefa: I'm not in the mood for your sarcasm.

Tomás: You will lead the procession tomorrow like the queen of the world . . . eh? You can spare a few centavos? A bottle? Do you keep some in the house when you get it for Clara?

Josefa: You're not getting any money.

Tomás [Starting to leave] :   What's in the pail?

Josefa [Indignant] :   I don't have to satisfy your curiosity.

Tomás: Cálmate . . . I was just asking. . . .

[*Josefa turns her back to him; he leaves through the kitchen door; his grumbling is heard as he helps himself to the food offered by Josefa.*

Josefa stares at the contents of the pail; she looks away and touches her temples with her fingertips. She sits in a rocking chair, leans back, closes her eyes, and grips the arms of the chair; she rocks back and forth.]

Josefa: There is no desert here . . . only light . . . to live each day with nothing . . . to sink. . . . [*She closes her eyes and rocks.*] The lonely, lonely struggle . . . then to emerge . . . to find the light. I have so much now. . . . I want to give so much now. . . . Alysea must understand! We must keep this world of light at all costs. . . .

[*She rises and walks to the window and stands absorbing the light; one can sense an obvious union between the light and Josefa.*]

Josefa [*Softly*] :   How moist your lips, my light. . . . Through me . . . through me . . . you live. [*She comes back from her intimate world and looks at the bird house with pleasure.*] The long flight . . . how tired they will be; how thirsty after the desert flight . . . here my swallows will find peace . . . home. [*As she looks at the tree, Tomás comes through the patio outside the window. He has a sack over his shoulder. Josefa does not seem to be mindful of him. Tomás calls.*]

Tomás: Hey Josefa! Are you casting a spell . . . so early? You don't scare me. I know you, querida. I know many things. You burn inside. . . .

[*Josefa stares at him unbelievingly, as if he has destroyed a beauty; then she turns away from the window.*]

Tomás: Hey, Josefa . . . don't run away . . . the great Doña Perfecta runs away from her good-for-nothing uncle. That's funny . . . ha, ha!

Josefa [*Firmly, but in an ominous tone*] :   Go home, Tomás, go home.

[*She closes the window and walks to an unfinished damask close to the window. She sits down, unhooks the needle, and begins to work on it. Her concentration is a fiery intensity; this is obvious in her finger movements. Alysea comes back into the room; she is now composed and refreshed; she has put on a pretty dress. She sees the pail and removes it, taking it into the kitchen; all this time Josefa remains absorbed in the damask. Alysea comes back. Josefa looks up.*]

Josefa: You look so nice! Every morning now . . . you look like the garden. . . .

Alysea: Nothing is as beautiful as your garden . . . paradise must look like that.

Josefa: A garden of light . . . perhaps it has a sense of paradise. . . .

Alysea: Tomás was here?

Josefa:　Sneaking around as usual. [*Pause.*] The pretty dress . . . for Eduardo again?

Alysea:　Yes. I'll bring in the morning coffee. Scones?

Josefa:　Fine . . . and honey. Suddenly I'm hungry. [*She leaves the damask and begins to clear the coffee table.*] By the way . . . ask Eduardo to have some morning coffee with us today. Don't run off for your usual morning walk.

Alysea:　May I? Thank you . . . he's been coaxing me. He's absolutely fascinated by you.

Josefa:　Do invite him.

> [*Alysea seems to be holding back tears, although she has pretended calm through the conversation.*]

Josefa:　What's the matter?

> [*Alysea is not able to answer; she just shakes her head. Josefa walks up to her. Alysea stands still and helpless. Josefa takes Alysea's face in her hands.*]

Josefa:　You are so dear to me. I don't like to see you like this. Alysea, don't dwell on what happened. Things will be all right. Haven't I always made things all right?

> [*Alysea still doesn't answer.*]

Josefa:　The tragic things in my life taught me one thing . . . calm. The waiting . . . that is harder than struggle. Alysea, learn how . . . to find a strength. This loveliness here . . . our world . . . isn't it worth it?

> [*Alysea begins to cry gently. Josefa comforts her. Alysea becomes limp; she places her head on Josefa's shoulder like a child. Josefa strokes her hair.*]

Josefa:　Your hair . . . your beautiful hair. Here, let me comb it. . . .

> [*Suddenly Alysea breaks away. She seems at a loss, then remembers the coffee.*]

Alysea:　I'll get things started in the kitchen. . . . Eduardo will be here any moment now.

Josefa:　About last night, Alysea . . . we must have a story.

Alysea [*She seems to shiver*]:　Story?

Josefa:　When I took David to the hospital . . . the doctors . . . everyone was sympathetic . . . I told them someone had broken in . . .

Alysea: And David?

Josefa: He will be all right.

Alysea: I can never believe that. . . .

Josefa: I will take care of him always. . . .

Alysea: You killed him!

Josefa: Don't. He'll be back with us in a few weeks. . . . I will make a fine life for him always. . . .

Alysea: He'll never . . . he'll never. . . .

[*She is overcome by emotion; she walks out of the room into the kitchen. Josefa looks after her. She remains standing for a moment; then she picks up a book of poetry from the lamp table.*]

Josefa: Santa Teresita . . . "El hombre toma . . . toma y hiere,
  La flor desnuda . . . temblorose . . ."

In her world of God . . . she saw what I see . . . she knew the light . . . beauty . . . truth . . . yes . . . in a cloister.

[*She looks around the room. Then she walks up to a workbasket and picks up a piece of lace. She holds it to the light and intently traces the pattern.*]

Josefa: The web . . . the beautiful web we weave! Anything . . . anything is worth this!

[*End of Scene 1.*]

Scene 2

[*A few minutes later; Alysea comes from the kitchen with a morning tray; coffee, scones, juice. She places the tray on the coffee table. There is a knock. Alysea goes to the door. It is Eduardo.*]

Eduardo [*A young man of mixed heritage*] :   I came through the path. . . .

Alysea [*Drawing him in*] :   I'm glad. Josefa wants you to have morning coffee . . . in here . . . with her; you always come for me in such a hurry . . . you hadn't seen this room . . . had you?

Eduardo: No . . . never! [*Looking around.*] Well . . . you were right . . . what a room! . . . for women.

Alysea: What do you mean?

Eduardo: It is a dream of gentleness . . . peace; it is not a man's room . . but it is beautiful.

Alysea: You're right. Josefa made this haven . . . away from the world of men.

Eduardo [*Looking at her quizzically*] : You like that?

Alysea: After what I've lived through . . . yes; this was heaven . . . when she brought me here. Sit down . . . she'll be here any moment.

[*Eduardo watches Alysea as she arranges napkins, spoons.*]

Eduardo: Have you told her . . . about our plans?

Alysea: No . . . she suspects something between us.

Eduardo: And?

Alysea: It is hard to understand her feelings . . . there is a stillness in her.

Eduardo: She dotes on you . . . I don't think she will be pleased. . . . After all, I'm taking you away to a wilderness . . . mountain, pines. My squaw . . . living and loving in the open.

[*He goes to her, gathers her in his arms; they kiss; Alysea clings to him.*]

Eduardo: It won't be like this . . . you know!

Alysea: I'll be with you . . . isn't that everything?

Eduardo: And the gentle life you love?

Alysea: What you will share with me . . . will be so much more. [*They embrace again.*]

Eduardo: Say! Have you seen the morning? It is a conspiracy . . . sun, clouds, green fields . . . and the pines from the distance . . . I can hardly wait. Let's leave right now . . . pack the horses . . . take the mountain trail past the lake . . . the way of my people.

Alysea: Not now . . . you crazy Indian!

Eduardo: We'll find a clearing . . . plow . . . build a cabin . . . have babies. . . .

Alysea: Sometimes I think you have to be out in the open . . . no matter what. . . .

Eduardo: That's where my God is.

[*Eduardo sits down; Alysea stands behind his chair and gently traces his cheek.*]

Alysea: Your world! A beautiful God exists . . . in your world . . . when you talk. . . He is free . . . green . . . open. You know something?

Eduardo [*Catching her hand and kissing it*] :   What?

Alysea: Father Prado understands your God too. At confession . . . I told him about not attending Mass because we go exploring . . . to find the tallest pines. I told him about your God. He smiled and told me I had found a holier temple.

Eduardo: Let's take him with us.

Alysea [*Laughing*] :   You know better. His life is the barrio . . . the people.

Eduardo: He will marry us . . . before we leave. . . .

Alysea [*Pulling away*] :   No . . . we must wait . . .

Eduardo: Why? Listen, woman . . . no one in her right mind turns down a marriage proposal. . . .

Alysea: I want you to be sure . . . after a while . . . after we have shared. . . .

Eduardo [*In jest*] :   You shameless hussy . . . you wish to live in sin, eh?

Alysea: Don't jest. . . . There was so much ugliness . . . before Josefa brought me here. I remember . . . they brought a bunch of us from the country . . . they promised jobs as seamstresses; my barrio was poor . . . we went hungry . . . so I came . . . the city was a nightmare . . . they locked us up in an old house . . . they gave us disgusting soiled dresses to wear . . . then we found out.

Eduardo: Stop torturing yourself.

Alysea: No . . . let me finish. I've never told you. I hid in the closet of the room; an ugly man with fat hands asked the girls where I was . . . they didn't know . . . he cursed; I was trembling underneath a pile of dirty dresses suffering with the sweat of lust. I closed my eyes. Then, I decided to run . . . I simply got up . . . and ran . . . down the stairs . . . into an open hall . . . where men . . . men with hard, dead looks stared . . . no one expected me to try and escape through the front door . . . but I did. I got as far as the street . . . then he caught up with me; his hands were at my throat . . .

Eduardo: That's enough. . . .

Alysea: All of a sudden . . . Josefa appeared . . . with her walking stick. She raised it over her head and beat the man. He cried out in pain. She never faltered. Then, she brought me to this world of light. . . .

Eduardo: We shall marry tomorrow night . . . that's it!

Alysea: No . . . no . . . there's something else. [*She becomes very agitated.*] Eduardo . . . last night . . .

    [*Josefa enters.*]

Josefa: Good morning . . . am I late? Is the coffee cold?

Alysea: No . . . no . . . you are just in time.

Eduardo [*Drawing out a chair for her*] :   Our great lady!

   [*Alysea becomes busy with the food.*]

Alysea [*To Josefa*] :   Juice?

Josefa: Yes . . . thank you. Eduardo, what are you up to . . . charming the
   women so early in the morning?

Eduardo: What better time?

Josefa: You are different! Alysea . . . give Eduardo . . . some of this orange
   . . . it's delicious . . .

Eduardo: No! No! Just coffee . . . and what's this? [*He picks up a scone,
   tastes it.*] Wonderful! I had heard about all your wonders . . . but . . . cook-
   ing too!

Josefa: Alysea baked them . . . from an old recipe of mine. . . .

   [*Alysea hands Eduardo some coffee.*]

Eduardo: Thank you, Linda. . . .

   [*Alysea serves herself. Josefa looks intently from one to the other.*]

Josefa: All these walks you two take . . . into forbidden country . . .

Eduardo: How can beauty be forbidden . . .

Josefa: I feel the same way . . . but the desert mind forbids it . . . many times.

Alysea: It won't be forbidden tomorrow. All the young girls will bathe in
   the lake at noontime . . the promise of a perfect love. . . .

Eduardo: I hear it is your year. Josefa . . . you will lead the church procession. . . .

Josefa: My people enjoy planning for it. . . .

Alysea: Josefa is as bad as Father Prado about the barrio people. . . . All is
   to please them. . . .

Eduardo: And what pleases you, Josefa?

Josefa: To make them happy!

Eduardo: I can see why they talk of you with awe. . . .

Josefa: I am Indian you know . . . yet not of desert, not of them, in a way.
   Yet . . . totally theirs.

Alysea [*Rising*] :   Well . . . I shall leave you for a few moments; Josefa . . . the
   lace for the capitol . . . must make the morning express . . . excuse me.

[*Alysea leaves. Eduardo finishes his coffee.*]

Josefa: She's falling in love with you. . . .

Eduardo: It's mutual. . . .

Josefa: For how long, Eduardo?

Eduardo [*Stands, hands in pocket, somewhat ill at ease*] :   Love is not timed.

Josefa: Isn't it?

Eduardo: What do you mean?

Josefa: Clara.

Eduardo: You know?

Josefa: She has described to me . . . your every mood . . . your every gesture . . . in love. . . .

Eduardo: I don't know what to say!

Josefa: Guilt?

Eduardo: Ridiculous . . . there's no guilt in love!

Josefa [*Laughing as if to herself*] :   The way you men justify . . . the word "love" doesn't it really mean . . . take? . . . destroy?

Eduardo: It isn't that. . . .

Josefa: Of course not! Disguised in a man's words . . . in a man's promises. . . . Oh, I know, you make a dream of your deadly game.

Eduardo: Alysea's happy.

Josefa: Is she? For how long . . . until you find another fancy?

Eduardo: What I feel for her is different. . . .

Josefa: I remember Clara telling me the same things about you and her . . . how easily you put her out of your life.

Eduardo: Clara understands.

Josefa: No, Eduardo . . . she just accepts . . . she knows nothing else.

Eduardo: You make me feel guilty . . . why?

Josefa: I'll tell you why. Alysea has love here; she is happy . . . she has found her place in the world . . . safe with me . . . there is a constancy here . . .

Eduardo: All right! I don't think one should have Conditions . . . I know I love her now . . . I want to love her forever . . . but it is not for me to know. . . .

Josefa: She belongs here . . . with me. You men explain away all your indiscretions, so easily . . . after all, you make the rules and enjoy the abuses!

Eduardo: That's not fair . . .

Josefa: That's funny. When has a man been fair to . . . women?

Eduarda: You are distorting . . .

Josefa: What I offer her is not a violence. Man's love is always a violence.

Eduardo: I'm sorry.

Josefa: For what . . . the evil in the world?

Eduardo: I love Alysea.

Josefa: Oh, yes . . . you love, he loves, they love . . . how convenient the word "love"!

[*Eduardo remains silent. Josefa suddenly realizes he is a guest.*]

Josefa [*In an even pleasant voice*] :   Come, Eduardo, you must forgive me for such an outburst. What a terrible hostess I am! Don't mind me, when there is concern for the people you love. Here let me refill your cup! [*She pours him some coffee and hands it to him.*] There is a special happiness in this house you know. . . .

Eduardo [*Reassured*] :   I know. It is the soaring sea in you.

Josefa: What?

Eduardo: You carry things, people with you . . . when your strength is washed away . . . you leave beauty behind.

Josefa: How lovely . . . you are easy to fall in love with. . . .

Eduardo: So are you . . . if a man is brave enough.

Josefa: Brave?

Eduardo: You are a whirlwind. . . .

Josefa: I have always sought the calm. . . .

Eduardo: Ah . . . but your depths! Josefa, I sense them. You are not of the barrio.

Josefa [*Amused*] :   Such discernment! But then, you are right. I am of the lake.

Eduardo: I've heard . . . I hear you dare the lake alone . . . in solitude. . . .

Josefa: The barrio stories are myth . . . primitive fears. What most of the people fear is instinctive. . . .

Eduardo: In what way?

Josefa: Out in the lake . . . out in the pines . . . they see themselves too well . . . they have become the desert . . . it is too much to accept . . . so monsters are created . . . but for me . . . ah . . . for me!

Eduardo: Tell me. . . .

Josefa: When I was young . . . when I refused to go bathe on San Lorenzo's day . . . when I chose the moonlight in any season . . . it was defiance. . . .

Eduardo: What did you defy?

Josefa: What defied me . . . the world! Yes, I would go . . . to defy . . . then . . . but it became something else.

Eduardo [*Looking at her intently*]: Why didn't you ever marry? No one good enough?

Josefa [*Shrugs it off*]: I never saw the dream . . . I never felt the hope. . . . There was always too much clarity for me. [*Pause.*] Do you think me beautiful?

Eduardo: Yes . . . very . . , mixed in with a dangerous excitement. . . .

Josefa: You are making love to me.

Eduardo: I make love to all things beautiful . . . don't you?

Josefa [*In a whisper*]: Yes. Oh, yes. . . .

[*Alysea comes in breathless.*]

Alysea: Well . . . you two. That wasn't long was it? [*Looks at both of them.*] You two must have found marvelous things to talk about . . . it shows!

Josefa: I tell you, Eduardo . . . this girl has possibilities. . . .

Eduardo: I know. . . .

Alysea: Did she tell you about her magicians?

Eduardo: She was about to . . . when you came.

Josefa [*Looking at him intently*]: How did you know . . . I was about to?

Eduardo: The light in your eyes . . . the sudden magic in you. . . .

Alysea: I know what you mean, Eduardo . . . such a mystical thing . . .

Josefa: You have laid the setting . . . so kindly. [*She walks to the window and looks out with her eyes closed as she speaks.*]

Josefa: The magicians are real, you know! I found them . . . long ago . . . the night of the Festival of San Lorenzo. The virgins had bathed by the noon day sun . . . I . . . I went after the Rosary bell . . . I went when they were all celebrating; the silence was perfumed . . . desire was heavy . . . painful. Does it surprise you that I speak of desire? Oh, yes . . . I felt it . . . to my fingertips . . . it was so real, the beautiful need . . . the lights of the barrio were far off in another world . . . this always affected me . . . I became another being far from my kind . . . even my desire was a special suffering. . . .

Eduardo: You still did not marry.

Josefa: What does that have to do with desire? My desire . . . like my being
. . . became a purer grain. It was more than someone to see or touch . . . or
embrace. It was a need for a pouring of self . . . a gentleness . . . a faith. I
did not want the callous Indian youth . . . with hot breath and awkward
hands . . . a taking without feeling . . . no, not that! I wanted so much
more. . . .

[*Josefa turns to look at Alysea and Eduardo caught in her spell.*]

Josefa: Look at you . . . children . . . listening to fairy tales. . . .

Eduardo: Children believe. . . .

Josefa: So do I! Isn't it funny?

Eduardo: No . . . it is like that with some people.

Josefa: For me . . . it came true! The wonder was my magicians. That night
at the lake there was a different music . . . the stillness sung inside me . . .
the moonlight grew in me . . . it became my lover. . . . There by the lake, I
felt the light finding its way among the pines . . . to me . . . It took me . . .
then . . . perhaps it was my imagination . . . it said to me: "We are one . . .
make your beauty . . . make your truth." Deep, I felt a burning spiral . . . it
roared in my ears . . . my heart. . . . [*Pause.*] It was too much to bear . . . so
I ran and ran and ran until I fell, opened my eyes, and found myself calmly
looking up at the stars . . . sisters of my love! The moon had followed me;
it lay a lake around me, on the grass. . . .

Eduardo: Were you afraid?

Josefa: Afraid? There was no room . . . the joy was too great. I had the secret of the magicians . . . the wine of love . . . the light was me; I knew that
I would bear the children of light . . . the moon . . . the burning lake.

Alysea [*In a whisper*] :   I believe her . . . look around you, the children of
light . . . her garden . . . the lace . . . her love for the barrio people . . .
her bright, bright calm. . . .

Eduardo [*Taking up the pace*] :   Her person. . . .

Josefa: Hush . . . you two . . . don't go on so!

[*The voice of Tomás from outside window breaks the spell.*]

Tomás: Josefa! David's horse! I found it out in the pasture . . . without a
bridle . . . Josefa!

Josefa [*Goes to the window*] :   David's horse?

Eduardo [*Going to the window*] :   Need any help?

Josefa: He didn't hear you . . . he's coming in. . . .

[*Alysea all of a sudden loses all her brightness; she seems frightened and lost. She looks at Josefa's every move; Josefa shows no reaction; she calmly begins to pick up cups, napkins.*]

Josefa: It is getting late . . . my! The morning has flown . . . such a wonderful time. I hope it isn't too late for you two to go for your walk.

Eduardo: No . . . no . . . there's plenty of time.

[*Tomás comes in through the kitchen door.*]

Tomás: He must have broken out from the stable. I thought I would tell you before I took him back to the hacienda. . . .

Josefa: Yes . . . take him back. Horses will do that.

[*Eduardo taking Alysea by the hands. He looks at her intently.*]

Eduardo: What on earth is the matter? You need some morning air. I'll tell you what. I'll take you to a place where I can trace the path of the swallows any day now.

[*Alysea doesn't seem to be listening to him; Josefa notices this and promptly suggests.*]

Josefa: Yes . . . I insist on it . . . take her; right now . . . enjoy this lovely day. . . .

[*Eduardo takes Alysea by the shoulder.*]

Eduardo: Come on. . . .

[*He stirs her to the door; Alysea does not resist. They exit.*]

Tomás [Shyly]: I guess she feels bad about David . . . what happened last night. . . .

Josefa: What?

Tomás: I heard the talk in the barrio . . . someone broke into the house . . . that is . . . that is what you claim.

Josefa: What do you mean?

Tomás: You didn't tell me earlier. . . .

Josefa: Tell you? Why should I tell you anything.

Tomás: The blood in the pail . . . you didn't tell me anything about that either. . . .

Josefa: So?

Tomás: Well . . . I remember . . . all those times . . . you save the poor, inno-
cent, helpless ones . . . you never say anything . . . it's always the barrio
who puts the story together . . . you are clever. . . .

Josefa: Don't be ridiculous. . . .

Tomás: Yes . . . people have no idea how clever you really are . . . la doña
Perfecta! You saved Alysea from the evil man . . . you saved David from a
drunken father; the barrio tells the story of an angel . . . but it's funny
somehow . . . they never remember to tell that you crippled one man and
the other died on the road where you left him. . . .

Josefa: You are pitiful . . . like those two men . . . destructive and pitiful. . . .

Tomás: Perhaps you'll get your hands on me too.

Josefa [Calmly, with disdain]:   Hadn't you better see about that horse?

Tomás: Now the town is busy making you out a heroine . . . an intruder?
That's hard to believe . . . the girl looked too guilty a while ago. [*He studies
Josefa who is straightening up.*] But you . . . it's amazing! Such grace . . .
such pious silence . . . yes . . . you are a dangerous one, all right!

Josefa: All this . . . this foolishness, I know, is leading up to some sort of
blackmail . . . you want money . . . don't you?

Tomás: You know me so well! After all, I'm on your side . . . we are of the
same blood. . . .

Josefa: Get out of here . . . and be careful about what you say . . . you
clown! Who's going to believe anything you say? Be careful . . . or I may
let you starve.

Tomás: Didn't work . . . eh? No money?

Josefa: You've tried my patience long enough. I have better things to do
with my time. Go and see about that horse. . . .

[*Josefa picks up the tray and starts toward the kitchen.*]

Tomás: Not even a few pesos?

[*Josefa looks at him contemptuously and walks out into the kitchen without a word.*]

Tomás: She'll break! She'll break . . . once I lay all my cards on the table. . . .
Stupid women! [*He looks around the room.*] I know they keep the household money somewhere around here . . . yes.

[*He begins to look in the drawers.*]

[*End of Scene 2.*]

Scene 3

[*Later the same morning. The room is empty, full of light, when Clara
enters. She is the wife of Don Esquinas, owner of the hacienda. She
has the grace and elegance of good living. But, at closer scrutiny, one
can see that this once beautiful woman is dissipated. Her blond beauty,
although meticulously enhanced by great care, has the flavor of fading
youth. She carries a knitting bag. Although she has been in this room
many times, she is each time overwhelmed by the unusual light. She
walks up to the table, lays her bag on it, opens it, searches for a cigarette; she finds one, lights it, and draws its flavor leisurely. She catches
sight of Josefa's workbasket; she also sees the damask; she traces the
design; then she picks up a piece of lace from the workbasket and examines it admiringly.*]

Clara: Angel filigree . . . how lovely. It's unearthly. . . .

[*As she examines the lace, Alysea walks into the room breathlessly. Her
arms are full of freshly cut flowers. She glances at Doña Clara apologetically.*]

Alysea: Doña Clara . . . am I late?

Clara: No, no . . . I just got here.

Alysea [*Going to the vase and setting the flowers next to it*] :   I always linger
too long in the garden. . . .

Clara: What a garden! What incantations does Josefa use?

Alysea: It's marvelous, the way she does it. . . .

Clara: She talks to the flowers. . . .

Alysea: She talks to all living things. . . .

Clara [*Looking at Alysea as she arranges the flowers on the vase*] :   You too. . . .
How you have blossomed in this house.

Alysea: Me?

Clara [*In a deliberately contained voice*] :   Of course, this time it could be
Eduardo. I hear he loves you.

Alysea: Love does that . . . doesn't it?

Clara: It's true then! And you love him too?

Alysea: Yes.

Clara: Well. [*She puts out her cigarette.*] That's that! Where is my dress?

Alysea [*Coming out of her reverie*] :   Oh, I'm sorry . . . of course, your fitting.

[*Alysea goes to a wardrobe and takes out a simple gown. She hands it to Clara. Clara goes behind the screen.*]

Clara: I suppose you'll go away with him?

Alysea: He wants me to . . . I haven't quite decided. . . .

Clara: About love?

Alysea: Am I good enough for him? I have to use reason. . . .

Clara [*Almost impatiently*] :   You don't have to reason love . . . my God!

Alysea: Will it be fair to him!

Clara: What love there is . . . you take. Don't reason it away . . . take it!

[*She comes from around the screen and gives her back to Alysea so Alysea will fasten the dress. Both are facing the mirror. Clara looks Alysea directly in the eyes.*]

Clara: Love is always fair just because it is. [*She can't look in the mirror any longer.*] What's the matter with me . . . look at me . . . an expert on love . . . ha! [*She bites her lip.*]

Alysea: You are beautiful and wise. [*Clara doesn't answer; she deliberately becomes absorbed with the gown. She surveys herself in the mirror.*]

Clara: It seems to lack something. Alysea, what do you think?

Alysea: Of course. Josefa made something very special for it. [*She looks around.*] Where is it? Oh, yes . . . I'll be back in a minute.

[*Alysea goes through the bedroom door. Clara goes to the mirror and traces the lines on her face. She then walks up to her knitting bag; takes a flask, opens it.*]

Clara: Well, my girl . . . what's in store for you? He's left you . . . you always knew he would leave you. What is there now, my girl . . . except time? [*She covers her face with her hands.*]

[*Alysea comes in from the bedroom with a beautiful lace shawl. Clara quickly recovers and looks at the shawl.*]

Alysea: Look . . . isn't it beautiful . . . a duende design.

Clara: Superb!

[*Alysea drapes it over one shoulder and claps it on Clara's waist.*]

Clara: Oh, thank you . . . but . . . these days I need the right lights . . . not all things are kind to me anymore. Yes, it is beautiful. . . .

[*She turns and contemplates Alysea.*]

Clara: Look at you . . . you are so young . . . your beauty so sharp. Only yesterday, my dear, only yesterday, I was young like you. Mark that well!

[*Josefa comes in through the outside door. Clara sees her. She goes to Josefa and kisses her cheek.*]

Clara: I missed you this morning. You didn't come.

Josefa: Didn't I tell you? There's a million things to do before tomorrow.

Clara: The shawl . . . it's beautiful . . . only Josefa!

Josefa [*Surveying her handiwork*] :   The design . . . the delicacy against the dark dress. It is impressive . . . you wear it well.

[*Josefa notices that Clara is somewhat too gay; a little bit unsteady.*]

Alysea: Shall I get the combs?

Clara: Combs?

Josefa: Mantilla combs . . . made by the gypsies. . . .

Clara: To go with the gown.

Alysea: I'll get them.

[*She walks back to the bedroom. Josefa looks at Clara realizing what the matter is.*]

Josefa: You must have started early. . . .

Clara: What? [*She busies herself at the mirror.*] You worry too much . . . just a little courage . . . I needed a little courage. . . .

Josefa: Eduardo?

Clara [*Turns and faces Josefa; pain in her eyes*] :   He loves her.

Josefa: I know. . . .

Clara: You see . . . I needed a little courage this morning.

Josefa: If you start again. . . . Promise me you won't!

Clara [*With false gaity*] :   I promise! [*She closes her eyes.*] I wish . . . I wish I were young for one day . . . just one day . . . so he would love me the way I love him.

Josefa: Men don't love . . . they take . . . haven't you learned that by now?

Clara: Oh, Josefa . . . you are wrong . . . you are wrong . . . a woman was made to love a man. To love is enough for a woman . . . if only they would let us love them without negating, without negating. . . .

Josefa: Why, Clara? Why must you give . . . so easily? Not to them . . . Clara
. . . not to men!

Clara [Shrugs] : My downfall? *[In a whisper.]* My life?

Josefa: Here . . . enough of that. There are beautiful things to love. . . .

   *[Alysea returns with the combs. She hands them to Josefa who goes to
   Clara and expertly places them in her hair.]*

Clara: Without mantilla?

Josefa: It would be too much with the shawl. . . .

Clara: Yes . . . of course . . . you're right . . . a gypsy with majesty!

Alysea: Yes . . . that's what you look like . . . a gypsy queen.

Josefa: El espíritu duende. . . .

Clara: Like your magicians?

Josefa: Perhaps. . . .

   *[The church bell rings midday; suddenly two swallows are seen outside the
   window.]*

Alysea: Look!

Josefa: They're coming . . . the advance guard . . . every year.

Clara: You love them . . . don't you? Your magicians let you find so many
things to love . . . lucky . . . lucky Josefa.

Josefa: The swallows are safe here . . . after the long, long, lonely flight. . . .

Clara: Lonely? They come in droves. . . .

   [The three look outside the window for a minute. Choir practice begins.]

Josefa: Look at the lake. It shimmers with love. *[Turns to Clara.]* I said
lonely, Clara, because finding direction . . . is lonely. It is too personal a
thing. . . .

Clara: I see what you mean . . . Josefa. *[Looks out the window pensively.]*
Why don't I see the love shimmering in your lake?

   [Josefa smiles.]

Alysea: Her magicians . . . isn't it, Josefa?

Josefa: Yes . . . my magicians.

   [End of Act I.]

ACT II

[*It is early afternoon of the same day. Josefa comes through the outside door. There is a small injured bird in her hands. She cradles it gently and examines it.*]

Josefa: You poor little thing . . . a broken wing . . . don't worry, you'll be fine in a little while. [*She puts the soft piece of life against her cheek.*] There will be no second pain . . . Alysea!

Alysea: [*Comes in through the kitchen door*] :   Yes?

Josefa: Look . . . I found it in the garden. It lay there . . . small, helpless. Look, he's thirsty. Quick get some water and an eyedropper.

[*Alysea goes into the bedroom. Josefa sits in her rocking chair and places the bird gently on her lap. Alysea comes back with a cup and an eye-dropper. Josefa picks up the bird, fills the eye-dropper, and patiently feeds the bird water. The bird drinks.*]

Josefa: See . . . oh, he has life . . . this one!

Alysea: Just a baby . . . let us set the wing. I'll get some small twigs and a bandage. . . .

[*She leaves again; Josefa continues feeding the bird.*]

Josefa: How did you find the bird-house . . . eh? My magicians must have led you here . . . before the others . . . every year . . . the sky is black with their wings . . . here they rest . . . and eat . . . you will be safe . . . until you join your brothers and sisters . . . yes. . . .

[*Alysea comes back; together they carefully set the small wing.*]

Josefa: There!

Alysea: Let's put him in the birdhouse . . . he's tired. . . .

[*Josefa kisses the bird; then both of them go to the window, lean out to the tree, and place the bird in the tree house. Satisfied, Josefa and Alysea look at each other. Josefa reaches out and begins to stroke Alysea's hair.*]

Josefa [*Softly*] :   We share so much . . . just wait . . . the magicians will come to you . . . I know. . . .

Alysea: What?

Josefa: Remember how much you wished for the magicians?

Alysea: No . . . no . . . I don't want them anymore. . . .

Josefa: But. . . .

Alysea: When you brought me here . . . all that's happened . . . it is so unreal
. . . a year of mists and deep sinking dreams . . . but not any more!

Josefa: Hush . . . you're just upset . . that's all.

Alysea: No . . . last night . . . no . . . never again. . . .

Josefa: Poor little girl . . . you've tired yourself out all morning . . . I forgot.
I don't know why . . . but I just forgot about . . . about last night.

Alysea [Looking at her with horror] : Josefa . . . no! Forgot? How could you?

Josefa [Becoming slightly agitated] : Habit . . . to keep strong . . . since I was
little . . . to keep strong . . . I put ugliness away.

Alysea: Where? Where?

Josefa: What do you mean?

Alysea: If you have a conscience . . . where could you put it away?

Josefa: There will be atonement. . . .

Alysea: No . . . that's impossible . . . you think . . . it will . . . disappear? The
blood . . . the knife . . . *[She runs to the table where she had placed the knife.]*
Look . . . I'll show you. You make it disappear! *[She opens the drawer and
stares unbelievingly.]*

Alysea: The knife . . . it's gone!

[She begins to look frantically everywhere.]

Alysea: Did you hear me?

[Josefa seems almost unaware of Alysea's frenzy.]

Josefa: Yes . . . of course. . . .

[Alysea begins to look again and this time finds the money box gone.]

Alysea: The money box . . . it's gone too.

Josefa: Tomás . . . of course. He took the money and the knife.

*[Alysea collapses into a chair and covers her face with her hands. Tomás's
voice is heard singing a barrio love song; Alysea looks up in fright. Josefa
goes to the door of the kitchen and calls out into the patio behind the
kitchen.]*

Josefa: Tomás! Come in here. . . .

*[Tomás comes into the kitchen still singing. He walks into the room. Josefa
watches him warily. Alysea in terror.]*

Tomás: Well . . . well . . . Did you call me, querida? [*He strokes Josefa's arm intimately. She breaks away.*]

Josefa: Don't you ever put your hands on me!

Tomás: Ha! ha! ha! Doña Perfecta. [*He looks around the room.*] You know . . . I think I'll move over here . . . I like this house . . . ah! It is time I had a little elegance in my life . . . yes. [*He sprawls out in a chair.*]

Josefa: You've been drinking. . . .

Tomás: Yes . . . I have been drinking . . . and I shall drink some more . . . you can afford it. . . .
[*Alysea begins to cry.*]

Tomás: What's the matter with her?

Josefa: She is tired . . . and I . . . have had enough of your insolence. . . .

Tomás: Qué maravilla . . . how long . . . Josefa . . . how long . . . can you keep it up? [*He paces in front of her; she remains calm.*]

Tomás [*Practically shouting in her face*]: I took the knife! Do you understand . . . I took the knife! Aren't you afraid, Josefa?

[*Alysea begins to cry desperately. Josefa goes to her. She tries to comfort her.*]

Josefa: Don't Alysea. Remember . . . it's late . . . we have to pack for David . . . he'll need his things in the hospital . . . compose yourself. Why don't you go and start packing. I'll talk to Tomas.

[*Alysea nods her head in agreement; she rises and leaves as if she wanted escape.*]

Josefa: [*Turns and faces Tomás*]: Have you ever . . . have you ever . . . done anything kind for anybody?

Tomás [*Sarcastically*]: No . . . just you . . . querida. You are the angel. . . .

Josefa: All right . . . what do you intend to do?

Tomás: Nothing . . . you see . . . we . . . you and I . . . must have a clearer understanding. I know much more than you think . . . about you and [*nods towards bedroom.*] her!

[*Josefa stiffens.*]

Josefa: All right . . . you win . . . I'll give you money. . . .

Tomás: No more crumbs . . . dear niece. I call the play . . . from now on.

Josefa: You're bluffing . . . lying . . . as usual.

Tomás: Am I?

[*There is a knock at the door; with alacrity Tomás springs up and goes to the door and opens it. It is Don Esquinas, Clara's husband.*]

Tomás: Ah . . . Don Esquinas, won't you come in?

[*Don Esquinas brushes past Tomás totally ignoring him. Tomás makes a mock gesture of humility.*]

Don Esquinas: Josefa, the worst has happened. . . . I warned you!

Josefa [*Placing her hands on her heart*]:   Clara . . . let me go to her. [*She starts to go; Don Esquinas stops her.*]

Don Esquinas: It's too late.

Josefa [*Savagely*]:   It isn't. I can take care of her.

Don Esquinas: How? By giving her more drink? You've done enough harm.

Josefa: Harm? I have been her sole companion for years. I have suffered with her . . . nursed her. . . . Harm?

Don Esquinas: Do you know how I found my wife this afternoon when I got home? She was lying in bed . . . stark naked . . . screaming about crawling . . . crawling, dark . . . she slashed everything in sight . . . broke the mirror. . . . There were bottles . . . everywhere. . . .

Josefa: My poor, poor darling . . .

Don Esquinas: I . . . the servants . . . we were helpless. . . . It was dreadful. She kept screaming and sobbing that your magicians had . . . had no faces. . . .

Josefa: She's so alone. . . .

Don Esquinas: Your lies . . . the liquor and your lies . . . both supplied by you! I'm taking her to the sanitorium . . . this time for good.

Josefa: She is so alone. . . .

Don Esquinas: Stop saying that! You . . . you supplied her with liquor. . . .

Josefa: All that unhappiness. . . . She is so lost. There was nothing else. She promised me this afternoon.

Don Esquinas: Promised? You stupid woman . . . you know she wouldn't keep the promise. . . .

Josefa [*Suddenly in anger*]:   I tell you . . . you won't listen. . . . You men never listen. All she had was hopelessness. . . .

Don Esquinas: You don't know what you are talking about. . . . She always had everything . . . . since the day she was born . . . never, never, did she have to lift a finger . . . anything she desires. . . .

Josefa: Except her husband!

Don Esquinas: What in damnation?

Josefa: She wanted you to love her. . . .

Don Esquinas: Love her? You women are insane! I married her . . . didn't I?

Josefa: She knew all about your . . . your women. . . .

Don Esquinas: That is a man's way! You have no right to question. Tell me, how much liquor did you give her? When did you give it to her?

[*Josefa remains silent.*]

Don Esquinas: Well?

Josefa: She wanted a baby. . . .

Don Esquinas: Nonsense! We settled that long ago. That was past and forgotten. . . .

Josefa: No . . . it was never forgotten. She cried every night. . . .

Don Esquinas: Silly tears of a drunken woman . . . adopt a baby . . . a baby not of the Esquinas blood? For my heir? Absurd!

Josefa [*Bitterly*] :   Which of your bastards are you going to choose as your heir?

Don Esquinas: You ungrateful peasant . . . let me tell you . . . you influenced her too much. This is probably all your fault. I don't want you around the hacienda now that she is gone. Do you hear?

[*Josefa turns her back on him; Don Esquinas is somewhat at a loss. Her calm towards his anger is disconcerting. He stands for a moment; then, he walks out of the room. On his way out, Tomás follows him, still assuming a pose of mock humility.*]

Tomás: It is terrible, Don Esquinas, what my niece has done. . . . If I can make up for it in any way . . . please call on me.

[*Don Esquinas ignores him and leaves. Tomás turns to Josefa.*]

Tomás: See what you have done to your friend . . . the wife of our Don?

[*Josefa too ignores him. Tomás's attitude of humility is now gone. His attitude is again cunning and sly. He walks up to Josefa.*]

Tomás: Tch, tch, tch . . . Doña Perfecta is not perfecta . . . eh?

Josefa [*Not listening to him*] :   She's gone . . . the light of my magicians never came to her . . . poor, poor lost child.

Tomás: You are insane about those magicians. [*Josefa walks away from him;*

Tomás grabs her arm angrily.] I'm sick and tired of you ignoring me! You think I'm scum? I don't matter . . . do I? Well, you listen, Doña Perfecta, you listen to me!

[*Josefa waits silently for him to let go of her arm. When he does, she touches her temples with her fingertips.*]

Josefa: I have a headache. . . .

Tomás: None of your tricks . . . listen to me! I saw you . . . do you hear? I saw you. Last San Lorenzo's day, I remember. I left the fiesta . . . I was too drunk; I walked toward the lake . . . I remember, it was a clear, clear night; the moon lighted everything. As I came near the lake, past the back of this house, I saw two figures come from the water's edge. They ran. One caught up with the other!

[*Tomás watches her maliciously and intently wishing to get a reaction; her surface is still calm as he scrutinizes her face.*]

Josefa: What are you trying to do?

Tomás [*Laughing slyly and triumphantly*] :   It was you and the girl . . . you and the girl . . . wasn't it? Now I begin to put things together. It all fits!

Josefa: Your drunken hallucinations. . . .

Tomás: I know better, reina del barrio..You are a . . .

Josefa: If you have nothing else to threaten me with. . . .[*She walks away from him with disdain.*]

Tomás [*Practically screaming with exasperation*] :   You think you can always win, with you calm; you're not made of stone. You'll break, milady; I'll be back. Inside you're trembling with fear. . . .

[*She turns abruptly and faces him haughtily. Tomás falters first; he turns and leaves. As Josefa looks after him, Alysea comes from the bedroom wearing street clothes.*]

Josefa [*Turns and sees her*] :   Finished?

Alysea: Yes, I'm ready.

[*Josefa walks up to her and puts her arm around her.*]

Josefa: The ride will do you good; after you come back from the hospital . . . after you see my little David, we'll have supper here. Then, we can have one of our little chats.

Alysea [*Gently breaks away from Josefa*] :   I'm not coming back.

Josefa: Not coming back?

Alysea: I meant to tell you earlier. I'm going away with Eduardo.

Josefa: Because of what happened last night?

Alysea: Many reasons, but mostly because I want to be with him.

Josefa: You are like all the rest. You insist on being a useless, empty sacrifice!

Alysea: I love him.

Josefa: Love him? Tell me, how long will your precious Eduardo love you? [*Pause.*] You know who was here? Don Esquinas! Clara drank herself insane because your Eduardo left her. What do you think he'll do to you?

Alysea: I can't believe that. There's more to love.

Josefa [*Ironically and bitterly*] :   Love! Remember the brothel? No different. . . . You choose darkness. All your pains are still to come! Haven't I taught you anything?

Alysea: It all fell apart . . . last night. All I can remember are David's eyes. [*She breaks down sobbing.*]

Josefa: He'll be all right. I'll take care of my little love . . . as long as he lives. . . .

Alysea: His eyes told me. You and I were all the terror in the world.

Josefa: No. The terror is in the world out there. Don't say that!

Alysea: The violence . . . the useless violence. . . .

Josefa: I forbid you to go on like this.

[*She walks to the window and reaches into the birdhouse until she finds the crippled bird. She picks it up, fondles him, and holds him against her cheek.*]

Josefa [*With eyes closed*] :   Remember how he came . . . crippled, starved, half dead?

Alysea: The way I came?

Josefa: It will be safe here and happy; you have always been safe and happy! We have so much, Alysea.

[*Alysea remains silent.*]

Josefa: You know why I built the birdhouse?

[*She seems to be remembering something painful; she goes to the rocking chair, places the bird on her lap, and strokes it gently.*]

Josefa: When I was seven . . . the swallows came. They came one hot dry dawn . . . and continued all day . . . on the edge of the desert that still hotter afternoon. . . . I saw noisy boys with desert time on their hands . . . playing.

I watched the playing become a violence . . . they were catching birds . . .
now it became a killing . . . they stoned them . . . plucked them . . . laughing
with a fearful joy. The sand was a sea of dead birds . . . I . . . I . . . couldn't
stand it. . . . I ran . . . I hit them . . . I said, "Stop! Stop!" [*Pause.*] They
laughed; then for a joke . . . for a joke, they said . . . they held me down, the
burning sand against my back. In spite of all my terror, I opened my eyes
. . . a boy . . . a big boy . . . held a swallow over me; he took a knife . . . cut
the bird . . . Oh, God! so much blood . . . all that blood. [*Josefa strokes the
bird gently and shakes her head, closes her eyes.*] It spilled . . . spilled into
my face . . . ran into my mouth . . . warm . . . warm . . . salt warm . . . was
it my tears? The blood?

[*She stands and goes to the window, still with the bird; she caresses the bird
with her cheek and places it gently in the birdhouse. The rosary bell begins to toll. It is sunset. Josefa looks out in silence.*]

Josefa: Alysea, look; the lake is screaming with life. Look . . . the colors of
love . . . then . . . the day went. [*She turns to Alysea.*] Out there . . . the
beauty is lost in fears. What do you expect out there? Stay with the radience.
Alysea, stay with me!

Alysea: I won't be coming back.

[*Alysea turns and leaves, going into the bedroom; Josefa looks after her for
a moment, seems to start after Alysea, then changes her mind. She turns
to the unfinished damask; she unhooks the needle and begins to work on
it in deep concentration. Alysea returns with a suitcase. Josefa does not
look up, although she is aware of Alysea. Alysea comes close to Josefa
rather hesitantly. Josefa looks up and smiles.*]

Josefa [*In a casual tone*] :   Look, do you think I ought to give the design a
name? I saw it in a dream the other night . . . so vivid! Perhaps I should call
it "Swallow Song." What do you think?

Alysea [*Looking intently at the design over Josefa's shoulder*] :   It looks like
flowing grain . . . with . . . with a streak of lightning . . . so well intermingled
. . . how strange! Beauty and terror as one . . . see? [*She traces the pattern
with her finger.*]

Josefa: How foolish of you. That is not lightning. It is . . . it is sweet rain.

[*Alysea looks intently at the pattern, then at Josefa.*]

Alysea [*Softly*] :   Lovely Josefa. No, no . . . you could never see the lightning
. . . only your gentle lights. [*She picks up her suitcase and starts to leave.*]
Goodbye, sweet lady of light!

[*Josefa looks up but does not answer. Alysea moves towards the outside door.*]

Josefa [*As if in afterthought*] :   Alysea?

Alysea: Yes?

Josefa: On the way . . . please stop by the rectory . . . will you? Tell Father Prado I cannot make rosary tonight. Tell him . . . if he would be so kind . . . to come later this evening. . . .

Alysea: Of course. [*She hesitates for a moment, as if at a loss for words. Then, with one last look of love for Josefa and the room, she departs. After Alysea leaves, Josefa continues putting the final stitches on the damask.*]

Josefa: There! Finished . . . another birth of light!

[*She stands and stretches as if very tired. She rubs the back of her neck and breathes deep. She goes to the window again. It is now dark.*]

Josefa: My lover! You look like morning crystal in the water . . . so still . . . so deep. . . . I ache for you so! You beckon me shamelessly. . . .

[*She stands at the window as the curtain drops for Act Two.*]

ACT III

[*Late the same evening. The church bells are announcing the end of rosary. Josefa is sitting in her rocking chair saying her prayer beads. Every so often she pauses in thought. There is a knock at the door. Josefa rises and goes to the door. Father Prado enters.*]

Father Prado [*Kissing her on the cheek*] :   My dear , , . how are you this evening? We missed you at rosary. You always lead prayer with the confidence of an angel. A hundred things to do before tomorrow . . eh?

Josefa: It's good to see you! [*She leads him by the arm to a settee.*]

Father Prado: Tell me . . . can I help with anything?

Josefa: You are here. That is more than enough.

Father Prado: You must give me a chance. You do so much for the church, for me. Now let me do something for you.

Josefa: Father . . . you are my kindred spirit . . . the oasis in the middle of the desert.

Father Prado: You spoil me. . . .

Josefa: I finished the boys' surplices for tomorrow.

Father Prado: See what I mean? Your lovely little hands [*Kisses them.*] produce such lovely wondrous things for us. [*Looks around.*] And this place! A sanctuary . . . who would think? To find such a place as this in our desert barrio? Ah . . . all things and all people here are too mindful of the desert . . . except you.

Josefa: My magicians, Father!

Father Prado [*In jest*] :   Of course, your magicians!

Josefa: I wonder if you take me seriously? Come . . . would you like some coffee? Tea?

Father Prado: No . . . no, it is late; I ate too much at supper. I tell myself every night it seems . . . but I go on eating just the same.

Josefa: The way you work for the barrio people! Every church festival is such a chore for you. You work yourself to death. . . .

Father Prado: So do you!

Josefa: We can't help it . . . can we, Father? You love the people as much as I do.

Father Prado: It means so much to them . . . these festivals. They are just ritual to you . . . aren't they?

Josefa: Maybe . . . but what blossoms from the barrio people because of the festival. That is not ritual. There is a rebirth. They come to life for a little while.

Father Prado: Tomorrow will be very special for them . . . a day to honor their Josefa. Such a legend you are!

Josefa: If it makes them happy.

[*Father Prado looks at her intently.*]

Father Prado: Are you feeling all right? You look a little pale . . . of course! How stupid of me . . . so many things have been happening today . . . even in the rectory life seeps in. . . .

Josefa: You know about Clara?

Father Prado: Unfortunate . . . pobrecita . . . such a beautiful child.

Josefa: She won't be coming back this time.

[*Josefa begins to cry softly. She brushes a tear from her cheek.*]

Father Prado: There . . . there, don't cry! [*Comforts her.*] I know how you feel. You two were so close. She depended on you so!

Josefa: When life is a farce. . . .

Father Prado: In her own way . . . there was so much meaning. Alysea has
   found something special too. She and Eduardo stopped by the rectory.

Josefa: One by one . . . like leaves from a tree. . . .

Father Prado: I know! Then . . . the terrible thing. I heard in the village . . .
   the terrible thing that happened to David. I hope they catch. . . .

   [*Josefa interrupts violently.*]

Josefa: Father!

Father Prado: What is it, Child?

Josefa: May I have confession now?

Father Prado [*Puzzled*]:   Here?

Josefa: Please, Father!

Father Prado: Of course, if that's what you want. . . .

   [*He comes near her; as he does, she falls to her knees and leans her head
   against his body.*]

Father Prado: What is wrong?

Josefa: Forgive me, Father, for I have sinned. [*Father remains silent.*] I have
   sinned . . . I have sinned. . . .

Father Prado: God forgives. . . .

Josefa: Oh, Father . . . I'm lost. . . .

Father Prado: All of us . . . at one time. . . .

Josefa: I am guilty of grievious sins. They are beyond forgiveness. People
   will judge them so! Father . . . before I tell you . . . you must know . . . I
   do not feel sorry . . . I want . . . I need . . . the calm . . . to keep things as
   they are.

   [*Father simply nods his head.*]

Josefa: David was hurt last night. I lied about the intruder. There was no intruder . . . I was the one.

Father Prado [*Incredulously*]:   You . . . did that to David?

Josefa: Yes. [*She braces herself as if to accept the fact.*] I did that to David.

Father Prado: I can't believe it . . . you! Not you!

Josefa: Me, Father, Me!

Father Prado: It was inhuman. . . .

Josefa: Oh, Father! I . . . I don't know. . . . Why? Why?

Father Prado: Tell me, my child, there must have been a reason.

Josefa: Last night . . . last night . . . after supper . . . David helped Alysea and me put the last touches on the bird house. David was so excited. [*Pause.*] The moon . . . the reflection of diamonds in the lake . . . life . . . all were too much for me. I was overflowing . . . I felt the sweetness of the night with every fiber . . . every fiber. [*Lost in memory; then she resumes her story.*] David didn't want to go to bed. He insisted on staying up all night to wait for the swallows. Of course I said, "No!" He left for bed reluctantly. [*Pause.*] Father?

Father Prado: Yes?

Josefa: Have you ever felt as if you were one total yearning . . . it roars and spills. . . .

[*Father Prado remains silent.*]

Josefa: Alysea and I are lovers.

Father Prado: What?

Josefa: A year ago tonight we became lovers. If you remember she had been with me for some months before San Lorenzo's day. She was something new in my life. She felt and responded to my every mood . . . my every act. Oh! To have someone in your life! I had repulsed all the men in the barrio . . . the coarseness! The taking! No . . . no . . . I could never surrender to that . . . but when she came, she filled my life in so many ways . . . so many ways . . . it was natural that the yearning grow for more . . . the body too is master. . . .

Father Prado: Yes, my child, of course it is!

Josefa: A year ago I took Alysea to the lake on the eve of San Lorenzo. She had heard about the Bathing of the Virgins at noon the next day. Could she go . . . she asked! I was angry . . . I knew all the hope . . . all the dreams of those girls would turn to jagged violence. It was a lie . . . the whole ritual is a lie!

Father Prado: No . . . no, Josefa . . . to those girls the dream of a perfect love is true as long as it gives meaning to their lives. . . .

Josefa: I know what men are!

[*Father Prado remains silent.*]

Josefa: I told her . . . go with me when the moon comes out. . . . When the lake waits for just me . . . it is my lover! [*Pause.*] She believed me. It is true, Father. The lake is my lover. . . .

Father Prado: Oh, my child!

Josefa: We bathed . . . and then . . . it happened. [*Pause.*] Last night, after David went to bed . . . I felt the nymph magic. I took Alysea. Suddenly . . . there was David . . . in the middle of the room. The horror in his eyes. Why? Why? There was horror in his eyes. . . .

Father Prado: He did not understand. . . .

Josefa: Oh, Father! Now . . . I can see why . . . now! But . . . last night . . . it was not the Josefa he loved that David saw. I could not stand what he saw! I could not!

Father Prado: God forgive you!

Josefa: Something happened in me. I don't know what it was. I ran. I ran into the kitchen and found a kitchen knife. Somehow . . . somehow I knew David would tell . . . the barrio people would look at me that way too. . . .

Father Prado: I never thought you would care about what people . . .

Josefa: Oh, Father . . . until last night I never knew my fears. I went back to where Alysea was holding the frightened child . . . then . . . then I made Alysea hold him tight. Father, it was not her fault! There have been so many furies in her life. She drowned in my agony. She trusted me. What else could she do? [*She goes to the window, looks out at the lake for a moment.*] Father . . . look . . . come look at the lake. Maybe you can understand the power it has over me. Look. . . .

[*Father Prado goes somewhat reluctantly to the window. He also looks out, but remains silent.*]

Josefa: I took the knife and cut David's tongue. . . .

Father Prado: Jesucristo, perdona a tu hija. . . .

Josefa: I was silencing the world from reprimand. I knew I had to silence the world from reprimand. I felt no guilt. All I knew . . . the life I had . . . the faith of the barrio people . . . this house of light . . . must be preserved. I silenced all reprimand with my terrible deed. [*She covers her face for a moment. Then, she gathers strength and continues talking.*] With the light of day . . . I knew better . . . others had not my eyes . . . others had not my eyes . . . others had not my reasons . . . or my magicians. . . . [*She looks at Father Prado intently.*] Can you ever understand?

Father Prado [*As if talking to himself*]: I don't understand. . . . I don't understand why I didn't see . . . detect what was happening to you. . . .

Josefa [*Puzzled*] :   Happening to me?

Father Prado: All your beauty . . . your calm . . . your giving was . . . your talent . . . what a splendid canopy for the twisted fears of so many years . . . so many years. I'm an old fool . . . forgive me, my daughter, I have never really seen you. I pride myself in knowing you so well. I claimed I loved you. How blind . . . how blind. . . .

Josefa: Don't blame yourself, Father. I am what you see. That is really what I am. Not what you discovered this moment. . . .

Father Prado: My poor, poor child. . . .

Josefa: No . . . father . . . don't pity me . . . anything but that! That is one thing I shall never suffer. . . .

Father Prado: I have never seen you cry . . . Josefa . . . until tonight. . . .

Josefa: The past . . . the dark gnawing . . . such hungers! I must not be a desert . . . now they are harmless ghosts. . . .

Father Prado: Are they?

Josefa: You don't understand . . . do you?

Father Prado: I want to. . . .

Josefa: The magicians created "me"! The blight of meniality never touched me. The magicians gave me the purity of light . . . and the wisp of beauties at my fingertips . . . so . . . I really am . . . what you always thought I was.

Father Prado: There is so much God in you!

Josefa: God in me? No, Father . . . no. I failed goodness. I wanted, I prayed, . . . to save my soul as the church instructed . . . as your faith believed. . . .

Father Prado [*Somewhat taken aback*] :   But . . . you are the most pious . . . the most constant . . . in the barrio. Faith shines in you. All the beauty you create. . . .

Josefa: Faith? Oh, no, Father, no. It was not faith; it was the light of my magicians. I bear the children of light! I am its high priestess. . . .

Father Prado: I . . . I. . . .

[*He can't go on; he sits down and places his head in his hands. Josefa looks at him and is full of concern. She goes to comfort him.*]

Josefa [*She says this as if she does not believe it herself*] Don't grieve for me, Father . . . for what I have done, I am willing to atone . . . David will be my whole life . . . I will create beauty for him . . . for you . . . for the barrio people . . . longings will fade away with commitment . . . Father . . . father

[*She kneels in front of him.*] Forgive me, Father, for I have sinned . . . I have grieviously sinned.

[*Father Prado, with tears in his eyes, strokes her hair in silence.*]

[*Curtain drops for Act III.*]

Final Scene

[*Dawn the next morning; the sitting room is a pastel paradise; there is life in the birdhouse, a roar of bird sounds; Josefa comes from the bedroom with a white gown over her arm. It is the gown to be worn at the procession. She goes to the window and looks at the tree with great happiness.*]

Josefa: I waited for you . . . before dawn I heard the flurry of the sea. Oh, what a sight you were over my burning lake . . . straight . . . straight. You came to me . . . to this temple of peace . . . no more songs of pain for you.

[*Church bells sound morning vigil. The procession will follow in the freshness of the early morning. Josefa remembers the barrio world.*]

Josefa: My day . . . my day . . . but, oh, my people! It was not meant to be shared with you. My day was planned by my magicians . . . long before you planned this one for me. I must get ready. . . .

[*She goes behind the screen, puts on her gown, comes back and looks in the mirror. Her dress is white. She looks unusually young and beautiful. All of a sudden she touches her rather severe hair-do. Then she lets down her hair.*]

Josefa [*Looking at herself intently in the mirror*]:   Yes . . . yes . . . this way. There is a wildness in me. [*She laughs in joyous delirium.*]

[*Then she becomes the usual Josefa for a moment. She remembers the boys' surplices. She goes to the wardrobe and takes them out. She lays them carefully over a chair.*]

Josefa: There . . . something of me will be at the procession. Yes, even that . . . the boys will find them here. . . .

[*She takes a final look in the mirror; then she goes to the window and looks out to the lake.*]

Josefa: So still your water . . . . but I know your passions underneath. Deep . . . deep . . . for all time. Hush! I'm coming. . . .

[*As she turns to leave, she touches the lace; the damask now finished, the fresh flowers on the table . . . with love . . . with a tender regret . . . but a secret within her. . . .*]

Josefa: My magicians will let me come back as light. Yes, yes!

[*She goes to the door and gives the room one final glance.*]

Josefa [*In a whisper*] :   Wait for me. . . .

[*Church bells begin to toll for the gathering of the procession. Voices are heard outside the window.*]

Voices: Here! The starting will be here . . . in front of Josefa's garden. Has anyone seen Josefa this morning?

[*The sitting room seems alive even without people, then, two boys enter. They have come for the surplices.*]

1st Boy: Hey . . . look . . . they're over there. [*Each of the boys takes one.*]

2nd Boy: Aren't they something . . . grand . . . like at the cathedral. . . .

1st Boy: That's what he said. . . .

2nd Boy: Who said?

1st Boy: Father Prado. He said Josefa was like a cathedral. . . .

2nd Boy: 'Cause she makes all this grand stuff?

1st Boy: I guess so . . . 'cause she's different . . . don't you think?

2nd Boy: Ah . . . ha! She made all the altar linen. . . .

1st Boy: Yeah. Father Prado said she was like the silence of the cathedral . . . and you know those glass-stained windows?

2nd Boy: Yeah. . . .

1st Boy: That's her soul. . . .

2nd Boy: You think something is wrong with Father Prado?

[*They laugh in jest; shove each other around in horse play, then stop when the church bells ring again.*]

1st Boy: Hey, come on . . . the procession is going to start. . . .

[*The room is empty again; this time the voices of the choir beginning the procession hymns are heard. They are as ethereal as the room. Combined, the room and the voices have a cathedral-like awesomeness. Clemencia breaks the atmosphere. She is in her Sunday best.*]

Clemencia: Josefa! Where are you? [*She looks in the bedroom; then she peeks through the kitchen door.*] Mmmm . . . where could she be? Everybody's waiting. Josefa! Oh, dear, oh, dear! They've started without her. [*She goes to the window.*] Look at those birds! Every year! They come straight to this tree. Ah . . . God's morning . . . the lake . . . the green pines. [*Suddenly something out in the lake catches her eye.*] What is that . . . floating in the lake? Mmmm . . . looks like a girl dressed in white. That's foolish! It is too early for the Bathing of the Virgins yet . . . yes . . . wearing clothes?

[*As she hears the choir, she loses interest and goes to the mirror and straightens her hat.*]

Clemencia [*With a sigh*]: Why do we all end up looking like scarecrows? [*She turns to leave and catches sight of the open window.*] I better close the window . . . the room will be covered with birds!

[*She goes to the window again; as she starts to close it, she gazes out into the lake, again fascinated by what she saw before.*]

Clemencia: Yes . . . it is a body! A body floating in the lake. I'm sure of it!

[*She gasps, but at this moment the church bells ring again. Out of habit she starts to hurry off, shrugging off what she has seen.*]

Clemencia: The sun is too bright. It is my imagination! I better hurry. What a day this will be. . . .

[*She leaves the room. The voices of the choir, the church bell, the birds on the tree in full life, and the almost unearthly light streaming through the windows gives the essence of a presence in the room . . . of something beautiful.*]

Bibliography

A. BOOKS

Acuna, Rudy. *A Mexican-American Chronicle.* New York, 1971.
Campa, Arthur L. *Spanish Religious Folktheatre in the Southwest.* 1st Cycle. Albuquerque, 1934.
Campa, Arthur L. *Spanish Religious Folktheatre in the Southwest.* 2nd Cycle. Albuquerque, 1934.
Carson, William G. B. *The Theatre on the Frontier.* Chicago, 1932.
Valdez, Luis. *Actos.* Fresno, 1971.
Wright, Edward A. *Understanding Today's Theater.* 2nd ed. Englewood Cliffs, N.J., 1972.
Zurita, Marciano. *Historia Del Genero Chico.* Madrid, 1920.

B. PERIODICALS

Aisenman, Leslie. "El Teatro Campesino," *Tenaz* 5(March 31, 1972), 7.
Covarrubias, Miguel. "Slapsticks and Venom," *Mexican Life* 13(January, 1939), 21–22; 57–59.
Duel, Pauline B. "Commedia del 'Arte' in a Mexican Folk Theater: Padua Hills Theatre, Claremont, California," *Hispania* 20(Fall, 1969), 537–39.

Englekirk, John E. "En Torno Al Teatro Popular Mexicano," *Hispania* 52(Fall, 1969), 405–11.

Huerta, Jorge A. "Chicano Teatro: A Background," *Aztlan*, 1972, pp. 63–71.

Savage, R. Vance. "Rodolfo Usigli's Idea of Mexican Theater," *Latin American Theater Review* 4(Spring, 1971), 13–19.

Tilles, Solomon. "Rodolfo Usigli's Concept of Dramatic Art," *Latin American Theater Review* 3(Spring, 1970), 31–38.

Underhill, John Barett. "The Modern Spanish Drama," *Drama League Monthly* 15(December, 1917), 553–65.

Ybarra, Tomas-Frausto. "Teatro Chicano: Two Reports," *Latin American Theater Review* 4(Spring, 1971), 51–55.